J.Q. Hunnicut
3700 N Capital St NW #025
Washington DC   20011-8400

A SOCIETY *of*
Gentlemen

Midshipmen at the
U.S. Naval Academy
1845–1861

MARK C. HUNTER

Naval Institute Press
291 Wood Road
Annapolis, MD 21402

Library of Congress Cataloging-in-Publication Data
Hunter, Mark C.
  Society of gentlemen : midshipmen at the U.S. Naval Academy, 1845-1861 /
Mark C. Hunter.
     p. cm.
  Includes bibliographical references and index.
  ISBN 978-1-59114-397-0 (alk. paper)
  1. United States Naval Academy—History—19th century. 2. United
States. Navy—Officers—Training of—History—19th century. 3. Military
education—United States—History—19th century. I. Title.
  V415.L1H86 2010
  359.0071'173—dc22
                                        2009052947

Printed in the United States of America on acid-free paper
14 13 12 11 10   9 8 7 6 5 4 3 2
First printing

CONTENTS

FIGURES AND TABLES

ACKNOWLEDGMENTS

I would like to thank several people and institutions that have helped with this book and my career. First, I must acknowledge the encouragement of Professor Lewis R. "Skip" Fischer, Memorial University of Newfoundland; Dr. David J. Starkey, University of Hull, United Kingdom; Dr. Andrew D. Lambert, Department of War Studies, King's College London; and Dr. Roger Sarty, Wilfrid Laurier University.

Other people have also made helpful suggestions as the book's focus has solidified. I must thank Dr. Harold Langley, who read a very early draft of this book, and Dr. Bruce Vandervort, editor of the *Journal of Military History*, for his suggestions and those of the journal's reviewers. They helped me center the summer cruise essay that appears in the journal on professionalization, and it served as the basis for this wider study.

I would also like to thank the staff of the Lauinger Library, Special Collections and Government Documents section, Georgetown University; Naval Academy archivist Gary A. LaValley for his assistance with academy regulations and candidate data; and academy archivist Dr. Jennifer A. Bryan for her help in obtaining pictures for the book.

Finally, I must thank Naval Institute Press editor Adam Kane for his commitment to this project.

Elements from this manuscript have previously appeared as "The U.S. Naval Academy and Its Summer Cruises: Professionalization in the Antebellum U.S. Navy, 1845 to 1861," *The Journal of Military History* 70, no. 4 (October 2006): 963–94, and "Youth, Law, and Discipline at the U.S. Naval Academy, 1845–1861," *The Northern Mariner/Le Marin du nord* 10, no. 2 (April 2000): 23–39, and are incorporated into this book with the kind permission of these journals.

INTRODUCTION

American naval history has concentrated primarily on battles, tactics, strategies, and the roles of great commanders in battle. It has rarely focused on sailors as a group, their social backgrounds, their training, or the society of which they were a part. Yet, there is debate about the relationship between the armed forces, the state, and the rise of professionalism. While most historians agree about the characteristics of a professional, they differ over when these characteristics emerged in the American armed forces. Samuel P. Huntington concludes that the professional soldier or sailor needs a type of specialized knowledge, or expertise, different from the public, gained through special training at institutions.[1] Similarly, Allen R. Millett believes that a profession is autonomous from the rest of society and entails a full-time commitment to service and identification with a "job subculture." To "do other people's unpleasant tasks," a profession serves a client and refrains from passing judgment on the morality of the job. To uphold these standards, professions developed their own "ethical codes" and did their own recruiting and education to transform "an initiate into a fully-accepted member of a profession."[2] Morris Janowitz notes that a "professional group develops a sense of group identity and a system of internal administration."[3] While Donald Chisholm explains that "occupations that achieve professional status do things full-time."[4]

Huntington asserts that the main symbols of a professional American armed forces emerged between 1865 and 1914. This trend meant that Annapolis and West Point reduced their amount of "technical instruction," and both services established graduate schools for technical and "advanced military study." By 1884 Stephen Luce established the Naval War College, and by 1901 the Army created the Army War College. Moreover, professional military journals, promotion by merit, and greater bureaucratic organization also emerged in the postbellum era as further signs of professionalization.[5] Connecting the military and civilian worlds, others surmise that professionalization in the late nineteenth century "fit well with the Progressive era's emphasis on efficient management and scientific planning."[6]

Frederick Winslow Taylor, a progressive-era engineer, was the pioneer of scientific management.[7] He urged businesses to collect data, use it to develop rules for operations, and "scientifically select and then train, teach, and develop the workman."[8] Under this theory, the U.S. military adopted scientific management practices similar to those developed in the civilian world. Millett, for instance, opines that late-nineteenth-century generals eventually appreciated civilian management practices, underwent education, and used their experience to be a "hero, gentleman, student of human psychology, and manager." The Civil War permitted this development because it killed many "amateurs," allowing professional officers to rise through the ranks.[9]

Others, like William B. Skelton, surmise that U.S. armed forces professionalization emerged before the Civil War. Beyond West Point, the Army already had professional boards, officers wrote treatises, and the War Department established "schools of practice, training encampments, and other programs." In sum, the army's efforts "reflected an emerging professional culture in the antebellum officer corps."[10] This professional culture, Skelton argues, then attracted recruits from the commercial sector: those with political connections but a modest income, who desired an acceptable professional career.[11] Unlike the Army, the Navy had a clearly defined role even during peacetime: protecting diplomats and businessmen from threats like pirates and competitors along the Gulf of Mexico, the West African coast, and in the Pacific before the Civil War. Therefore, as Millett admits, the Navy "manifested more professional autonomy than the Army" and faced fewer impediments to the greater professionalization of its officer corps.[12] This study asserts that the U.S. Navy, through the U.S. Naval Academy, exhibited some of the characteristics of a profession in the antebellum era and sowed the seed for later developments after the Civil War.

Janowitz theorized that military professions use service academies to "set the standards of behavior" for their members. Moreover, service academies are important instruments that instill in recruits "'like-mindedness' about military honor" and help their students develop "the sense of fraternity which prevails among military men."[13] As a result, the Navy believed that its future officers needed structure, discipline, and appropriate role models to be an effective force and often tried to quantify these qualities during the midshipman's stay at the academy. Annapolis took its lead from West Point's system of classroom education, drill, and summer encampments. Training ashore over the academic year from October to June, the summer practice ships, established in 1851, then rounded out the young officer's introduction to naval life. Annapolis selected and trained midshipmen as potential officers and then tested them at sea in a systematic and almost "scientific" manner. Here they were supervised by academy authorities and shown the at-sea responsibilities of those who commanded others and worked on foreign stations. By 1859 this system was fully integrated with the shore-based system, with a school ship tied up at the academy during the academic year. In these safe and formal settings, instructors taught the midshipmen the corporateness and special requirements needed to fulfill their duties. The antebellum U.S. Naval Academy reveals that, before the Civil War, the Navy applied many of the criteria that historians have looked for in a professional organization.

Because of the changes that began at the institution at Annapolis in 1849, this study is divided into two periods: the school and academy eras. The former encompasses the time when the Navy founded the Naval School and catered to older midshipmen with prior sea experience (1845–49). The latter time, from the school's reorganization during the 1849–51 period, was when Annapolis educated younger students without prior sea experience until the outbreak of the Civil War. During both of these eras, vignettes will largely expand upon statistical data dealing with student backgrounds and discipline. Chapter 1 discusses how the Navy educated its officers before the foundation of the Naval School and Academy at Annapolis in 1845 and reveals that the new institution was a consolidation of efforts the Navy already used to educate its midshipmen. Still, the new structure, discussed in detail in chapter 2, was influenced by that of the Military Academy at West Point as the Navy brought forward plans for greater structure for officer education and development.

Chapter 2 shows that during the school era, students were older and had prior sea experience, but beginning in 1849 and into 1850 and 1851, the Naval School was reorganized. Under internal pressure from the Navy Examining Board, the Navy Board, and those who saw the success of the Army during the Mexican-American War, the Navy concluded that change was needed to educate its officers in truly a more professional manner. Annapolis supporters contended that the Navy's needs would be better served if new officers were taken directly from civilian schools while still youths and first educated at a naval academy similar to cadets at West Point before being sent to sea. This meant that only when the Navy educated a young man, often just in his early teens, on shore, did the Navy send them to sea to gain practical experience. All the while, the Navy assessed their suitability as officers and expunged those found deficient professionally in skill or character. To those ends, chapter 3, combined with statistical analysis, reveals the backgrounds of the academy-era students and how they were educated.

The program of studies and student supervision illustrates that the Navy considered it paramount to instill the organization's values into its young officer recruits, while realizing that they were learning the skills and ethos required of a professional officer. Nevertheless, the academy weeded out those who were unsuitable to the

Navy's needs. This was particularly shown in how the students were treated under school and academy discipline, the subject of chapters 4 and 5. Naval authorities believed in gradually introducing young students to the rigors of naval law and tried to reason with them as they taught them the expectations of their career. In turn, the school-era students were generally older and, contrary to myth, statistical analysis will show that they were generally well behaved. Meanwhile, during the academy era, students were much younger, often in their early teens, and academy officials concluded they should be given some leeway for simply acting as mere "boys." The institution often gave them warnings when in the real naval world they would have been severely punished. But in the end, the Navy still used discipline to teach the young recruits professional expectations. Ultimately, those who failed to meet them suffered a court martial.

The most remarkable change in naval officer education, to be discussed in chapter 6, was the establishment of summer cruises and the institution of school ships tied alongside the academy. Where new midshipmen were once educated on the job at sea, academy midshipmen were sent to sea under the supervision of academy officials. Here they were introduced to practical seamanship, navigation, and other skills to serve them in their future careers. On these cruises they also visited foreign ports and experienced a naval life all in the safe confines of their ship without the danger of active duty. Clearly the Navy no longer saw its young midshipmen as simply miniature officers, but also as recruits who first needed guidance and a clear introduction into naval life. Unfortunately, the Civil War interrupted this education and left Southern students to choose between upholding professional expectations and remaining in the Navy, or resigning and "going South." Meanwhile, the conclusion shows that many students failed to graduate, and many others spent little time in the Navy after graduation, moving on to other careers. But those who remained were the professional officers, like George Dewey, Alfred Thayer Mahan, and others, who contributed to the Navy's exploits and development after the Civil War.[14] As James Calvert concludes, professionalism and academic need were pivotal in the Naval Academy's creation in 1845. Still, the institution's history was cyclical as it coped with the intertwined nature of congressional support, the Navy's duties, evolution, and periods of "high professionalism and productivity at the Academy."[15]

A SOCIETY *of*
Gentlemen

CHAPTER 1

The Foundation of a System

During the nineteenth century, Americans started to place greater emphasis on formal education for a professional career.[1] Engineering, for example, moved from shop training, apprenticeship style, to sustained education in universities like Yale and Rensselaer Polytechnic.[2] Meanwhile, the Naval Academy, established in 1845, was where young men went to become naval officers. However, change in American naval officer education was gradual. Those who advocated a centralized naval school faced a conservative officer corps that believed in tradition and a nation wary of powerful federal institutions. Consequently, before Annapolis, midshipmen attended several tenuous shore schools at naval yards, or on ships attached to the yards, and were educated at sea. Secretaries of the Navy, and some members of Congress, advocated more-structured naval education, but disagreements over its nature stalled change. Therefore, when he became secretary of the Navy in 1845, George Bancroft reorganized the system by using existing resources to show Congress that a new school at Annapolis worked. The idea built on existing trends, with support from naval officers who backed a formal way to educate naval officers for the growing needs of the country.

The duties and training of naval officers had a long tradition in the Atlantic world. As captains, officers commanded warships in accordance with government's instructions, while other officers ensured efficient vessel operations. The modern naval officer profession originated in Europe as states monopolized sea power, expanded their navies, and competed with each other. Before the development of a standing national navy, the British monarch, for example, called on private maritime resources, if needed. The monarch's officers gave the vessel's master a heading but played no part in the ship's operations: military and maritime operations were separate, and the relationship was temporary. While sufficient for hand-to-hand fighting and boarding the enemy's ships, where land tactics were essentially transferred to sea, the command structure was problematic as ship battles involving guns emerged. On a practical level, a naval officer, with both military and seamanship skills, was born to coordinate effectively ship movement, gunfire, naval tactics, and strategy.[3]

Historically, as with army officers, European governments generally preferred naval officers who were from and loyal to their own class, often the nobility and upper class—from the elite. Norbert Elias contends that officers were gentlemen, and, at minimum, it was unseemly for them to have "done manual work at any time during" life.[4] Elias asserts that the conflict in Britain between the upper and lower classes gave rise to "a new kind of officer corps," with professional status that allowed middle- and upper-class Britons to embark on a seafaring career, in command of others, without the working-class stigma of a seafaring job associated with manual labor.[5] The problem for many governments was developing methods to control who were officers, while fusing together the qualities of a gentleman and an expert seafarer.[6]

When England created its own state-sponsored navy, several methods emerged for becoming an officer. Established officers took young boys as servants, as apprentices at sea, to learn the officer's ways, and someone could also become an officer by first serving as a rating and working their way up as a midshipman. After the Restoration, the Admiralty and Charles II, with the support of Samuel Pepys, secretary to the Admiralty and naval administrator, instituted reforms to cultivate better officers, allow the Admiralty more control over their numbers, and ensure their obedience and diligence to duty. Beginning in 1677, potential lieutenants spent three years at sea—one as a midshipman—and were examined to prove their navigation and seamanship skills.[7] By the eighteenth century, a potential lieutenant first spent six years at sea—at least two as a midshipman—presented journals and good conduct certificates from their commanding officers, and proved proficiency in practical navigation and theory. The reforms would also allow lower-class seafarers to become officers, but "the skills required in navigation and keeping journals excluded those without some formal education."[8]

The methods of officer selection meant a bias toward officers from the higher classes. By 1794 the Admiralty eliminated the servant-style of officer entry and established First-Class Volunteers, but it took until 1830 before they eradicated the ability of admirals and captains to recruit future officers.[9] Other European nations had similar patterns of officer selection. The Dutch navy had few requirements to become a naval officer at first, and the nobility dominated admiral-level ranks. On a practical level, Jaap R. Bruijn notes, anyone could become an officer, but the "higher classes" had a better opportunity.[10] The French naval officer corps was also largely aristocratic, and the *Code des armé navales* (1689) stipulated that commissions were solely for the nobility. French naval reform was impossible; when Commodore Charles Henri d'Estaing, for instance, made suggestions to bring greater professionalization to the service in 1763, other officers opposed it and any notions of egalitarianism.[11]

Beyond learning their profession at sea, the European tradition of naval officer education varied. As Anglo-Dutch rivalry led to larger navies and at-sea confrontations, the Dutch navy expanded and the requirements to become an officer evolved. By the 1650s, Dutch officers followed formal written instructions, and by the 1780s, all five Dutch admiralties forced officers to undergo examination before promotion. Regardless, the Netherlands only established a formal shore school for naval officers in the early nineteenth century.[12] Meanwhile, France established naval schools on shore in 1682 to educate officers in theory and practice, but the École Navale opened only in 1830.[13] Nearby, in 1701, the Royal Danish Navy required its officers to graduate from the Royal Danish Naval Academy, which provided theoretical education in mathematics, writing, navigation, geography, and languages. By the 1740s, cadets also took summer cruises, where authorities tested their skills, and in 1763 the Danish introduced officer promotion exams. Jacob Seerup opines that the Danes equated the creation of a naval academy with a professional navy, composed of Dano-Norwegian citizens rather than foreigners, and the facility was important in bonding citizenship, the profession, and the state.[14]

In Britain officer education was confined largely to sea, learning on the job with the assistance of shipboard schoolmasters.[15] The Admiralty still wanted officers from the upper classes and thought that shore-based training would help control officer corps composition. In 1733 the Royal Naval Academy at Portsmouth opened and limited enrollment to students aged thirteen to sixteen, of a noble background, in an attempt to recruit a good class of boys. The navy allowed the Portsmouth students three years to prepare for their examinations and complete their studies. By 1806 the program consisted of fortification, gunnery, physics, naval history, and astronomy education, but it failed to attract many upper-class sons of noblemen and gentlemen, who continued to obtain their naval appointments under the patronage scheme.[16] The navy closed the Portsmouth academy in 1837. A new shore-based officer education program waited for later in the century, and until then naval instructors taught new officer recruits at sea.

In 1839 the Admiralty instituted more promotion examinations and in 1857 ordered all officer recruits first to a training vessel, regardless of their initial method of appointment.[17] In the end, the British Admiralty had to overcome the centuries-old patterns of naval appointments and patronage. European nations had a tradition of selecting their naval officers for the specific needs of the profession according to the desires of the government that owned the navy, but once ensconced, change was difficult as organizational inertia and the desires of existing officers emerged.

European naval officers had a "gentleman's" temperament and social origins, and American naval tradition is rooted in European antecedents. When Congress authorized a naval force to protect U.S. shipping from the Barbary corsairs in 1794, it assumed the navy was "temporary" and authorized the president to appoint officers, subject to the Senate's confirmation. As the Navy became permanent, members of Congress petitioned the president to obtain midshipmen's appointments, although the secretary of the Navy handled the process on a practical level. The Navy only examined midshipmen candidates to see if they were literate and could do basic mathematics. After seven years service, with two to three years spent at sea, and if a midshipman was eighteen or twenty years old—depending on the regulations at the time—an idiosyncratic board of two captains, a commodore, and a naval teacher examined the midshipman in seamanship, navigation, and morals before promotion to lieutenant—or passed midshipman if no lieutenant's commission was available. After 1841 passed midshipmen underwent reexamination if, after three years, they had not been promoted and had not been to sea for two years. If they failed, they lost seniority and another failure meant dismissal.

Once appointed, officers saw their commissions and promotion by seniority as a right. But for the Navy Department, efficiency meant having the correct officers in the proper location at the right time, in a system where officers joined decades earlier and the special responsibilities of the service meant that the Navy was unable to "hire its top executives from [the] outside."[18] For the U.S. Navy, a good start for a new officer was important for the future of the service.

John Paul Jones was one of the first Americans to consider formal naval officer education. He believed officers should be taught the theory and practice of officership, for efficiency and culture, and that only "gentlemen" should obtain commissions. In linking the concepts, Jones declared that commanding officers should be able to put their ideas to paper in a manner suited to their role. John Locke, who wrote on the education of gentlemen, likely influenced Jones' thinking, because the latter encountered Locke's work while moving among an educated circle.[19] A naval education was to instill certain values. Officers were to be merciful, empathic, and humble: heroes like Oliver Hazard Perry rather than embroiled in personal scandal like Britain's Horatio Nelson and his infidelity.[20] Their behavior, according to Secretary of the Navy Robert Smith, had to be free of self-destructiveness and vice. The officer had to be clean, neat, and friendly with his fellow officers, a philosophy that would be echoed at Annapolis.[21] Moreover, each frigate-class vessel needed a little academy for training, and President John Adams agreed that there should be a school on every frigate of the U.S. Navy. When in port, seamen would be required to attend shore academies to learn more about science and art needed for character formation.[22] Henry L. Burr concluded that "naval education of the period, then, was socially realistic in preparing for a practical career, disciplinary in inculcating the military virtues, and idealistic in being a means to an end."[23]

Samuel P. Huntington concluded that the professional officer had a duty to society, was more than a wage laborer, and extolled expertise, responsibility, and "corporateness"—in naval terms, the Band of Brothers' philosophy.[24] As tradition dictated, the American officer's first introduction to sea life was on the ocean, where he learned the officer's role while on the job. In their sea duties, midshipmen did everything from commanding to being personal servants. At times, if needed, they were promoted to acting lieutenant, master, or sailing master, and experienced midshipmen were made officers of the deck. The youngest might be responsible for giving the captain his pistols and belt when the crew was called to quarters. Older midshipmen were posted about the ship to provide general supervision. They ensured that the lieutenant's orders were followed, helped the officer of the deck, mustered the men on deck at night, and kept them awake. Other midshipmen manned the guns, or the tops, and experienced lads were sent to the foretop. Finally, while ashore, midshipmen worked in the Navy Department and with the secretary of the Navy and others were clerks. More often than not, older officers acted like parental figures.[25]

Key to the professional socialization of young men into the early U.S. Navy were role models. When Midshipman Lynch arrived on his first ship, for example, an older midshipman showed him the ropes. In another case, Captain Bolton found Farragut asleep on deck and he put a pea jacket over him rather than discipline the future hero.[26] But it was generally accepted that small gunboats were an inappropriate place to train young men. The commanders of the smaller vessels were usually sailing masters or older midshipmen and were unsuitable role models for young midshipmen because they were too close to their crews; real officers, in the British tradition, were a class of their own. The small gunboats also stayed close to shore, and their small crew complement and small number of officers—usually one or two—were insufficient to instruct the new midshipmen in how to work as a team, or learn shared values and attitudes through a common routine. The gunboat failed to instill, it was thought, the proper sense of "corporateness" into the new midshipmen.[27]

While new midshipmen were looked out for, they were still sent to sea at a tender age, were exposed to the rigors of naval life with a minimal transition period, and were expected to fit in with the crew. Stephen Bleecker Luce, eventually one of the nineteenth century's most famous advocates of naval education, was born in Albany, New York, on 25 March 1827. On 4 November 1841, Luce was ordered to report to the receiving ship *North Carolina* at New York after obtaining a midshipman's appointment. Luce wrote that "to be suddenly cut adrift from one's mother's apron strings and landed on the deck of such a ship was . . . a tremendous change" at fourteen. First, he reported to the commodore, then to the captain, then to the first lieutenant, and finally to the officer of the deck. His name was put in the ship's log, and the midshipman of the watch escorted him down a maze of ladders to the gun room, then deeper "where it was so dark that I had to grope my way along, and was in constant fear of falling through into some nameless abyss." His escort, his own age, had been on board for about four weeks and showed Luce his locker and where his hammock was to be hung.[28] Luce wrote that "I was appalled at first by the very idea of living in such a dreadful place, but my eyes adapted themselves in a little while to the darkness, and as the humorous remarks and cheerful voice of my companion reassured me, I soon began to think it might be possible to become reconciled to such life if others could."[29]

Luce's education began immediately. He learned the ropes, how the sails were set, and other practical information. The most important was his sense of initiation into the world. The "captain of the top," Luce described, looked like he had a good, solid, English education, but he had unique characteristics. He sported gold earrings and a tattoo of *Constitution* on his chest. He told the young midshipmen that they all must have a tattoo of an American national emblem on their arms, and the initiates went through this tattoo ritual, their only solace a ration of grog. Moreover, the receiving ship was the site of hazing. The new arrivals would band together to stave off hazing from the older midshipmen, then haze new arrivals themselves. Luce wrote, "the gun-room was the mess-room of the passed midshipmen, the youngsters being admitted on sufferance. The passed midshipmen we regarded as belonging to a superior order of beings."[30] Luce spent six months on *North Carolina* and concluded that the experience "added a chivalric sense of honor . . . [we] were [all] being educated all the while, silently, unobtrusively and in a manner according to each individual character effectively. Two educational processes were in continual operation—absorption and habituation."[31] A chronicler later wrote that Luce's journals of this period "are filled with notes and neat pen and ink sketches relating to damages to spars and rigging; how to avoid accidents, what to do in cases of emergency, and how to effect repairs, all of which were later embodied in his great work on practical seamanship." The young midshipmen were learning at sea.[32]

The Navy spawned other great leaders whose backgrounds provided an example of the best qualities of a future officer. John A. Dahlgren, for instance, was of Swedish ancestry; his father Bernhard was an immigrant to Philadelphia who supported Thomas Jefferson and made connections with the city's elite as a small businessman. John, Bernhard's eldest and future U.S. naval ordnance expert, was born in 1809. John attended Rand's Writing Academy, while Quakers instilled scientific and linguistic knowledge in the boy. Topics ranged from mathematics to Latin, Greek, moral philosophy, geography, and navigation. John was studious, and his teachers marveled at his character and conduct. However, the death of his father in 1824 disrupted John's life and left the family's finances in chaos. In response, John joined the Navy and became an officer.[33] Dahlgren was an ideal potential naval officer, and, as will be discussed, his education was similar to the training that the Navy sought to implement at Annapolis.

Tales of the heroic exploits of men like Oliver Hazard Perry, the Philadelphia dockside, and a youthful encounter with a young Midshipman Samuel Francis DuPont—whose father was a business acquaintance of Bernhard—inspired Dahlgren. Bernhard's careful cultivation of social connections brought returns, and influential city residents, including forty-seven members of the Pennsylvania General Assembly, wrote letters and signed petitions to the secretary of the Navy to obtain John an officer's appointment. But the secretary initially rejected the request because the area had its quota of appointments. Undeterred, John went to sea as a merchantman and finally obtained his naval appointment in 1826. Robert J. Schneller Jr. concludes that a "naval career offered him [Dahlgren] a chance to recoup or perhaps transcend the status and security he had lost when his father died."[34]

Dahlgren made few comments on daily ship life, but he visited ports populated by American merchants, who he felt made money in their new abodes but lacked the social graces of the upper-class society he grew up with in Philadelphia. Dahlgren also resented fellow midshipmen who had obtained their appointments just because of their connections, but who lacked the education he felt they needed to be gentlemen officers. Illness plagued Dahlgren's career, but it allowed him to return home in 1831 and attend the Norfolk Naval School, discussed below, where he studied for his passed midshipman's examination. From 1819, the test covered mathematics, gunnery, seamanship, and navigation, and Dahlgren placed ninth out of thirty-one examinees in 1832. Dahlgren next served with the U.S. Coast Survey, as "close as the navy came to providing graduate education in science" and by 1847 agreed to teach gunnery at Annapolis but declined a permanent appointment as head of the department. Instead, his reputation grew at the Bureau of Ordnance and Hydrography, as inventor of the Dahlgren gun and Civil War leader. Andrew Hull Foote, fellow officer and naval reform advocate, believed that Dahlgren's scientific mind and character was an "example for 'young men just at the turning point of character'" and attending Annapolis.[35]

Although new midshipmen were educated at sea, there was a rudimentary shore-based system meant for young officers, like Dahlgren, preparing for promotion examination. Secretary of the Navy Robert Smith was an early advocate of shore-based naval education. In 1802 he ordered Chaplain Robert Thompson to the Washington Navy Yard to educate midshipmen in navigation and mathematics. Smith felt that the little shore academy was an important step in better naval education. He required Thompson to send regular reports on the progress of the midshipmen to the yard's commandant, John Cassin, who forwarded them to the secretary. Meanwhile, imprisoned sailors from *Philadelphia* opened one oddly placed naval shore school in 1803 in Tripoli after the loss of their vessel. The Danish consul supplied books, and some of the officers studied mathematics, history, and French. However, education at the Washington Navy Yard was interrupted from 1804 to mid-1806, when Commodore Samuel Barron's squadron was ordered to the Mediterranean along with all the midshipmen. Smith tried to get congressional recognition for the Washington Yard academy by getting Congress to change Thompson's title from chaplain to naval mathematician. Congress killed the proposal, thinking that Smith was attempting to create a new office, but Smith instructed Thompson to continue his instructions. The yard's academy eventually offered a four-month program of study for a wide age range of pupils, with short bursts of intense study interwoven with periods of work. Thompson died in 1810 and was replaced by Andrew Hunter.[36]

The persistence of Secretary of the Navy Paul Hamilton attracted Hunter to the post. A graduate of the College of New Jersey in 1772, he had been an army chaplain and later a Presbyterian minister. Hunter ran two academies in New Jersey and in 1804 was appointed chair of mathematics and astronomy at his alma mater. After discussing the offer with friends and family, Hunter, now in his sixties, accepted the naval appointment and continued the program's astronomy and mathematics instruction with a slant toward naval operations. About one hundred midshipmen completed the program during Hunter's tenure, spending approximately sixty-five days at the school. Approximately two-thirds attended just three to eighteen weeks, and 40 percent stayed for less than five weeks, but they already had a mathematics and astronomy background and attended to test their competency. Secretary William Jones closed the academy in 1813 as he purged the Navy of Hamilton's appointments. Later, Commodore Isaac Chauncey and Chaplain Cheever Felch opened a mathematical school at Sackets Harbor, New York, in the 1814–15 period, during the War of 1812, for officers stranded at Lake Ontario during winter ice. But, with peace, the school closed in 1815.[37]

Naval schools were subject to the ebb and flow of the prerogatives of secretaries of the Navy and supportive officers. Perhaps inspired by the Tripoli Naval School, opened during his fight with the Barbary corsairs, Commodore William Bainbridge, on *Independence*, opened a naval school at the Boston Naval Yard on 10 December 1815. The school, which remained operational until 1845, ran classes daily from 9:00 AM to 1:00 PM, except for Sundays. Pupils studied Nathaniel

Bowditch's *Navigation*, took daily latitude and longitude observations, and learned Spanish, French, advanced mathematics, and science. Finally, they studied tactics, naval battles, steam engines, and maritime and national law and were encouraged to observe the ships under repair or construction at the yard. The scattered naval schools were ad hoc, and their organization and rigor varied considerably. One new school that opened in New York sometime between 1821 and 1825 had relaxed discipline, and when the midshipmen had free time, they often jumped the yard walls and headed into town. Still, they learned Spanish, French, and mathematics, and the Navy required them to attend church on Sundays.[38]

The Norfolk Naval School, where Dahlgren studied, first opened on *Guerrière* in 1821, replaced by *Java* in 1833, and probably remained open until 1845. The school taught mathematics and some languages but originally just history, geography, naval tactics, and laws. It was like the other shore schools for students that officers felt had the right characteristics for their profession, if they were monitored. Captain Arthur Sinclair, the commander at Norfolk, speaking of lads like Dahlgren, believed they had "the character of gentlemen—have generally been bred as such—and as such you know how to treat them—I must, however, observe that the more a Student absent himself from study, the greater inclination he feels to continue" absenting himself. Consequently, Sinclair asserted that the students should remain active on shore to avoid attracting negative commentary from the local population, although the pupils often roughhoused aboard ship and about the nearby forest.[39]

Benjamin Sands was another midshipman who attended the Naval School at Norfolk. Like other midshipmen of this era, Sands also spent time at sea before attending Norfolk. Sands, from Baltimore, grew up in Louisville, Kentucky. His brothers entered the business world, and "it became a question as to my future career." Sands later explained that the medical and legal professionals were expensive. Instead, he went to live with his uncle, Major Joseph H. Hook, in Washington, where the Sands family also had political connections. Consequently, by 1828 Secretary of the Navy Samuel L. Southard appointed Sands a midshipman, and he reported to the New York Naval Yard to learn "the rudiments of navigation." But Sands explained that "there was no schoolhouse, so our class, with another of older midshipmen, preparing for their final examination for promotion, was located in the loft of one of the ship houses." Moreover, the midshipmen were housed in scattered locations "amongst the boarding-houses near the Navy Yard gate in Brooklyn." Sands, for instance, lived on Sands Street, and then on York Street. Soon thereafter, the Navy sent young Sands to sea. He had hardly received quality education in New York; he noted that once aboard ship he climbed aloft and "thought I never should be able to learn the uses of the numberless ropes around me when I was informed that each had its appropriate name and use, known to those who were initiated."[40]

Sands spent about five years at sea before receiving any further formal officer education at Norfolk in 1833. His objective in applying to the naval school was to help prepare for his examination in navigation, nautical astronomy, and mathematics. His experience at Norfolk reveals the rudimentary nature of officer education before Annapolis. At Norfolk, the Navy housed and educated Sands and the other midshipmen on *Java*, and it was an informal setting. The onus was also on the midshipmen to attend to their studies. Sands contended that "with all of our fun and mischief, which we carried on at proper hours, we were reasonably assiduous and did well for youngsters who had only their own sense of propriety to spur them on in their studies." Norfolk was a Navy town, and Sands exclaimed that when not studying, the midshipmen romanced the young ladies of the community. Nevertheless, by June 1834 a "board of gray heads" assembled in "a parlor of Barnum's Hotel in Baltimore" to examine the young men from the Norfolk and New York schools. Sands declared that "it was a trying ordeal to most of us who had endeavored to make good use of our time, and who were devoted to the Navy as a profession." Sands succeeded, and was declared a passed midshipman on 14 June 1834.[41]

The Philadelphia Asylum Naval School was the most influential naval shore school before Annapolis was established, and administrators at Philadelphia supported a sustained effort to educate young officers. The Naval Asylum School was founded in 1839 and originally taught eleven midshipmen mathematics during an eight-month academic year. At Philadelphia, midshipmen were allowed outside the asylum until sunset, or at night with special permission, such as on Sundays. They could also go to evening parties in the city, but were not allowed into Philadelphia often and lights out was at 9:00 PM. The Navy also required the school's administration to submit monthly progress reports on each student as they developed toward professional naval officers. Finally, the Philadelphia school was the only one devoted to a finishing course for officers; the others offered both introductory and finishing programs. The establishment of a finishing course appears to have occurred sometime in the 1820s, when the midshipmen began to request extra time to study before their promotion examinations.[42] The Philadelphia school was an unintentional prototype for Annapolis, and many former instructors at Philadelphia later taught at Annapolis.

The last two years of the Philadelphia school were a mixture of success and failure. In 1843–44, Professor William Chauvenet, by then the school's head, planned to institute a two-year program of study, but Secretary John Y. Mason canceled it. The Navy instead wanted the midshipmen freed for duty. Chauvenet attempted to provide more teachers, and in the last year of the school, Henry Lockwood joined and one Mr. Belcher arrived to teach maritime law. Lieutenant James H. Ward taught gunnery, and Passed Midshipman Samuel Marcy taught navigation. Chauvenet, Ward, and Marcy would go on to teach at the Naval School at Annapolis when it opened in 1845. But despite Chauvenet's efforts, a report to Secretary Mason on 16 February 1845 indicated that one midshipman had committed suicide and another had gone insane. On 25 February 1845, another midshipman was reported missing and only returned on 3 April 1845.[43] The old system, spread over several facilities, was faltering, and calls for a new naval school grew in the early 1840s as the use of steam power developed in the Navy, and the *Somers* mutiny focused attention on how young officer recruits were introduced to life at sea.

Shore naval training could provide important technological skills for officers so inclined, and many, like Lieutenant James H. Ward, saw steam technology as an important subject that officers should grasp. The Navy's first steam vessel, *Fulton*, was built in 1814, and another *Fulton* began construction in 1836. The late 1830s and the 1840s saw a U.S. Navy steam warship construction boom. Four ships began construction in the late 1830s, another ten in the 1840s, and thirty-four were laid down in the 1850s. The U.S. Navy experimented with several steam configurations—paddle or screw-driven vessels—before settling on screw-driven vessels. In 1839, for example, construction began on *Mississippi* and *Missouri*, both side-wheel, bark-rigged frigates. Another steam warship was *Allegheny*, designed by Lieutenant William W. Hunter, laid down starting in 1844 and launched in 1847. *Allegheny's* horizontal wheels were eventually replaced with a screw propeller, while *Princeton* began life at the Philadelphia Naval Yard in 1842 and was the first warship built exclusively with a screw propeller. By 1845 the secretary of the Navy warned not to experiment with "doubtful novelties," and warship designs settled largely on screw propellers before the Civil War. Still, William H. Thiesen concludes that U.S. naval advancement stagnated after the Civil War, only to reemerge rejuvenated in the 1870s and 1880s with a cadre of formally educated naval engineers who brought a more scientific approach to ship design and construction.[44]

In his annual report for 1841, Secretary of the Navy Abel P. Upshur discussed the establishment of naval schools. He concluded that, with the increased use of steam power, officers needed more scientific training. Upshur concluded that "this important object can be best attained by the establishment of naval schools, provided with all necessary means of uniting practice with theory." Upshur recommended mathematics professors be given a rank so that they would not have to mess and live with their students, because "this close and constant association is well calculated to weaken the respect and influence which their relation to the young officers ought to inspire, and which is absolutely necessary to give due effect to their instructions." Upshur asserted that "the advantages which the army has derived from the Academy at West Point afford a sufficient proof that a similar institution for the navy would produce like results."[45]

Despite calls for better officer education, congressional debates centered on the best age for midshipmen and whether shore naval education was practical for the service and the nation. Secretary of War James McHenry proposed a military academy in 1800 that would also include a naval school, but instead Congress only authorized the establishment of the Army's West Point in 1802. Opponents of a naval academy asserted that history was replete with heroes who succeeded without classroom naval education. Others felt that academy training would create "effeminate leaders" or become the domain of the elite. Moreover, anti-Federalists asserted that military and naval academies were just another way the national government would use to strengthen its power.[46] By the 1840s, as American politics fractured further, it was also Whig versus Democrat and it led nowhere.[47]

On 8 August 1842, a Senate debate about the establishment of five new, permanent, naval schools is revealing. Those arguing for the establishment of the schools, Whigs, had little to say, but those against, the Democrats, felt they were too expensive, would give too much power to the secretary of the Navy, and would educate just the rich. Still, advocates believed that on-shore training would produce professional officers more useful to their client, the state. Virginia Whig senator William Segar Archer told his colleagues that these schools would not cost the government much and would benefit the Navy. To bolster his argument, Archer reported that young men could already become midshipmen at fourteen and asked the senators, "how far can he be qualified to make an able officer at that age?" He believed that an efficient naval officer had to be trained in more things than simply running a ship: "Very often the highest questions of diplomacy are necessarily referred to the officers of the navy." It was shameful, in his view, that the government had failed to provide the best possible measures to ensure the adequate training of these young men for their duties.[48] The nation, embarking on the world stage, needed professional officers skilled in the needs of their nation and who could be trusted to act far from home.

The main opponents of the naval schools were Democratic senators Reuel Williams, Maine; William Allen, Ohio; Perry Smith, Connecticut; and James Buchanan, Pennsylvania. Williams, ignorant of the existing naval schools, believed that they would be too expensive if more than one were opened. Meanwhile, Allen believed that naval schools would become like West Point, which he felt had deteriorated into an institution of political patronage and education at public expense. Allen believed that if the naval schools were established, they should be for the benefit of "sons of poor widows, or of officers who have fallen in the service of their country." But Allen felt that once the young men had received their naval education, they would enter law, or some other profession, and not serve their country in return for their free education. He felt that the present system was sufficient and reminded his colleagues that young men entered the Navy at thirteen or fourteen and then traveled the world and that this gave them all the knowledge they needed. He did not understand how putting young midshipmen in "cloisters" or a "college cell" would teach them how to manage a ship in a storm. Allen told his colleagues, "send him to sea, and there let him learn how to control the elements."[49]

In a later heartfelt speech, Senator Allen declared that the naval schools would not be for the poor or helpless, or the "obscure" and "powerless citizens" of America. Nor would they be for the poor orphan child. Allen declared, "no, sir, all experience is against such a belief. The sons of the great, the powerful, the wealthy men of the nation—they who can speak with authority and effect to the appointing power—their sons will, with few, if any exceptions, be the chosen objects of this national gratuity."[50] Allen then questioned the practical education that was taught at West Point. He declared that the taxpayers of the nation were unaware that they were funding a "dancing school." Allen read to the Senate a letter he received from a West Point cadet:

> We rise in the morning at a quarter before 5 o'clock; at a quarter past 5 o'clock we police; at half past 5 until half-past 6 o'clock, infantry drill; from half past 6 o'clock till 7, recreation, or cleaning arms; from 7 to 8, breakfast; from 8 to half-past 8, dress parade and guard mounting; from half past 8 until 9, recreation, from 9 to 10, artillery drill; from 10 to 1, recreation; from 1 to 2, dinner; from 2 to 4, *dancing lessons* [emphasis in original]; from 4 to half past 4, recreation from half past 4 until 5, police; from 5 till 20 minutes past 6, infantry drill; from 20 minutes past 6 till 7, dress parade; from 7 till 9, supper; from 8 till half past 9, recreation; from half past 9 till a quarter of 10, prepare for bed; at a quarter of 10, signal for extinguishing lights.[51]

Allen was aghast that these men were taught to dance for two hours. He told the Senate that West Point ought to be a place "where men are to be taught to fight."[52]

Senator Buchanan, ironically formerly a Federalist, was concerned about the power that would be transferred to the Navy Department. The Navy would now be solely responsible for running these facilities originally constructed as forts for the Army to defend the people. Buchanan questioned the costs and believed the estimate of $400 to renovate each of five forts under consideration was unrealistic, as was spending $1,000 to purchase a steam engine, to be placed on shore, which would cost $5,000 to operate. Buchanan concluded: "Get these fortifications into the power of the Secretary of the Navy, and, ere long, there will be a magnificent establishment, and the Secretary soon clothed with the power to send whom he pleases to these schools, to be educated by the Government."[53] It would just be a system of patronage.

Finally, Senator Levi Woodbury, New Hampshire Democrat and former secretary of the Navy under President Andrew Jackson, pledged his affinity with the old style of educating midshipmen. He thought naval education should concentrate on practical matters. He told the Senate that the deck of a vessel was the best training ground for the sailor. It was optimal to send him to sea to prove his worth first, then, if he was fit, continue his training on shore when he happened to be there. Woodbury opined that "it was no more proper to send the army officer or the cadet at West Point to sea, than to keep the naval officer much on shore, and attach him strongly to shore pursuits. The most abhorrent idea to a genuine tar is a land-lubber." Despite opposition to funding naval schools, a bill passed the Senate twenty-two to five and was received by the House on 13 August 1842, but appears to have died in committee.[54]

Beyond politics, Craig L. Symonds concludes that by the 1840s mothers of young midshipmen soon worried about sending their children into a "life of debauchery" in the Navy. He found that one publication, the *Southern Literary Messenger*, in 1842, believed a naval academy was gravely needed. Undoubtedly, the *Somers* mutiny—in which a young midshipman, Philip Spencer, son of the secretary of War, was executed—pressured the government to consider a safer way to indoctrinate new young officers into the demands of their profession. While ostensibly on a training cruise from September to December 1842, Captain Alexander Slidell Mackenzie heard reports that Midshipman Spencer, along with other crew members, was planning to seize *Somers* and turn to piracy. With little evidence, Mackenzie ordered Spencer and two others—a seaman and a boatswain's mate—in shackles and soon determined to execute the cabal, fearful that the rest of the now-agitated crew would rebel. The three protested their innocence but were hung nonetheless. When the vessel returned home, newspapers soon reported the executions, and New York's elite were stunned. Frances Seward, wife of future Secretary of State William Henry Seward, then governor of New York, exclaimed that "the men all seem to think it just right to hang a boy of 19 without an hour for preparation, and some of the women too." Mackenzie suffered a court of inquiry and then a court martial over his handling of events, but both cleared him. Still, Captain Charles Stewart, head of the court of inquiry, recommended that a naval academy train midshipmen to prevent a similar incident in the future.[55]

By December 1842, as the *Somers* mutiny stunned the nation, the secretary of the Navy renewed calls to improve naval education. Although not mentioning the mutiny directly, Upshur believed that the Navy exhibited as many abuses as in any other society; those on shore simply failed to attract the same public attention. Upshur believed that reform must first begin with the midshipmen. He told his audience that "after a time, these boys become men, and these midshipmen become lieutenants, and commanders, and captains." Consequently, he believed that only those young people who were qualified should be appointed. Instead, he wrote, "it is a notorious fact, that wayward and incorrigible boys, whom even parental authority cannot control, are often sent to the navy, as a mere school of discipline, or to save them from the reproach to which their conduct exposes them on shore." He hoped permanent shore schools would remedy the problem. To those ends, Upshur proposed that admission to a naval school would be regulated like at West Point and "no boy shall receive an acting appointment in the navy, until he shall have passed a certain period of diligent study at a naval school" or received the proper certification.[56]

Upshur also believed that the modern U.S. naval officer had important duties abroad and were most often the only representatives of the United States in a foreign land. The West Point cadet, he explained, was "well-founded in the principles of solid and useful learning, and fully prepared to engage with advantage in any pursuit, whether of civil or military life," but the naval candidate was simply asked if he could read and write. Given the important duties of naval officers, Upshur believed the government had a responsibility to elevate their character and equip them for their careers. He explained that "this can be best done by giving him a suitable preparatory education, and by providing proper and ready means of removing him from the ranks of his profession, whenever he may be found unworthy to occupy a place."[57] Yet despite the demands of naval advocates for a more professional way to select and train future officers, Congress made little headway in the 1840s, and the 1844 election cycle interrupted further developments until the new secretary of the Navy, George Bancroft, with a bold mentality, achieved progress.

George Bancroft was born into the family of a New England minister, Aaron Bancroft, on 3 October 1800. Bancroft graduated from Harvard and obtained a Ph.D. at Georgia Augusta University of Göttingen. Later he and some colleagues founded a school for boys between nine and twelve years old, at Round Hill, Connecticut, in 1823. Their plan was to enroll wealthy lads to prepare them to enter Harvard or Yale. The school was a limited success, but Bancroft grew tired of looking after the pupils and moved on to marry Sarah Dwight, to help with her family's business, and to begin writing his multivolume *History of the United States*.

Figure 1. George Bancroft. *(George Bancroft, LC-BH82-5157, Brady-Handy Photograph Collection, Library of Congress Prints and Photographs Division, Portrait Photographs 1850–70)*

In the end, the only political office he held before becoming secretary of the Navy was running the customs house in Boston until he resigned on 8 March 1841. All the while, Lilian Handlin concludes that Bancroft supported reform "without violent upheaval."[58]

Bancroft became secretary of the Navy under President James K. Polk in March 1845, soon learned of the previous attempts to create a naval school, and realized that he had to prove any new system to Congress using existing funds.[59] He met with Professor William Chauvenet of the Philadelphia Naval Asylum School and decided to circumvent Congress. The Navy's budget for 1845 included $28,272 allotted for "Instruction"; Bancroft took this, and Fort Severn in Annapolis, which the Army had abandoned, to create a centralized location for officer education.[60] Based on the good aspects of the previous shore-based system, the new school would ensure that when midshipmen were ashore, they were occupied in the "study of mathematics, nautical astronomy, theory of morals, international law, gunnery, use of steam, the Spanish and French languages," and any other task required of a naval officer. Bancroft felt that the new system would be a better, more rigorous affair than that which currently left midshipmen on shore to their own devices.[61]

Undoubtedly, Bancroft drew on his previous experiences with schools, but he also turned to West Point for inspiration. James L. Morrison concludes that the Military Academy at West Point reflected the attitudes and "socioeconomic composition" of the commercial and mercantile sector of America. He believed that key to understanding West Point graduates was an understanding of their experiences at the school and the "forces at work on their minds and personalities in the years they were passing from adolescence to manhood" and being made into Army officers. West Point was founded in 1802, Major Jonathan Williams was its first superintendent, and the facility fell under the jurisdiction of the Army Corps of Engineers. Its first students studied surveying, mathematics, and fort construction. Joseph Swift succeeded Williams and remained the school's head until 1818. Under Swift's leadership, students were examined twice a year, a board of visitors was established to inspect the school, and a four-year program was introduced in 1816. Still, West Point found its students spent varying times at school and were often called into Army service.[62]

Sylvanus Thayer, West Point's next superintendent, left a lasting mark. Under his leadership, an academic board of school administrators was created that oversaw the school's curriculum. The Academic Board examined and ranked the students and suggested what branch of the Army best suited them. Thayer molded his reforms on the École Polytechnique in France and emphasized engineering, science, and mathematics. Many in the Army criticized West Point's emphasis on science because they felt it taught officers little about battlefield life. Boards of visitors

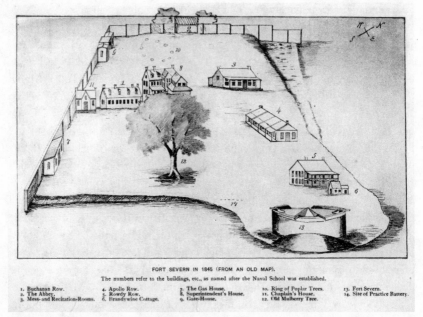

FORT SEVERN IN 1845 (FROM AN OLD MAP).
The numbers refer to the buildings, etc., as named after the Naval School was established.

1. Buchanan Row.   4. Apollo Row.   7. The Gas House.   10. Ring of Poplar Trees.   13. Fort Severn.
2. The Abbey.   5. Rowdy Row.   8. Superintendent's House.   11. Chaplain's House.   14. Site of Practice Battery.
3. Mess- and Recitation-Rooms.   6. Brandywine Cottage.   9. Gate-House.   12. Old Mulberry Tree.

Figure 2. Fort Severn, Annapolis. *(Fort Severn in 1845 [From an Old Map], Special Collections & Archives Department, Nimitz Library, U.S. Naval Academy, Annapolis, Maryland)*

were also critical of the overemphasis on engineering, but regardless, the school's curriculum remained virtually unchanged during the antebellum period. Beginning in the late 1830s, Joseph G. Totten was the chief of engineers and was West Point's inspector for a quarter century. Totten too wanted to broaden the school's focus and include ethics, geography, history, English, and law. Totten began making such recommendations in 1846, although it took him years to muster support for reforms to commence.[63]

In the interim, Thayer required professors to submit weekly reports and placed the students under strict discipline. The superintendent was ultimately responsible for discipline at West Point. He appointed an officer to investigate incidents, could convene a court martial, and could suspend or dismiss a student for serious offenses like drinking or obtaining the services of a prostitute. West Point also used a demerit point system whereby a student who obtained more than 200 points in a year could be expelled. Authorities issued different demerits for different infractions, depending on the severity of the offense. For example, mutinous conduct, a first-grade offense, was worth ten points, while tardiness for roll call, an eighth-grade offense, could be punished with one point. A student could also be suspended or put in a darkened barracks room for more severe offenses. Nevertheless, students could appeal demerits and had up to twenty-four hours to write an excuse. If accepted, the demerits were expunged, or they could stand if the administration rejected the excuse. As a last resort, if the student felt his punishment was unfair, he could appeal the decision to the secretary of war. In 1855 new discipline rules were instituted that accounted for a student's experience. Senior students were only permitted a maximum of 100 demerits within a six-month period, while first-year students were allowed 150 demerits. While secretaries of war intervened to varying degrees, Joel Poinsett, President Martin Van Buren's secretary of war, believed in the institution's autonomy and only overruled disciplinary actions after a full investigation.[64] It brought a level of professionalism to the Army in training, discipline, and governance.

Students reported to West Point in June and September and were assigned a room and an upperclassman as a mentor during for the first weeks. The new student was tutored for four hours a day on academic and military topics and examined for mental and physical attributes. Students also underwent hazing at the hands of older cadets. This often involved extra duties and jokes, but it also involved more "sadistic" practices that often verged on torture. Finally, during the summer, students, both old and new, encamped and learned military skills in the field under the auspices of the Department of Tactics. The junior classes enjoyed a furlough over their summer, while the senior class practiced captains' and lieutenants' duties. The sophomores took on the roles of noncommissioned officers, while the plebes, or new students, learned a private's life. By 30 August summer encampment and activities ended, the second, or junior class, returned, and the academic year began again. Finally, during summertime, parents could visit West Point, and the students attended dances on Saturday evenings and celebrated the Fourth of July.[65]

West Point regulations stated that students could only spend ten hours a day in academics, while the rest of the day was spent on military drill. In all, West Point instilled in young officers the skills needed for their future profession and weeded out those unsuited to the life. In practice, about 70 percent of classroom time was spent on practical aspects like engineering, chemistry, mathematics, and other fields. Dennis Hart Mahan, father of Alfred Thayer Mahan, future Naval Academy student and naval analyst, taught civil engineering and a nine-hour course on the science of war. But with a set proportion, modifying the curriculum was difficult, and it bred a degree of conservatism. Students were ranked by academic merit based on course scores, but the administration often treated students laxly, for many believed that there was no need to prevent a boy from becoming an Army officer just because he understood geology or chemistry poorly. Professor Robert W. Weir, who taught drawing from 1833 for over forty years, would pass a student even with bad drawing skills.[66]

The Army deemed practical drawing related to maps and engineering-related objects important. Chemistry, mineralogy, and geology courses were also useful if an officer needed to find things like water while surveying the Western frontier. But French, although taught, was weighted lower than mathematics or engineering for a student's final grade. Meanwhile, although West Point had a Department of Ethics that taught law, English, and rhetoric, they were "ornamental" courses and, with the set hours for academics, were dropped when time was needed for other topics. In all, the Academic Board, largely dominated by professors like Dennis Hart Mahan, set the institution's "intellectual tone," which focused on practical military matters. Still, there were accusations from within and outside West Point that the institution lacked an emphasis on military skills, with too much focus on science and engineering. The solution was a proposed fifth year. The new five-year program allowed additional courses on military law, geography, Spanish, and history in addition to those courses already offered. It took until 1854 for a large enough first-year class to arrive, and for a secretary of war to support the plan. Even then, Secretary of War John B. Floyd suspended it in 1858, under pressure from politicians and parents, only to overturn his decision in 1859. Congress then studied the program and recommended legislation to enshrine the five-year program, but the Civil War disrupted any further discussion.[67]

The foundation of the Naval School at Annapolis in 1845 owed much to the structure at West Point. An opportunity to obtain support from older members of the Navy for a new naval school occurred in June 1845 at the examinations at the Naval Asylum School. The members of the examining board included Isaac Mayo, E. A. F. Lavellette, Matthew Perry, Thomas Ap. C. Jones, and George C. Read. In addition to their regular duties, Secretary Bancroft also tasked the board to study moving naval officer education to Fort Severn, Annapolis. Bancroft phrased his desire for establishing a new naval school in such a way that it only left the board to argue over where it should be founded. Captain Isaac Mayo lived in Annapolis and favored it as the new school's location. Commodore Perry sided with his friend Mayo, but it took time to convince the other members. Commodore Jones wanted the facility established in Virginia, while other members thought some island in Chesapeake Bay would be suitable. After twelve days, the board members, some of the best known men in the Navy, sided with Mayo and Perry.[68]

The board recommended that appointments to the new school be made like those at West Point and the "rank" of naval cadet to be created. The facility was to be headed by a captain, while the students would be taught infantry tactics, English, French, law, steam engineering, chemistry, and geography. For practical seamanship, they felt that a frigate should be stationed at the school. Students would be required to stay at the school for two years, then be promoted to a full midshipman and sent to sea for three years before they would return for a year to study for their next promotion examination. The board recommended that the school follow West Point's class structure and entry requirements. Furthermore, the students were to be no older than fifteen and no younger than thirteen years old.[69] The students would be young so the Navy could train them early in a structured and consistent fashion before habits were instilled at sea.

Other Navy officials also reported their observations of West Point as that institution stood in the early 1840s and recommended the Navy adopt its structure. While those, like Senator Allen, decried West Point, Bancroft sent Passed Midshipman Samuel Marcy, son of the then-secretary of war, to study its training methods. Marcy reported that West Point was a fine institution and thought that the Navy would benefit from creating one along similar lines.[70] While he pointed out the training scheme at West Point as of 1845, he also emphasized the need to create a new naval school able to keep pace with the technological developments needed specifically for the Navy. Marcy recommended using existing naval resources and developing a three-year program for students before they were sent to sea. He echoed former Secretary Upshur and wrote that "for the most of them enter at an age when habits are most easily formed and take deepest root and upon going on board ship they are thrown among associates much older than themselves to whom they look for their precept and example for guidance in the service."[71]

Marcy concluded that with a preparatory course completed, the young midshipmen would better be able to serve the Navy. They would have more "mature judgements" and be attuned to bettering themselves during their free time rather than going ashore and getting into trouble. Marcy asserted that if they were instilled with the values of self-improvement through a preparatory course, then "'the young gentlemen' will learn more practical seamanship and navigation" when put to sea. Whatever was decided, Marcy concluded that West Point was a good example and the Navy could substitute the lessons for soldiers with lessons for sailors; instead of a summer encampment, a summer cruise could be instituted. Yet, it would be at least five more years before all the elements of naval training aimed at making better officers would be fully in place.[72] The Philadelphia board's plan and Marcy's recommendations were sound, but Bancroft knew that to carry it out to that extent required additional congressional funding that they would undoubtedly withhold. Therefore, he took a more gradual approach.

In 1845 the task of establishing the new system came first, and Bancroft centralized the existing professors in Annapolis so that this resource would not be wasted. It was Bancroft's goal to put them to the best possible use. Furthermore, he pointed out that current naval regulations classified midshipmen as officers as soon as they were appointed, and they could be called back to sea at any time,

Figure 3. Franklin Buchanan. *(Franklin Buchanan, LC-B813-1428 A, selected Civil War photographs, 1861–65, Library of Congress Prints and Photographs)*

rather than being students at an introductory school like the cadets at West Point. Therefore, when midshipmen returned from sea, regardless of the time of year, they would have to be detached to the naval school. Under these conditions their classes were to be arranged "in such a manner as will leave opportunity for those who arrive to be attached to classes suited to the stage of their progress in their studies."[73] To govern the new institution, Bancroft selected Franklin Buchanan as its first superintendent.

Buchanan lived on Scott Street, Annapolis, and was probably aware that Bancroft called him to Washington about a new naval school. Bancroft chose Buchanan because he was a lower-ranking commander with sea experience, who would help the secretary maintain the institution's "low profile" until it found its footing within the political and naval establishment. Additionally, Buchanan was a known disciplinarian, and Bancroft gave him a free hand to organize the new school. Still, Bancroft knew that the Navy would often call students back into service, and he recommended that Buchanan take that into consideration when formulating the curriculum. In response, Buchanan recommended that "every applicant for admission to the school must be of good moral character," between thirteen and seventeen years old, and pass medical examination. An academic board of school officials would examine them and assure the school that the applicants were fit for service, literate, and able to do basic math and geography. Organizationally, Buchanan recommended that the secretary of the Navy appoint the superintendent of the naval school, responsible for managing it, from a list of naval officers no higher in rank than commander, but he failed to specify his reason for this belief. Meanwhile, two captains, appointed annually, would compose the examining board. The professors and instructors were also to be selected from the Navy and, when the superintendent ordered, constitute a board for the purposes of examining the midshipmen in their courses and make suggestions as to the improvement of the school.[74] In this way, the Navy instituted some symbols of a profession: setting basic entrance requirements, selecting potential recruits, and assessing their worth in a structured manner.

Once an acting midshipman received his appointment, he was to be sent to the school "subject to the exigencies of the service." There he was to be subject to semiannual exams; those who failed would be "dropped from the lists and returned to their friends." Only those whose "conduct and proficiency" were suitable to the Academic Board and the superintendent would be sent to sea. They would remain at sea for six months and "receiving a favorable report of his conduct during that time from his commander . . . will be entitled to a warrant bearing the date of his acting appointment." Buchanan concurred that all midshipmen on shore were to report to the school. After three years service at sea, and being allowed a leave of absence to return home, they were to report to the school to prepare for their final examinations. Buchanan recommended that their course of studies encompass "English Grammar and Composition; Arithmetic, Geography, and History; Navigation, Gunnery, and the use of Steam; the Spanish and French Languages," and any other subjects required of a naval officer. He also recommended that a sloop of war or brig be attached to the school "as a school of practice in seamanship, evolutions, and gunnery." In total, the education program centered on the students' role as a junior officer and the requirements of "the final examination for promotion [to lieutenant] will embrace all the branches taught at the School."[75]

The midshipmen would be examined by a board in Annapolis every 15 July. Professors were to examine the midshipmen on their courses before the board, but the board was also to take into consideration the averages submitted by the professors. The board was to be responsible for ranking the midshipmen and letting the Department of the Navy know of their progress. The board was also to take into consideration such factors as the general and moral character of the midshipman, as well as his academic abilities. For each branch of study, the board was to assign a merit scale of between one and ten. Averages were to be used for assigning rank, but in seamanship a "multiplier of five" was to be used. Buchanan concluded that "as a much higher value is thus placed on seamanship than on the other branches, the board is directed to exercise a sound judgement in deciding upon the numbers to be given to the candidate before them previous to the examination of another."[76] The system was almost scientific in its qualities, albeit with some major caveats at this early stage.

A student could fail other subjects if he passed seamanship and navigation with high marks; otherwise, he would be dropped from the Navy. But the board could grant a reprieve if he proved he could be valuable and provided a good excuse for his poor performance, such as sickness. If he failed a second time, he would be dropped from the list without any further consideration. The rules for examination were to be virtually the same for the junior classes of raw acting midshipmen as for those midshipmen being examined for promotion to lieutenant, although the examination would be more "cursory" and "seamanship will be omitted." The board was also responsible for reporting how the midshipmen spent their time at the school and whether they "show[ed] a clear incapacity for the naval service" and would be dropped.[77] From 1845 to 1850, the Naval School was a hybrid institution to serve the needs of both the older students and the raw appointees. The older students would acquire the education needed to supplement their sea experience before becoming lieutenants, while the younger acting midshipmen would find in the school a transitional place to introduce them to naval life and the requirements of the Navy.

The internal operating rules for the new school composed by Franklin Buchanan on 10 October 1845 were straightforward. He ordered that all at the school were to abide by the regulations and any subsequent rules that might be issued by the superintendent. All officers were required to treat each other with respect, and anyone with a complaint against another would present it before the superintendent. But the seventh article declared that "as obedience and subordination are essential to the purposes of the School, all therein are required to obey the commands of the Professors."[78] On 15 October 1845, Buchanan promulgated some additional regulations. Students were to stay in their rooms unless given permission by the superintendent to leave. They were also ordered to "prepare their clothes for the wash women before recitation hours on Monday morning." And finally, the superintendent decided to give one midshipman in each room added responsibility: "the duties of superintendent of the room for one week: and he will be held responsible for the cleanliness and general neat arrangements of the room."[79] Command responsibility in miniature.

The Navy Department formally adopted Buchanan's recommendations on 28 August 1846, and they were little different from the best of the previous scattered shore schools. But Annapolis was one central location that the Navy would use in which to select and train its officers. It would take another four years for the Naval School to evolve into a facility that was markedly different from the previous system of naval education. Yet, the new school would be similar to West Point. In George Bancroft's Annual Report of the Secretary of the Navy, December 1845, he told Congress that previously professors were stationed at the Naval Asylum in Philadelphia or they went to sea with the midshipmen. He concluded that this was ineffective and that a ship was unsuited to educate midshipmen. The teachers on the receiving ships were in a similar position and provided little or no instruction to incoming midshipmen. This was not the fault of the professors but rather the system; now he told Congress the Navy had a new educational facility at Annapolis.[80]

Although shore schools existed for some years, it was a tenuous existence. Congress had provided a budget for teachers, but they were scattered about naval facilities and had to rely on educationally inclined commanders to let them teach for any extended period. These old "schools" were informal at best, with the most structured at Philadelphia. Before 1845 there were calls for the establishment of more permanent facilities to provide better training for the young midshipmen, but congressional inertia stalled any progress. Bancroft hoped to make the system better. He told his audience that it would be more efficient to instruct midshipmen on shore between cruises. The instructors would be paid out of funds already allotted, and combined with the use of old Fort Severn, the school "was immediately organized, on an unostentatious and frugal plan."[81] Finally, Bancroft hoped the school would provide a transition to naval life. He concluded that "by giving some preliminary instruction to the midshipmen before their first cruise, by extending an affectionate but firm supervision over them as they return from sea, by providing for them suitable culture before they pass to a higher grade, by rejecting from the service all who fail in capacity or in good disposition to use their time well, will go far to renovate and improve the American navy."[82]

CHAPTER 2

The Naval School, 1845–49

When the Naval School opened at Annapolis in October 1845, most students were midshipmen with sea experience (see table 1). Many young people had queried the secretary of the Navy, their local congressmen, or the Navy, to obtain midshipmen's appointments, and those who attended Annapolis from 1845 to 1849—and some as late as 1853—were appointed between 1840 and 1849. Meanwhile, the 1845 naval appropriation's act stipulated that the president had to appoint midshipmen in proportion to each state's and territory's congressional representation, the midshipmen had to be residents of those places, and until the distribution of midshipmen reflected the law, the government had to favor underrepresented areas.[1] Consequently, most midshipmen who joined the new institution at Annapolis were connected with some sort of government employee and lived near the nation's power centers. Still, at the new facility, the Navy tried to train them in a more professional manner, round off the practical experience they had gained at sea, and rid the service of unsuitable individuals. For the students, Annapolis gave even experienced midshipmen the opportunity to bond with comrades and share stories about their careers to date.

Table 1. Annapolis Alumni by Date of Appointment 1840–49

1840	1841	1842	1843	1844	1845	1846	1847	1848	1849	Total
55	173	8	0	0	6	24	65	0	34	365

Source: Calculated from U.S. Naval Academy Alumni Association, *Register of Alumni, Graduates and Former Naval Cadets and Midshipmen*, 91st Edition (Annapolis, Md.: The Naval Academy Alumni Association, 1976). Hereafter, Register of Alumni.

The geographic breakdown of the residence from which appointed, for 284 midshipmen for whom data could be found, shifted from the period earlier in the nineteenth century studied by Christopher McKee perhaps as appointments began to better reflect new requirements. While McKee's officers generally came from the

Table 2. Geographic Origins 1800–14 and 1840–49 (Percentage)

State	1800–14	1840–49	Birth State	15–24-Year-Old White Males (1840)
NH, VT, MA, RI, CT	17.4	7.1	7.3	13.0
NY, NJ, PA, DE	29.4	20.0	20.2	35.1
MD, DC, VA	35.2	15.1	22.5	6.9
NC, SC, GA	12.6	6.6	6.6	4.9
OH, KY, TN, MS, LA	5.4	14.8	9.4	20.2
Other		14.2	9.1	19.9
Missing Cases		81 (22.2%)	91 (24.9%)	
Total Cases		365	365	

Source: Calculated from Register of Alumni and Records of the United States Naval Academy, Registers of Candidates for Admission to the Academy, Oct. 1849–Oct. 1860, National Archives (NA), Record Group (RG) 405. Hereafter, Registers of Candidates for Admission. Percentage of white males between 15 and 24 years old calculated from Ben J. Wattenberg, *The Statistical History of the United States from Colonial Times to the Present* (New York: Basic Books, Inc., Publishers, 1976), Series A 195–209, "Population: Population of States," 24–37 and Christopher McKee, *A Gentlemanly and Honorable Profession: The Creation of the U.S. Naval Officer Corps, 1794–1815* (Annapolis: Naval Institute Press, 1991), table 2.

Note: For consistency of comparison, McKee's geographic breakdowns by state, and his statistical methods are employed to compare the Naval School students with their immediate predecessors. Only McKee's known state residences are used, hence the 0% unknown cases.

mid-Atlantic states and from New England, by the 1840s there was greater representation from the South and the central states (table 2). For instance, as a share of the total of all those states that sent appointees to the school, the percentage of white males, age fifteen to twenty-four, from Ohio was 11.8 percent in 1840, while the percentage of appointments from Ohio was only 6.8 percent between 1840 and 1849; McKee found that in the period between 1800 and 1814, only 0.4 percent of the midshipmen were appointed from Ohio. The increase in the number of appointments from Ohio was probably a function of its representation coming into line with its population of white males and because some candidates simply relocated to Ohio long enough to claim residence and an appointment; only 4.1 percent of the midshipmen appointed from Ohio were born there. A much more accurate reflection of the true origins of the midshipmen is their birth states. In the Ohio, Kentucky, Tennessee, Mississippi, and Louisiana cases, the proportion of midshipmen born there is much lower than those appointed from that region. The largest portion of appointees came from Maryland; Washington, D.C.; and Virginia—most likely a function of those regions' proximity to the government and the ease of contacting those responsible for midshipmen appointments.[2]

In the pre-1815 Navy, it was only immediate family connections, like a father, brother, or uncle, that helped a young man acquire an appointment.[3] Unfortunately,

Table 3. Family Occupational Background of Midshipmen 1840–49

Occupation	Number	Percent of Known	Free White Males 1850 (%)
Agricultural	6	15.4	45.2
Farmer	3	7.7	
Planter	2	5.1	
Carpenter/Farmer	1	2.6	
Commercial	7	18.0	30.2
Merchant	6	15.4	
Clerk	1	2.6	
Professional	9	23.1	2.5
Lawyer	6	15.4	
Physician	3	7.7	
Government Service	17	43.7	0.5
Army Officer	6	15.4	
Navy Officer	4	10.3	
Public Officer	3	7.7	
Judge	2	5.1	
JP	1	2.6	
Post Master	1	2.6	
Other			21.5
Total Known	39		
Total Unknown	326		
Total Cases	365		

Source: Calculated from Registers of Candidates for Admission and William B. Skelton, *An American Profession of Arms: The Army Officer Corps, 1784–1861* (Lawrence: University Press of Kansas, 1992), 100, table 9.5.

Note: Percentages are of total known cases. For ease of comparison, the table has been formatted using essentially Skelton's categories.

information on the occupational backgrounds of Naval School midshipmen's parents or guardians was hard to obtain, and the school's appointment records provided little information about family backgrounds in the 1840s. Information was only found for thirty-nine of the midshipmen (see table 3). Although definite conclusions cannot be drawn based on such a small sample, some comments can be made. Most were sons of government workers, more so than in the general population, followed by members of professional families. The next largest group was from the commercial and manufacturing arena, but far fewer in number than from the general population. Finally, the smallest group included sons of agricultural families, composing only 15.4 percent of Naval School students, while about 45 percent of the general population of free white males worked in the agricultural sector.

With a dearth of statistical information about the backgrounds of the common midshipman appointee, other sources for information must be employed. Young men went to sea for several reasons. Often from maritime areas, the attraction was natural: many of their relatives and their fathers had gone to sea. For these young men, maritime work was a natural way to find a job. Going to sea in the Navy was one option that young men had to see the world, gain different experiences, and meet economic needs. Under economic stresses, jobs in the civilian world were tenuous at best. There were many more applicants than there were government positions to be filled. Another reason young men joined the Navy, again related to economics, was the death of a father, which left families with little money. A naval career provided security and immediate income, as Dahlgren discovered. Alternative careers, like law or medicine, had substantial social and economic barriers to entry, while they required a substantial investment and the loss of income until the young man finished his training.[4]

Young men, or their fathers, wrote the secretary of the Navy asking for information or appointments once Annapolis opened. However, there is no record that the secretary granted their requests. Some applicants, like George Twiggs of Philadelphia, only saw joining the Navy as one way to bide their time while they finalized which career to choose. Twiggs, for instance, was studying law and had requested an appointment to "wile away the time that must elapse since my final examination before I can be admitted to the Bar." By June 1846, Twiggs was glad the Navy rejected him, because he asserted that his "prospects would have been damned for life" in the Navy. Instead, he got involved in politics and newspapers and was happy with his choice.[5] The Navy likely rejected some boys as too old, or because there were too many midshipmen after the large number appointed in 1841 in anticipation of a war with Britain over the Maine–New Brunswick border and tensions over British searches of suspected American-flagged slave traders off West Africa.[6] The war never materialized, but when conflicts emerged, some families held fast to the notion that a young officer's place was at sea. Others, with children already in the Navy, perhaps believed that Naval School attendance would give their sons an edge in a competitive officer marketplace. Finally, families with children in the civilian world hoped that a naval officer's career would provide their sons with meaningful employment.

Fathers of younger sons wanted a place for their boys. On 16 May 1846, Mr. H. Nutes of Harrisburg discussed his son Henry's fate. Henry was fourteen, generally well educated, and showed good progress in arithmetic, mathematics, and grammar. Nutes hoped that he could obtain a midshipman's warrant for the boy so that he could attend the Naval School. Nutes knew little of the regulations governing entry and wished more information.[7] The regulations that governed Fort Severn, until reorganization, set the age range for new appointees at between thirteen and seventeen, and likely excluded many older applicants.[8] John Parrish Jr. wrote the secretary of the Navy on 17 April 1846 and expressed disappointment over the age rules. Parrish was twenty years old, dismayed that no one over eighteen could receive a midshipman's warrant, and begged the secretary to make an exception because of his heartfelt desire to defend the American flag on a warship.[9] Marcus L. Dadley, meanwhile, was seventeen and wrote the secretary in September 1845 for an appointment to attend the new Naval School. Marcus, then in Baltimore, was born in Massachusetts, had sailed frequently between Boston and Maryland, and was attending civilian school. With his mother's support, he wanted a new career, because he no longer liked working for the merchants, and although poor, he believed that "a poor man with an education may rise to greatness for adverse fortune gives rise to sentiments that one would not feel were it not for adversity."[10]

Charles Trimbull Van Allen, nineteen, from New York, also had prior sea experience, and his brother wished to get him a midshipman's appointment.[11] The same was true of Montgomery Davis Parker, the son of Richard Parker, and an acquaintance of Secretary Bancroft from Boston. The elder Parker reminded Bancroft of their friendship and believed his son would make a good midshipman: he had an English education and sea experience. Montgomery had made two voyages to Samoa and one to St. Helena but was currently on the U.S. brig *Boxer*, serving as captain's clerk. Parker exclaimed that "I shall be exceedingly gratified" if with Bancroft's favorable attention and sense of "deep obligation in mature years" his son would receive an appointment.[12] Robert Taylor from Philadelphia wrote the secretary on 24 November 1845 to ask that his son, eighteen, receive a midshipman's appointment. Taylor told the secretary that he supported his son's efforts to seek fame and gratification in such an honorable profession, even though he believed that his son might be better off in seeking his fortune "among the mercantile class."[13]

Lawrence J. Reiss of Baltimore also wrote the secretary on 26 March 1846, telling him that he was twenty and had wanted to join the Navy since he was twelve but had been discouraged. Lawrence was fond of adventure and believed that the Navy was where it could be found. He was the son of a well-known Baltimore mechanic, who would soon give up his business and retire. Lawrence confessed that "this makes me acquaint you of my intent as I have no trade whereby I could make my bread." He wanted a career as a midshipman in order to be independent from his father.[14] Isaiah Townsend also wanted a better life for a relative and wrote Senator Daniel Dickinson, Democrat, New York, on 27 March 1846 on behalf of his uncle, a man with few political connections. Townsend's mother was an old friend of Dickinson, and Townsend told the senator that his cousin, Henry Townsend, sixteen, wanted to be a midshipman. Townsend believed that it was time that his family, and area, received a midshipman appointment and wanted Dickinson to use his influence with the secretary to obtain the berth for the young man. Townsend ended his letter hoping to appeal to Dickinson's sense of charity and informed him that his uncle was a farmer who had toiled hard on his farm to raise his family. Dickinson was moved enough by Townsend's request to at least forward the letter to the secretary.[15]

Sons from military families were also interested in joining the Navy. Representative Paul Dillingham Jr., Democrat, Vermont, wrote the secretary on 12 March 1846 and asked that a sixteen- or seventeen-year-old son of a now-dead soldier receive a midshipman appointment.[16] Meanwhile, other families wrote the secretary and requested that he send their sons, already midshipmen, to the new school. Washington Haxtun, for example, told the secretary that his son Milton had been at sea almost constantly since his appointment in 1841, except for one week of shore leave. According to his commanders, Milton's devotion to duty and moral standing were high, and Washington wanted Milton transferred to the Naval School.[17] John Davis, meanwhile, had a similar request and asked the secretary of the Navy to also transfer his son to the school.[18] Nevertheless, some inexperienced applicants clung to the notion that a midshipman's life was at sea.

Talk of war, for example, brought applicants, but they wanted the traditional young officer's life rather than detachment to Annapolis. On 13 February 1846, John Lawrence of Fredericksburg, Virginia, wrote the secretary of his desire to enter the Navy since he was sixteen. His relatives had discouraged his ambitions, however, because of the large number of junior officers already in the Navy; the odds of career advancement were low. Lawrence wrote his local congressman, who promised him a midshipman's warrant, yet Lawrence had heard nothing from him since. Now Lawrence wrote the secretary directly, because he believed that tensions between the United States and Britain, and the calls for naval expansion, increased

Table 4. Student Ages, When Detached to Annapolis, by Date of Original
Appointment 1845–47

Statistic	1845	1846	1847
Average Age	21.6	20.9	21.0
Minimum Age	20.3	17.6	16.3
Maximum Age	23.3	22.6	23.3
Standard Deviation	1.25	1.56	1.47
Missing Cases	0	8	33
Total	6	24	65

Source: Calculated from Registers of Candidates for Admission.

Note: The author was unable to find meaningful age data for the dates of 1840–42. There were no Annapolis Alumni for the dates of 1843–44 and 1848. The age data for the date of 1849 is so dramatically different that it is included in the next chapter's analysis.

the demand for officers.[19] John Davis, meanwhile, wrote the secretary on 13 May 1846 on behalf of his son, a midshipman, then at sea. This time the threat was from Mexico. But Davis declared that "the post of danger is the post of duty" and requested that his son remain at sea rather than be dispatched to the Naval School.[20] Another young man, George Springer also wanted a midshipman's berth; if that was impossible, he wanted a letter of marque to run a privateer so he could help make Mexico "smart for her impudence towards us."[21]

In the end, most who attended the new Naval School entered after being at sea in the Navy for some time and already had limited command experience. While age data are unavailable in the Annapolis records for midshipmen appointed from 1840 to 1844, data from 1845, 1846, and 1847 reveal that students were in their twenties by the time they reached Annapolis.[22] Meanwhile, the minimum age slowly fell, as expected, when younger students first went to the Naval School before going to sea as the new system of professionalizing young officers into the Navy took hold (see table 4). Such midshipmen entered the profession with some variation on a "good English education," or "very liberal education," meaning some schooling that would at least qualify them to have possibly been permitted to attend a higher level of schooling, such as an academy. Of the 885 midshipmen Christopher McKee studied, for instance, he found that the educational backgrounds for only eighteen could be traced to a known academy. Although there were only eighteen who could be confirmed as having an academy education, those who did not would "stand out from the crowd." McKee concluded that it enabled the midshipmen to be able to read and write effectively and gave them the wherewithal to succeed in their future career.[23]

The school's objective for these students was to round out their training as they prepared to become lieutenants. In addition, coming together at Annapolis, the young officers learned the expectations of their profession from each others' experiences. William Harwar Parker, born in New York in 1826, was one officer whose career bridged the old apprenticeship style of officer education at sea with the newer program at Annapolis. Although born in New York, Parker's family was from Virginia, where his uncle sat on the state's supreme court. William's immediate family was steeped in naval and military tradition. His father and one brother, Foxhall, were both officers, while his other brother, Richard, attended West Point. Consequently, a naval profession seemed a perfectly reasonable career choice for young William, who obtained a midshipman's appointment in 1841. Before attending Annapolis, William deployed to a number of stations—the Mediterranean, Brazil, and with Commodore David Conner's flagship during the Mexican-American War.[24]

The Navy ordered Parker to the Naval School in the fall of 1847. Parker, part of the large '41 Date—those midshipmen appointed in 1841—along with his comrades, were still fighting the Mexican-American War. Consequently, the secretary of the Navy broke them into three groups that attended Annapolis as circumstances permitted. Those in the first group, appointed from January to July 1841, began their studies in 1846; those appointed after July started Annapolis attendance in 1847; while a third small group of forty students arrived in 1848. Spread over several academic years, the '41 Date graduated in 1847, 1848, and 1849, respectively, and by the late 1840s, the mixing of these students with the newer raw recruits caused administrative problems, as will be discussed. Nevertheless, Parker believed that their time at Annapolis was well spent. The institution prepared them for the examinations for passed midshipman—equivalent to lieutenant—but also exposed them to older officers and instructors who served as role models. Parker, for instance, noted that Superintendent George P. Upshur was gentle and honorable and had a "pure character." Such an example was important, Parker explained, and if "we did not profit by it it was our own loss." Parker profited by the example, graduated in July 1848, and later returned to the academy as an instructor in 1860.[25]

Beyond the school's role models and educational program—discussed below—the facility also brought together young midshipmen and allowed them to share their stories about midshipman life. Such "yarns" reinforced professional and ethical expectations demanded of the young officers. Parker recalled that he and his classmates congregated on Saturday nights to swap stories of life on board the different ships with different commanders. One, Captain Percival, for instance, "always took a fatherly interest in his midshipmen." But the account served another purpose. It fortified for the midshipmen the qualities that experienced naval officers looked for in their future colleagues. Parker noted that the captain "wrote once to the father of one of them that his son had entered a profession 'where he would either go down to his grave wept, honored and sung, or unwept, unhonored and unsung.'" When the young midshipman disappointed Percival, the captain again wrote his father and explained that "your son is going down to his grave unwept, unhonored and unsung."[26]

Stephen B. Luce also had substantial naval experience before going to Annapolis, indicative of the experience of many pre-Annapolis appointees. While at anchor in the Canton River, Luce was assigned to get water, a difficult operation that required ship's boats to carry sixty-gallon casks. While getting the water, part of the crew he was supervising went missing, got drunk, and wreaked havoc in a local village. Luce and the coxswain went to retrieve the drunken sailors: "I had drawn my sword and was prepared to use it, for I was no match in a hand-to-hand conflict with those stalwart seamen, half crazed as they were by liquor. I was but little over sixteen at that time, of slight build and not particularly strong; so that I would have been a mere child in the hands of any one of the crew disposed to do me bodily harm." He took a long time to return to the ship, and the captain was furious, asking who had given him permission to return so late? Luce started to explain himself by stating that he was "thinking," to which the captain informed him that it was not his job to think. Later, Luce was assigned command of another task and rushed back to the ship so as not to be late. Hurrying during a storm caused his small craft to become swamped while docking alongside *Columbus*, killing the livestock he and his men had obtained on shore. Again, the captain was furious. Luce explained saying "I did not think, sir." To which the captain replied, "You didn't think? Why what was your head given you for?" The rest of Luce's voyage on *Columbus* was uneventful but for a cholera outbreak at Manila, when in six days twenty men perished. On 8 March 1848, *Columbus* arrived home at Hampton Roads, and Luce was reassigned to the Naval School.[27]

Luce reported to the school's superintendent on 1 April 1848; by this time Luce was twenty-one, with seven years' experience. Luce was near the top of his class from the outset, but by graduation had fallen somewhat because of disciplinary problems. When President Zachary Taylor was elected in 1848, Superintendent George Upshur was permitted to let the midshipmen attend the inauguration ceremonies, but he refused. The midshipmen were upset and one night protested by ringing the school bells and firing off guns. Luce was connected with the protests, and the secretary of the Navy decided that all those involved in the affair would be penalized. The punished midshipman, by August 1849, had finished his stay at the school and was assigned to *Vandalia*. A month later he was promoted to Passed Midshipman.[28]

The pre-Annapolis exploits of Francis Gregory Dallas, son of a naval officer, are similar. Between October 1837 and November 1841, Dallas and his father made several attempts to get the young man a midshipman appointment. Navy secretary Mahlon Dickerson, from New Jersey, wrote Lieutenant A. J. Dallas on 17 October 1837 and told him that his letter on behalf of his son had been received and filed, but "at present no more appointments can be made, but the case will be respectfully considered."[29] In 1838 another attempt was made, and Dickerson passed on the request for appointment to the president but warned that "there is not at present a single vacancy in the Corps of Midshipmen, and besides, the State of Massachusetts has the full share to which its population entitles it."[30] From 1838 to 1841, Dallas continued to press the new secretary, James K. Paulding, only to be told again that there were no vacancies. Francis' father even received a letter from a former congressman from New Hampshire, Samuel Cushman, who expressed his hopes that Francis would get his appointment.[31] Finally, on 8 November 1841, Secretary Abel P. Upshur wrote Francis, now about seventeen, and appointed him an acting midshipman. But in accordance with tradition, his indoctrination would be at sea: "after six months of actual service at sea, report favorably of your character, talents, and qualifications, a Warrant will be given to you, bearing the date of this letter."[32]

On 24 November 1841, the Navy ordered Dallas to report to the receiving ship *Columbus*; his commander would be Commodore John Downes. Downes then ordered Dallas to join *Columbia*, and by March 1843, Dallas received his warrant. He served on *Columbia* until January 1845, when Secretary John Y. Mason informed him that he was permitted three months leave, after which he was to report back to the Navy Department.[33] In April he was ordered to report to the Pensacola Naval Yard, and about one year later he was sent to duty with the Home Squadron, specifically *Mississippi*, under the command of Captain Andrew Fitzhugh.[34] Dallas then spent some time in the Pensacola Naval Hospital in 1846, before being released and assigned to *John Adams*. Over most of 1846, Dallas complained of illness and repeatedly requested reassignment. On 16 September 1846, Dallas once again wrote the Commodore to request that he be permitted passage on the U.S. Schooner *Flirt* to go home. Dallas complained that his health was so bad that in the previous fourteen months he had to be hospitalized three times. Dallas' condition deteriorated so much that at one point he tried to jump overboard while docked at Tampico.[35]

Dallas was ill and under stress after his father had passed away, leaving behind two orphaned sisters. Consequently, on 18 September 1846, Commodore Conner granted Dallas leave to return home.[36] On 4 November 1846, the secretary also informed Dallas that he was not required to attend the Naval School at Annapolis the next year, and by January 1847, the secretary renewed the sick Dallas' leave for another two months. But on 2 March 1847, Dallas asked to be put back in service on a vessel in the Gulf of Mexico squadron and a week later the secretary ordered him to report to Commodore Charles W. Skinner on *Saratoga*. By the end of the year, Dallas was reassigned to the store ship *Electra*. Finally, in 1848 Dallas was at the Naval School in Annapolis with seven years' experience under his belt.[37] During this time, Dallas had learned the expectations of a naval career on the job.

Parker, Luce, and Dallas were not alone. By the time other young men entered the Naval School, many had also spent much of their time at sea. Such students were like John W. Bennett, who was appointed on 10 February 1840 and warranted on 30 March 1841. At times he served on *Delaware* and *Congress*—the latter for almost two years—and was given leave for three months on 14 March 1845. It was only on 6 September 1845 that the Navy ordered him to report to the Naval School by 10 October. Allen T. Brown had a similar career. He was appointed a midshipman on 26 February 1841 and by 27 March was on a receiving ship at New York. On 16 October he was transferred to an ocean-going ship and appears to have remained there until 1 October 1844, when he was transferred to the store ship *Erie*. On 30 October 1844, he was detached to *Jamestown* and appears to have served on her for a time but was detached on 27 September 1845 from *Preble* and ordered to the Naval School by 20 October 1845. Joseph Seawell was appointed on 2 July 1842 and by 21 July was on *Marion*. On 29 June 1843, he was transferred to *Macedonian* and by 23 January 1845, was warranted as a midshipman. He then served on such vessels as *Cumberland* before eventually being sent to the Naval School.[38]

The Naval School system was tenuous at best, because midshipmen obtained appointments, went to sea, and continued to gain skills and experience in a less-structured and professionalized manner. Still, several, like William H. Smith, Felix Grundy, John Adams, Ralph Chandler, and John Hamilton, were appointed midshipmen and sent right to the school, but others were quickly detached only to return in the 1850s. Philip Carrigan Johnson, for instance, was appointed on 31 August 1846 and sent to the Naval School, but by 3 December he was detached to *Ohio* and warranted on 26 October 1847. In 1849 he served on *Dale*, until he was sent to the school again on 13 October, but by the following May he was once again detached to *Congress*. It was only on 12 July 1851 that he was detached from *St. Louis* and ordered back to Annapolis by 1 October, where he was warranted as a passed midshipman on 9 June 1852 and then sent to *Princeton*. Hudson M. Garland moved around in a similar manner. He was appointed on 20 November 1848, and by 12 May 1849, was detached from the school to *Mississippi* and warranted on

11 May 1850. Between 1852 and 1853, he served on *Independence, Dolphin*, and practice ship *Preble*, ironically the academy's practice ship, until he was sent back to Annapolis on 18 June 1853. Then, on 8 December 1853, he was turned back one year for misconduct and once again detached to *Albany*, then served on the Coast Survey Ship *St. Bibb* until returning again to Annapolis on 1 October 1854 and warranted as a passed midshipman on 12 June 1855.[39] Typically, these midshipmen were young when they joined, but by the time they entered the Naval School at Annapolis, they were in their twenties, with much of their "professional" outlook set by the ad hoc experience of the sea and the idiosyncrasies of their commanders.

Despite Marcy's recommendations after studying West Point, the school's program was structured in light of the fact that many midshipmen had prior sea experience and only provided the beginning of the structured environment to professionalize young officers. Bancroft's gradual plan for the new school also set low entrance qualifications. Academy alumnus Park Benjamin wrote that students were simply to be able to "read and write well and have a knowledge of geography and arithmetic." Bancroft hoped that by setting the entrance qualifications lower, simple boys from "the village school house" would qualify to enter the school and thus negate opposition arguments that the Navy was creating a patronage system for the rich.[40] Moreover, the Navy had yet to properly address the fact that the students were still pulled away, or not even sent to the facility, because of the needs of the service.

Despite the age of the students, the professors, under the direction of the superintendent and the supervision of Lieutenant James Ward, the school's second in command, drew up the academic program for the first year of the school. They hoped to further officer education and prove to Congress, and perhaps skeptics in the Navy, that the new system of professionalizing young officers could work. The school's Academic Board proposed that the school run a program of nine months ending in June and divided the training into mathematics, natural philosophy, chemistry, ordnance, gunnery, the use of steam, history, geography, English, French, and Spanish. The board also recommended that a qualified gunner's mate instruct the midshipmen in fencing, but this was optional. Finally, the board proposed that "manual exercise, or infantry-drill, be introduced" to "elevate the military character of the school" under the direction of Professor Henry Lockwood.[41]

The Academic Board also broke the school into junior and senior classes to bridge the gap between the old style of indoctrinating officers into the Navy and the new one they were promoting. Acting midshipmen who had just entered the service composed the junior class and were sent directly to the school. Meanwhile, those midshipmen sent to the school to study for their examination for promotion to lieutenant were members of the senior class. Finally, any student with sea experience in the Navy, but not studying for the lieutenant's examination, would be placed with those students the authorities deemed best suited their needs. Consequently, the program for the junior class was more introductory and composed of such subjects as geography, English, Spanish and French, mathematics, and "navigation as far as the sailings and the use of the quadrant." They were also required to attend lectures in chemistry, natural philosophy, and ordnance that would also be delivered to the senior class. The senior class learned more advanced skills and studied more complicated mathematics, like spherical trigonometry, as well as nautical and descriptive astronomy, mechanics, optics, steam, history, magnetism, and electricity. Finally, all the classes learned fencing and infantry drill.[42]

The Navy intended the students' timetable to almost replicate the rhythm of naval life applicable to their future careers. Students were in class from 8:00 AM to noon and then provided with dinner and "recreation" until 1:30 PM. School then continued until 4:30 PM, unless it was Saturday. Another break followed and dinner was from 4:30 PM to 6:00 PM, while study hours occurred from 6:00 PM to 10:00 PM. Specifically, the senior class' math and natural philosophy instructions were divided into two sections: 8:00 AM to 9:00 AM and 9:00 AM to 10:00 AM daily. This was followed by a study period from 10:00 AM to 11:00 AM. On Tuesday and Saturday, they were taught in steam, gunnery, and ordnance from 11:00 AM to noon. Chemistry was relegated to Thursday from 11:00 AM to noon, while history and writing were taught from 11:00 AM to noon on Monday, Wednesday, and Friday. Foreign languages occupied the senior class from 1:30 PM to 4:30 PM, a skill increasingly important for professional naval officers that dealt with foreign ports and navies far from home. Significantly, traditional maritime and practical topics, like instruction on navigational instruments, were relegated to periods that did "not in any way interfere with recitations in other branches, or with the preparation for the same."[43] With prior sea experience, the school wanted senior students to spend more time on complementary learning.

The junior class operated under a slightly different timetable. Their days were governed in the mornings by a class in natural philosophy from 8:00 AM to 9:00 AM, while they studied from 9:00 AM to 10:00 AM. Then the midshipmen learned math from 10:00 AM to 11:00 AM, while gunnery, chemistry, and any other subjects were slotted for 11:00 AM to noon. The junior classes spent less time on foreign languages, but still learned French and Spanish from 1:30 PM until 2:30 PM daily, except on Saturdays. After their foreign language instruction, they learned English and geography until dismissed at 4:30 PM. Finally, they were to study from 6:00 PM until 10:00 PM. Still, as with the senior classes, there was vagueness as to when they were to be instructed in navigation: "the class [is] to be exercised at suitable times in the use of the quadrant."[44] Those skills required to serve their client, the state, in overseas roles and learning that separated the officers from the men were emphasized the most, as was the emergence of new technology that might help the nation.

The mechanics and physics course was divided into several topics, which closely resemble engineering courses. Midshipmen first learned mechanics over five lessons and were taught the mechanics of liquids, pneumatics, acoustics, and optics, electrical, and heat theory. After they obtained a firm foundation, the professor then taught the pupils chemistry and steam. Meanwhile, the mathematics course was divided into eight parts, including arithmetic, which covered the "principles and practice of operations in whole numbers and in vulgar and decimal fractions." Finally, the Department of Astronomy, Navigation, and Surveying was, naturally, divided into the three fields of astronomy, navigation, and surveying.[45] This department also taught the midshipmen navigation: "Sailing by compass; sailing on a great circle; finding a ships [*sic*] place by dead reckoning; construction and use of charts; principles and use of the sextant and circle of reflection, and application of the glass prism to these instruments; the artificial horizon; variation compass; methods of correcting the compass for local attractions on ship board; construction of instruments for determining a ship's rate of sailing; [and] sounding instruments."[46] Instructors also instructed the students on finding their azimuth by variations in the compass, and in finding their latitude by meridian observations of the stars, planets, sun, and the moon. They were also taught the use of their chronometer and learned how to rate "the chronometer on shore by single altitudes and by equal altitudes, as seen by series of lunar observations."[47]

The administration had grand plans to make midshipmen well-trained officers equipped with the latest tools to advance the nation at sea. Nevertheless, in December 1845 the students found the physics course difficult and complained to their professor, Lockwood. They told him that their writing was no reflection on him, and they appreciated that he cared for their improvement, but they failed to grasp the material. They wished the textbook changed from "the present text book (Peschel's *Physics*) [to] one of a more elementary character, such as Lardner's *Mechanics*, or any others, the selection of which we leave to your judgement." They desired this change to help their studies, because up to that time they had met with little success in studying.[48]

After three months it was time to pass judgment on the school's success. On 30 January 1846, Superintendent Buchanan submitted his first quarterly report to Secretary Bancroft.[49] Buchanan was pleased with the progress of the school and its students. Since October, eight-five midshipmen had attended and their health was good, with only one serious illness. Meanwhile, visitors had made favorable remarks about the midshipmen's "gentlemanly bearing." Significantly, the school

had also monitored almost scientifically the midshipmen's professional development. The administration recorded each midshipman's merit level weekly, and
those with low numbers were deemed "hard students." Buchanan believed that
their standing reflected their poor prior academic experience, but they seemed willing to work. The secretary's decision to allow only one examination for promotion
had prompted those who had shown indifference to their studies to be more serious. Nevertheless, Buchanan had little hope for some students he expected to fail
their examinations; they were unsuitable candidates for the type of officer the new
system advocated.[50]

While the school struggled, Buchanan believed there was room for improvement. In particular, he wanted a sloop to provide students with a leisure activity
and instruction in the practical aspect of their careers. Moreover, Buchanan recommended a special two-month refresher course in seamanship for those midshipmen
scheduled to take their promotion exam. It might also help appease traditionalists,
because he concluded, after all, that seamanship was the most important branch of
their profession, despite its weighting in the academic program.[51] By April 1846,
Buchanan reported that the merit numbers of the midshipmen had generally
improved, although, as he predicted, there were several who, despite his efforts,
lacked the desirable qualities for the Navy.[52]

Table 5. Course Grading c. 1846

Course	Original Grade	Scale Factor	Scaled Grade
Mathematics	10	3	30
French	10	3	30
English	10	3	30
Natural Philosophy	10	2	20
Chemistry	10	1	10
Total	50		120

Source: Calculated from table A, in Lieutenant Ward to Buchanan, 25 April 1846, letters received by the
superintendent of the U.S. Naval Academy, 1845–87, Records of the United States Naval Academy, NA, RG
405. Hereafter, letters received.

The Navy formally tested the new scheme at the student examinations in April
1846. On average, the administration found that students did equally poorly in
each subject, although probably a little worse in chemistry. But the grades were
given different weights for the final analysis. Mathematics was multiplied by three,

as was French and English. Natural Philosophy was multiplied by two and chemistry by one. Lieutenant Ward reported that "these multipliers [were] being adopted by the board to express the degree of labor devoted to the subjects respectively, and their comparative importance in an elementary education." The sum of each student's grades, after multiplication, was then taken "to express relatively its estimate of each individual's proficiency" while at the school. Consequently, the academic report divided the midshipmen into three groups: good, indifferent, and bad. Ward wrote that "those named in the second column may by increased industry and attention exhibit more satisfactory proofs at the second examination of fitness for the service; but those in the third column give but little promise that it will find them prepared for its ordeal." Ward concluded that the exams and marking represented the "merits of each individual" and clearly indicated who had improved themselves "so as to afford some evidence of future usefulness to the service."[53] Still, at least one of the "bad" students of this group went on to prove himself worthy to the Navy. William Henry Smith graduated from the school, served his country, but was lost while still a midshipman in the Pacific Squadron.[54] Although in its infancy, by April 1846, the Navy had implemented a careful scheme to recruit, train, and assess those it hoped would forge its future professional officer corps.

In the middle of 1846, Buchanan ordered another report on the progress of those midshipmen appointed in 1841 who had prior sea experience and were then attending the Naval School. Lieutenant Ward reported that they were all progressing adequately, with the exception of one individual, Midshipman Robert Patton, who "wants capacity to acquire any of the branches taught in this institution."[55] And indeed, Patton failed to graduate, unable to meet the professional expectations of a future officer.[56] In this light, the Board of Examiners found that the breadth of the program of studies was "sufficiently extensive," it occupied most of the students' time, it and left only "short intervals" for recreation. As a result, the board's only suggestion for change was to find boats for the midshipmen to use to occupy their time and to give them exercise in rowing.[57] The board asserted that "these and other facilities of harmless relaxation would doubtless have a tendency to divert the young gentlemen from a practice of mingling too generally in the society and amusements of the Town, by which their minds are distracted from their studies, and expenses falls upon them, which their pay is inadequate to meet. The undersigned would not discourage a [*sic*] occasional intercourse with polite society, sensible as they are of its inestimable advantage to youth."[58] In training and living, the Navy wanted to keep its new professional officers as separate from society as decorum and friendliness with the host community allowed.

By the fall of 1846, Lieutenant James H. Ward gave his frank opinion on the school. At the outset, Ward was second in command at the facility and head of the gunnery department. Frank M. Bennett opines that Ward was something of a visionary and knew the importance that steam power would play in changing naval tactics. Therefore, Ward wanted Annapolis to focus much of its attention on training the young officers in the rising technology. As a result, Ward researched the emerging field, developed lectures, and tried to show the connection between naval gunnery and steam propulsion.[59] A year had passed since the Naval School opened, and with the summer to reflect, Ward had several suggestions for improvement. As president of the Academic Board, an officer, and technophile, Ward was in a unique position to note the troubles that were brewing. He asserted that the program of instruction had been developed by professors who "have spent their early lives in cultivating and promoting habits of mental application which render close study easy," while the midshipmen "led active lives, wholly adverse to habits of application, and tending to render close study irksome and discouraging." Ward believed that the midshipmen had become discouraged early in the last academic year and had relaxed or discontinued much of their study. He thought the main problems were poor study habits and a lack of appreciation of this by the part of the professors.[60] In reality, it was a discourse between the Navy, instructors, and students over what professionalism meant for the Navy and its future.

Ward disagreed with what had been done thus far to fix the program's problems. He concluded that "there has been in some cases too eager a disposition to push forward certain studies, and give them a prominence not due to their relative importance in a naval education and incompatible with the plan of instruction originally contemplated." He believed that only three subjects could be handled by the midshipmen at a time and suggested that they concentrate on mathematics, French, and gunnery and steam as a single course. He believed that mathematics should remain with the weight it currently had at the school, while "Gunnery and Steam" should be expanded from two days to three days a week, with battery exercises on Saturdays. Meanwhile, he suggested that natural philosophy instruction be reduced from three to two days a week. Theoretical aspects should be kept to a minimum, and the topic should be "taught popularly and so far as possible illustrated by experiment." Moreover, he asserted that mathematical analysis should be "forbidden altogether in the class, as calculated to occupy time which cannot be spared from other more important studies." Instead, he advocated more emphasis on the importance of steam and that the students occupy themselves with only "mechanical philosophy" of the type in "[Denison] Olmsted's small edition."[61]

Ward also felt there were some problems with the mathematical program. He asserted that the students should be experts in algebra, but he contended that traditional navigational skills take precedence over abstract mathematical abilities. Therefore, he suggested that the midshipmen should be thoroughly knowledgeable in Nathaniel Bowditch's work on navigation before progressing to algebra. Practical navigation, he believed, should be taught in a mechanical form, as it was a mechanical practice; learning navigation should come before mathematics.[62] He concluded that "no one, whether mathematician or not, would pass here [the school] without being a good navigator, and the Institution would consequently not be under the imputation of spoiling men capable of making good navigators in the frequently abortive attempt to make them mathematicians, or of sending men into the service as mere mathematicians who are almost useless as navigators."[63]

Ward concluded that his views went against the majority of the members of the Academic Board. Regardless, he asserted that he would continue to carry out his duties as the president of the Academic Board, but there was only one other member that he liked: Professor Lockwood. Ward concluded that "I entertain for that gentleman personally and officially sentiments of high respect, and trust that the Institution will long enjoy the benefit of his knowledge and skill in instruction."[64] Despite Ward's complaints, the academic program from 1846 through 1847 was little different from the previous year, however the school regulations for 1847 stated that students could fail other subjects as long as they passed seamanship and navigation with high marks; they would be rejected and dropped from the Navy list otherwise.[65] Ward left in 1847, when he was ordered to sea, probably a happier man until his death during the attack on Mathias Point in June 1861.[66]

By early 1847, Buchanan also found problems with the school. Since it reopened in October 1846, sixty-two midshipmen and twenty acting midshipmen had attended. Nine of the midshipmen and eight of the acting midshipmen had been detached from the school, while one midshipman had resigned. By January 1847 there were fifty-three midshipmen and twelve acting midshipmen still in attendance. After reviewing the professors' merit reports, Buchanan concluded that many of the midshipmen were deficient in their areas of studies. He believed, as previously, that this was still because many of the students had only encountered their subjects when they came to the school. Nevertheless, he was hopeful that the ambition and effort he saw in many of them would prevail, although he remained concerned. Buchanan specifically pointed out one Midshipman Cushman as an example. All efforts by both Buchanan and the professors to motivate Cushman were failing, and the superintendent saw little hope that he would graduate. He recommended that Cushman's father be notified and that Cushman be given a chance to resign from the Navy rather than be expelled for failing his examinations.[67] I have not been able to clearly identify Cushman, but there was a W. S. Cushman appointed a midshipman on 18 February 1841, who resigned on 31 July 1847, possibly excluded from the Navy via its new educational system as an unsuitable future officer.[68]

While the school still had problems, some improvements had occurred, and those who believed in the system tried to impose the more orderly way to professionalize midshipmen. Before Bancroft left as secretary of the Navy, he had authorized Buchanan to construct more rooms to house the midshipmen. In addition, a brick building was under construction for the mess hall, lyceum, and kitchen, as well as a wooden building for the sick. The new construction was nearing completion, and the midshipmen "will then be accommodated in 24 rooms calculated to contain 90 persons comfortably." Buchanan's request for money to buy standard works for the library had also met with success. In response, the midshipmen were generally well behaved both inside the school grounds and during their visits to Annapolis. Buchanan concluded that this was "evidence of their appreciation of the many valuable advantages given them by the Gov[ernment] to make themselves useful and accomplished officers." There had been only one case of misbehavior that Buchanan had to place before the department. Although he failed to give details, he believed the outcome had "a beneficial effect on that officer and his associates here."[69] By spring Buchanan had little to add to his previous report.[70]

In the fall of 1847, the Academic Board passed several resolutions for the superintendent's consideration. It suggested that instruction in steam be added to the course on chemistry, and that the same professor teach the subjects. In addition, it recommended that there be academic exercises before breakfast. The board also resolved "that in the opinion of this Board prayer should be introduced as a part of the exercises of the School, so soon as the hours of the other exercises can be arranged to admit of it."[71] In late 1847, Superintendent Upshur ordered the Academic Board to study the present allotment of time for various courses to see if they could be better arranged. In November, the Academic Board recommended that the total time devoted to each course remain the same, and Upshur told the Navy Department that the "all important course of gunning" was expanded by one month. Finally, once a midshipman completed a course, they would then embark on the next three courses as they progressed to higher levels in a systematic manner.[72]

From 1 June until they were examined, the midshipmen reviewed their studies. Meals were served along the summer schedule. The schedule was the same every day during these periods, except for Saturdays, when the students studied grammar for one hour every morning, then spent an hour on infantry drill, and had the rest of the afternoon off. But the professors also scheduled lectures in maritime and international law, critically important knowledge for professional naval officers who represented their nation overseas, often dealing with rivals like the British during tense situations. Significantly, the new course was "to be delivered once in two weeks in the place of a lecture in chemistry or steam, and the midshipmen are required to present written abstracts of the preceding lectures on that subject."[73] With their recommendations submitted, Upshur approved of the program for that academic year. Slowly, Annapolis was gearing its program on the needs of a profession as it tested and assessed the Navy's educational needs and program deployment at Annapolis.

Still, these early years were draining on the school because of the Mexican-American War, which erupted on 13 May 1846. The next day Superintendent Franklin Buchanan asked to be ordered to sea, but Secretary Bancroft denied his request and told him that his work at the school was much more important. The midshipmen had a similar desire to go to war, and fifty-six applied for active service, but most were denied. Still, some of the early midshipmen did ship out: John Adams, Thomas T. Houston, W. B. Hayes, and John R. Hamilton were ordered to *Dale*, while S. S. Bassett went to *Truxtun*, and H. G. D. Brown and Seth L. Phelps were sent to the New York Naval Yard. The rest of the midshipmen were forced to stay at the school and were examined in July 1846. Forty-seven passed, received their warrants as passed midshipmen, and went to sea. The remainder were sent home until October. The "youngsters"—or acting midshipmen with no prior sea experience—were also ordered to sea for the summer, but probably for training on various warships, rather than truly for war service. In the end, Secretary Bancroft decided to give in to some of the midshipmen's demands for a role in the war and pushed their examinations up by four months. The midshipmen from the next academic year during the war received similar treatment, and those who attended from 1846 to 1847 even raised money to erect a monument to their fallen comrades.[74]

By early 1847, the war began to disrupt the classes and Buchanan finally received permission to go to sea on 2 March 1847 and took command of *Germantown*. In the meantime, Lieutenant James Ward became the acting superintendent until George P. Upshur replaced him. Ward was then sent to sea in command of *Cumberland*. The 1847–48 academic year was a period of confusion. Attendance was poor, and the midshipmen were examined over a stretch of thirty-one sessions and then finally examined one at a time. Nonetheless, the school pushed on until the close of the war. Although it lost a number of midshipmen and personnel, and had its organization disrupted, school-trained officers helped show members of Congress that Annapolis had a beneficial role to play in training America's naval officers.[75] In January 1848, Superintendent Upshur concluded, like his predecessor, that most of the midshipmen were making good progress in their studies and duties because of their diligence, although there were some who still performed worse than others, as in any system.[76]

Early in 1848, the Navy Department, acting on the board's recommendations, hired a new professor, Charles W. Copeland from New York, to teach steam engineering, as the steam construction program moved forward. The Navy ordered Copeland to instruct "the midshipmen on the science and practice of steam and the use of the steam engine by a course of lectures and experiments." For this purpose, the department agreed to pay his transportation to Annapolis as well as the packing and shipping of the models used in his course. Secretary Mason expressed "the wish of the Department that your lectures shall consist of a full course"— three years after the foundation of the school, it finally had someone hired specifically to teach steam.[77] By 6 May 1848, Upshur was able to submit his report for the period 1 January to 31 March, in which he noted that Copeland taught a short course on steam and Professor Lockwood continued the topic as part of his chemistry course. Still, no grades were assigned. Regardless, Upshur was pleased with the progress of the midshipmen and reported only minor academic problems in the lower sections.[78]

Upshur felt that the biggest issue the institution faced was that the ages of students mixed too much between young and old. He asserted that the older midshipmen took the place of older brothers in this naval family, and Upshur worried about the effect of a "bad apple" on the professional development of the younger boys. One young man, Charles Cushman from Maine, posed an immediate problem. The Navy transferred Cushman to the school on 25 March 1849, but the next day Upshur wanted the transfer revoked. As soon as Cushman had settled in his room, he surrounded himself with young acting midshipmen and proceeded to misbehave. Upshur was particularly upset by Cushman's foul language, which he used to offend a midshipman, his mother, and the "memory of his deceased father." Cushman's language was so reprehensible that Upshur felt that it would be improper even to quote it in his report. His conclusion was clear: Cushman was a bad seed and he wanted him removed. He told the secretary that he feared "the corrupting influence of his [Cushman's] language and example upon the acting mid[shipmen] some of whom are only 13 year olds."[79] Cushman was not the honorable officer the professional Navy wished to cultivate.

Cushman's father, a judge, then wrote the secretary of the Navy, complaining about how his son was treated. Judge Cushman wrote that he believed Upshur misrepresented the facts of the case. In his defense, Upshur said that the testimony of witnesses supported his assertion and that he, contrary to Judge Cushman's contention, gave young Cushman every chance to defend himself. Upshur added that after Cushman finished his defense, he informed him that his use of vulgar language was still unacceptable. The superintendent added that he told young Cushman that "I can not in justice to boys of 13 and 14 years of age, or to their parents, consent to place him [Cushman] in a room with them. That as there was no vacant room at the School, it was proper that he should return to the Hotel and remain there until the decision of the Department upon his case could be received."[80] Later, one of the young midshipmen who heard Cushman use vulgar language came to Upshur's residence. The lad had received a letter of apology from Cushman and wanted Upshur's opinion as to whether he should accept it. Upshur told the secretary that because he was "very young I counseled him to accept it, but advised against personal intercourse with Mr. Cushman." Upshur concluded that if the department decided to reinstate Cushman, he should be sent to sea immediately. Upshur felt that he could go to sea because of the advanced stage of his training and because he was seventeen years old. He wrote that "I think he would not be cordially received by the young officers now at the School, and it would be difficult for him to establish an acceptable companionship with them."[81]

In the end, Cushman appeared to have been reinstated, since he graduated, served in the Navy for twenty-eight years, and retired as commander.[82] However, school administrators were wary of such men and felt that change was necessary so that the Navy could start training midshipmen on shore at an earlier, more uniform age. Despite its best intentions, the Naval School was too informal and hardly a "military institution at all." It had no formal battalions or formations, nor did it have cadet officers. Often the students didn't even wear their uniforms and considered the place simply a location to study for their promotion examinations. Even some in the Navy never considered that the Naval School would become a permanent place to educate young people for future careers as officers. Park Benjamin concluded that, if they had, "it would have met with a storm of opposition which might well have brought its [the school's] career to an untimely end."[83] The Naval School era was a time of establishing the institution and of negotiating what professionalism meant in the Navy, rather than stirring the waters with any revolutionary changes.

In the school era, midshipmen came together at Annapolis, often from different states, having deployed first to a variety of ships if appointed before 1845. Joined together, they shared a common experience and bonded as young officers. Yet Upshur was disillusioned and ordered the Academic Board to study the situation.[84] Students were still coming and going as the Navy required, and the Navy needed a longer program that took its students into the system at an earlier age before their habits were set in stone. In his annual report to Congress for 1848, Secretary Mason explained that creating a naval officer was a long process and proper education was important. Mason explained that to "qualify him [the officer] for the responsible duties of his profession must be the work of years." Moreover, he told congress that the naval officer's services were "more of the head than the hand." West Point's system, he asserted, proved the utility of sustained officer education, and it "will not fail to be confirmed in the navy." Beyond navigation, steam, and mechanics, Mason contended that naval officers also had to be familiar "with the languages of all nations with whom his duty brings him in contact, and with the laws of his own country and of nations." But rather than burden Congress with passing new legislation, Mason assured members that the Navy "aided by the learned and judicious professors on duty at the school, and by the officers of the navy who take a deep interest in the subject, will doubtless be prepared to present a more complete system" soon to train young boys for their professional responsibilities.[85] By then, Mason was a lame-duck secretary, but his successor, William Ballard Preston, in President Taylor's new administration, moved forward with the department's desire to reform Annapolis.

CHAPTER 3

The Naval Academy, 1850–60

T he changes that began at the Naval School in 1849 created the Naval Academy in 1850 under the jurisdiction of the chief of the Bureau of Ordnance and Hydrography.[1] The reforms also formalized the academy's command hierarchy and gave students the variety of courses needed for the modern naval officer. The result, by 1851, was a full-fledged four-year officer training program and a decrease in the average age of student admissions as recruits entered the academy after leaving civilian schools. Rather than a consolidation of the existing system, the new Naval Academy became a place where the Navy introduced young students slowly to naval life, rather than simply send them off to sea as the Navy's needs arose: Annapolis became a structured way to professionalize potential officers into the U.S. Navy, as had been first envisioned. Continually looking to West Point for inspiration, the Army's success in the Mexican-American War gave reformers the stimulus needed to enact a more professional naval officer training program at Fort Severn.

On 22 August 1849, a board composed of Professor Chauvenet; Surgeon William S. W. Ruschenberger; Commanders Upshur, Samuel F. DuPont, and Franklin Buchanan; and Commodore William B. Shubrick, along with Captain Henry Brewerton, Army Corps of Engineers and superintendent of West Point, told the secretary of the Navy that the school's structure should fully match that at West Point, because the latter had brought "glory to the army after the victories of the late War [Mexican-American]." In response, the board recommended that the probationary period for midshipmen be six years, with two spent at Annapolis.[2] It concluded that "they [would] then undergo a rigid examination; if this examination proves satisfactory they [would] be sent to sea under the present regulations as to recommendations from their Commanders, and after at least three years service at sea they [would] return to the School for one year and then be examined to ascertain their qualifications, professional and moral, for promotion and that any Midshipman rejected at this final Examination, [would] be dropped from the service."[3] Administrators, however, remained concerned about the quality of education at Annapolis if the regulations allowed midshipmen's time at the facility to be interrupted and recommended an uninterrupted four-year training program, established in 1851, as the students spent summers on an academy training ship to satisfy at-sea requirements, the subject of chapter 6.[4] The new regulations solved some of the old system's problems and kept the students at the academy for a sustained period as the Navy taught them professional skills.

Under the new academy regulations, beginning with the 1849 academic year, candidates for admission reported to the academy between 1 and 5 October and were examined to see if they were suitable to be made into officers. They had to be able to read, write, spell, be of "good moral character," as before, but also be between ages thirteen and fifteen. If they passed their admission exam, they received an acting midshipman's appointment and went straight to the academy. At first, after two years of service, they were ordered to sea for six months until the four-year program was instituted fully. If his commanding officer deemed his conduct proper, the acting midshipman received his midshipman's warrant; three years after leaving the academy he then returned to study for his lieutenant's exam.[5] With the 1850–51 academic year, acting midshipmen first completed their four-year program and graduated before they received their midshipmen's warrants.[6]

By the early 1850s, the academy divided education into nine departments analogous to West Point's: Practical Seamanship, Naval Gunnery, and Naval Tactics; Mathematics; Astronomy, Navigation, and Surveying; Natural and Experimental Philosophy (mechanics, including the steam engine); Field Artillery and Infantry Tactics; Ethics and English Studies (which included English grammar, descriptive geography, physical geography, outlines of history, rhetoric, ethics, and political science); French; Spanish; and Drawing and Draughting. The new academy also further developed its hierarchy—the superintendent, also the president of the Academic Board, and at least a commander, and was responsible for the government and discipline of the academy. His executive officer was the commandant of midshipmen, at least a lieutenant, and taught naval tactics, gunnery, and seamanship with three assistants—at least master's rank. The most senior was the principal assistant. Finally, midshipmen ranks were based on the date they enrolled in the Naval Academy. Unlike the naval schools, the academy regulated every aspect of academy life as the Navy brought more structure and formality to the students' existence. The academy introduced a dress code, with school uniforms, and enforced naval hair and beard regulations on the students. Furthermore, the Navy barred midshipmen from marrying while at the academy, which stifled romance with the local ladies, and introduced a curfew: the midshipmen were allowed out on Saturday afternoons but had to return to the academy at 8:00 PM in the winter and 9:00 PM in the summer.[7] Moreover, after 1851, the academy's grading scheme also employed a more scientific system to assess midshipmen's progress.

A midshipman could obtain up to 1,000 total points toward satisfying his educational requirements over four years (table 6), but no more than 275 could be for "subjects that did not have a strong practical or professional bent." The remaining points were devoted to topics that the professional naval officer required to carry out the nation's needs far from home. The points factored in training on navigating a sailboat or steamship "to distant lands," communicating with "the people you found there," and, naturally, "how to fight them" if needed. Weekly tests were scored out of four points, but the final exams were restricted to seamanship and tactics. However, the academy also linked education and naval discipline through a system of demerit points, similar to West Point's. As will be discussed in chapter 5, if a midshipman received 200 annually, he could be dismissed and the number of demerits was factored into the student's final grade.[8]

The aggregate point system of 1,000 points was balanced by the fact that individual subjects were marked on a different scale. By 1855, for example, drawing composed forty points, while ethics and English studies were graded out of a maximum of ninety. Seamanship was still given a high priority in the final grade, but the importance of the other "nonprofessional" topics were simply noted in the final record.[9] The academic weighting system affected George Dewey, for example. Dewey did poorly at his first examination in June 1855 and placed thirty-fifth out of thirty-eight. History and geography were weighted heavily compared to other topics, and history was Dewey's weakness. In 1856, when weighting changed, Dewey did better. History was given the lower weighting, and his problems with that subject "had but small influence on the general result, which raised him to No. 9 on the merit roll." By his last examination he ranked fifth out of fifteen.[10] A future professional officer of the Navy was saved.

The new Naval Academy also divided students into four classes and subdivided them into manageable sections according to its members' standing. The remaining "Oldsters" or midshipmen—as opposed to the "Youngsters" who were acting midshipmen—had a separate class. Each class was to study one course, but the most difficult were left for senior sections as students progressed from year to year. Professors and instructors were responsible for a class's discipline, students were forbidden to leave without a good reason, and they had to tell the instructor if they were unprepared for the class. The Navy also gave professors assistants, and the professor occasionally took over to assess the assistant's abilities. Finally, instructors were required to keep daily notes of the students' progress, and assistants had to make weekly reports to department heads. All reports were to be handed weekly to the superintendent, who in turn forwarded monthly reports to the secretary of the Navy.[11]

Table 6. Naval Academy Course Grading

Department and Branch		Maximum Grade at Graduation
Practical Seamanship		220
Seamanship	150	
Naval Tactics	30	
Practical Gunnery and Boat Armament	40	
Mathematics		100
Astronomy, Navigation and Surveying		110
General Astronomy	30	
Practical Astronomy, Navigation and Surveying	80	
Natural and Experimental Philosophy		120
Mechanics	60	
Physics	25	
Steam Engine	35	
Field Artillery and Infantry Tactics		85
Theory of Gunnery	40	
Field Artillery	20	
Infantry Tactics	25	
Ethics and English Studies		90
Moral Science and International Law	30	
Grammar and Rhetoric	25	
Geography	15	
History and Composition	20	
French		75
Spanish		60
Drawing and Draughting		40
Conduct		100
Total		1,000

Source: Adapted from U.S. Naval Academy, *Regulations of the U.S. Naval Academy at Annapolis, Maryland* (Washington, D.C.: A. O. P. Nicholson, Printer, 1855), 19–23; Edward Chauncey Marshall, *History of the United States Naval Academy* (New York: D. Van Nostrand, 1862), 137; and Charles Todorich, *The Spirited Years: A History of the Antebellum Naval Academy* (Annapolis: Naval Institute Press, 1984), 82–83.

The academy held examinations twice yearly in February and June to test student progress. Each department head examined students in the presence of the Academic Board and the class's instructor, and a student found deficient could be dismissed from the Navy or reexamined. There was even room for advanced students; a candidate could join any class if he proved qualified, and he could graduate at any annual examination.[12] Nevertheless, the professors questioned giving special weight to certain subjects and felt that those given less weight were often truer tests of a midshipman's mental abilities. Seamanship, they contended, professionally, was the most important subject, but even second-rate sailors could pass the exam, making it difficult to rank scientifically the classes and weed out unsuitable students. The same was true of practical gunnery, often taught at the academy's battery (figure 4), so testing theoretical gunnery might better assess which midshipman would make the best officer. The professors proposed a weighting system with maximum marks of 500, 400, 300, 200, and 100 points yearly, which allowed midshipmen to show improvement over time, but the existing system was maintained.[13]

Figure 4. Naval Academy Battery. *("View of the Battery from River," Frank Leslie's* Illustrated Newspaper, *26 March 1853)*

Selecting and educating recruits at an institution is an important sign of a professional organization, but so is instilling the profession's ethos. The Naval Academy, through its ethics department, instilled in midshipmen important officer values by teaching "moral science," two hours weekly, with up to four hours spent studying the subject in preparation for classes.[14] Moral science taught the midshipmen decision-making skills and that while they might disagree with the state's orders, professionals had to obey their client. Couched in Christian terms, with reference to biblical evidence, the academy used Francis Wayland's *Elements of Moral Science*, originally published in 1835 and based on the series of lectures he gave at

Brown University.[15] The earliest mention of Wayland's book in use at Annapolis was 1851, but it was likely used before then, and at least until 1858, when two copies appeared in the inventory of books of the Department of Ethics and English Studies.[16] Perhaps because of time constraints, the Navy failed to write its own ethics textbook and instead assigned a civilian text. Consequently, the government issued additional directives to interpret it based on the state's needs. Secretary of the Navy William A. Graham, for example, told Superintendent Cornelius K. Stribling that the department "directs that the [Ethics] Professor inform the young men that the objectionable parts, being upon a disputed question in this country, . . . are not [to be] taught as a part of the course."[17] Because the state might call upon naval officers to enforce the Fugitive Slave Act, the most problematic section was likely Wayland's support for slave freedom.

Key to understanding moral science is Wayland's definition. Moral law derived from God's laws as revealed in the Bible and established the connection between actions and consequences. Wayland warned his readers that a "higher authority has admonished us, 'Be not deceived, God is not mocked; *whatsoever* a man *soweth, that shall he* also *reap* [emphasis in original].'"[18] Consequently, Wayland believed that each person should judge his actions—personal, spiritual, or official—to assess whether they were moral, but also remember that conscience was imperfect. Meditation had to be impartial: "remember that you are liable to be misled by the seductions of passion and the allurements of self-interest. Put yourself in the place of those around you and put others in your own place and remark how you would then consider your actions." Finally, if a person found that he had done wrong, he must remember what led him to error and to guard against a recurrence.[19] Wayland believed that God gave everyone the facility to decide right from wrong: "It is an ever present faculty. It always admonishes us if we will listen to its voice, and frequently does so even when we wish to silence its warnings. Hence we may always know our duty if we will but inquire for it. We can, therefore, never have any excuse for doing wrong, since no man need do wrong unless he chooses; and no man will do it ignorantly unless from criminal neglect of the faculty which God has given him."[20] For Wayland, the Bible was the ultimate guide to right and wrong.[21]

While morally and religiously conservative, Wayland was socially liberal and often echoed John Stuart Mill. Wayland believed that a person could do anything as long as it did not interfere with the rights of another individual. But with rights came obligations. For example, Wayland believed a parent was obligated to make a "child a suitable member of the community" and to support the child in infancy. Moreover, Wayland believed that God's laws applied equally to all beings, including slaves. Wayland declared that slavery was immoral because it denied an individual freedom and choice and made slaves no different from animals. Furthermore,

Wayland asserted that slavery was contrary to the Bible's teachings to "love thy *neighbor as thyself, and all things whatsoever* ye would that men should do unto you, do ye even so unto them [emphasis in original]."[22]

For the Navy, the most important aspect of Wayland's textbook emphasized professional responsibility to the state. Wayland concluded that government derived its authority from society and God's moral laws bound officers to the state. They had a duty to carry out their assignments in accordance with this law. Significantly, Wayland believed that the military officer's duty was to carry out orders to the best of his ability, rather than judge their legality.[23] Wayland's definition of the officer's duty matches that of a professional. He wrote that "the officer has no right to question the goodness or wisdom of the law; since for these he is not responsible. His only duty is to execute it so long as he retains his office. If he believe the action required of him to be morally wrong or at variance with the constitution, he should resign. He has no right to hold the office and refuse to perform the duties which others have been empowered to require of him."[24] Moral science guided the individual in carrying out his duties, and he had to resign if unwilling to follow orders. As a professional text, moral science taught the young midshipmen to do their job rather than pass judgment on a client's policies. Moral science instilled shared values in officer-recruits, but some felt it had few professional applications. On 20 November 1852, twenty-seven midshipmen demanded to spend more time studying "drawing or some other branch, more practically useful in our Profession" than moral science and suggested that the Academic Board "take the necessary steps to relieve us of this study."[25]

To complete the students' ethical education, the Navy also required them to attend chapel.[26] Moreover, as Peter Karsten contends, church attendance also showed midshipmen they were a cohort even in spirituality.[27] The chapel held morning prayer for fifteen minutes daily before breakfast, and students also attended a full service each Sunday.[28] In 1859 the academy relaxed the regulation that required attendance at Sunday service, if officers declared "in writing that they cannot conscientiously attend."[29] The amendment failed to qualify what "conscientiously" meant, or whether the new exception applied to the midshipmen or just the staff at the academy. However, when Superintendent George S. Blake addressed the concerns of one Presbyterian parent in 1859, he told him that his son was permitted to attend the Presbyterian church in Annapolis on Sundays and communion days and would only be exempted from the academy chapel if Blake were informed in writing that their son could not conscientiously attend.[30]

The Board of Examiners and other academy officials observed the changes that occurred after 1850 and made recommendations, but they believed generally that the academy had found its place in the American military establishment. But the board believed that the system of still having midshipmen who received their warrants before 1851 harmed their development. The board found that these midshipmen, after spending time at sea, spent much of their time at the academy "constantly engaged in occupations which give them no time for study." Therefore, they took longer to learn those "branches of professional science" required to make an officer. Consequently, in 1852 the board recommended that midshipmen appointed before 1851 spend two more years at Annapolis, be examined in seamanship, and be awarded their merit numbers before returning to sea. Those found deficient would be dropped from the service as unsuitable officers. While disappointed with the old style of officer professionalization, and admitting that the older classes were foundering, the board concluded that "the younger classes commencing at an early age, are kept constantly at their studies, [and] with nothing to destract [*sic*] their attention [they] gradually advance step by step to the more easy attainment of the requisite knowledge."[31] The Board of Examiners, composed of visiting naval officers, believed that starting the officer's education immediately upon appointment from the civilian world showed the best results.

Until the mid-1850s, the academy operated under a two-tiered system. Superintendent Stribling reported in 1852 that the midshipmen of 1847 were at the academy, but those appointed in 1848, 1849, and 1850 had yet to attend. To clear the backlog, the academy permitted those midshipmen, who started schooling before 1851, one year to prepare for their promotion examinations, but Stribling estimated in 1852 that it might be 1856 before all these midshipmen graduated. He believed that only then would the new four-year system become fully effective.[32] By 1853 the Board of Examiners contended that the new four-year system of officer education was best for the needs of the nation. They wrote that "the Institution will annually furnish to the country which has so liberally sustained and fostered it, a Corps of Officers well prepared to uphold her interests and sustain her honor in times of War, and who, during the period of peace that we may be permitted to enjoy, will contribute largely to her growing greatness and improvements to the Arts and Sciences."[33] The years 1853 and 1854 were critical in the final establishment of the antebellum U.S. Naval Academy. The age qualifications were changed—candidates for admission had to be between fourteen and sixteen years old—and students attending under the old system regulations were told that after three years' service they were allowed to stay for only one more year. The academy would examine the older students in June; if they failed a second examination, they would be dismissed from the Navy.[34]

In July 1854, Superintendent Louis M. Goldsborough thought, and the Board of Examiners recommended, that the age of admission should be set between fifteen and seventeen years old, rather than between fourteen and sixteen. The board, "after witnessing the examination of all the classes throughout, & being particularly struck with the *remarkable* proficiency of the graduating class of Acting Midshipmen even in Seamanship & Naval Tactics [emphasis in original]," believed setting the age between fifteen and seventeen would be ideal. Moreover, Goldsborough believed that graduate midshipmen should only be required to spend two years at sea before taking their promotion examination, instead of the existing three and one-half, which included time on the training ship.[35] Goldsborough concluded that the "united effect [of the changes] would be simply to take one year from the Sea-Service now required after graduation, & to add that time to the limits of age at present imposed for admission; so that candidates would thus be able to join this establishment at a more befitting age than now, & then become Passed Midshipmen just about as early in life as the existing rules prescribe."[36] Goldsborough would have been pleased, because the age requirements in the 1855 regulations stipulated that candidates must be between fourteen and seventeen years old.[37] By 1855 the institution appears to have found its footing in several respects, because it selected some midshipmen and rejected those who were unsuitable for the new officer corps.

Notwithstanding what can be learned from their program of study, regulations, and texts, a true understanding of the dynamics of life at the new academy can only be understood through the students, their backgrounds, time at the academy, and how the academy viewed their progress. As in the Naval School era, only so much can be learned of the backgrounds of academy students from the records of the famous. The students' ages, for which data are available, varied with the admissions regulations, but they were generally between thirteen and eighteen years old. The average ages of the students dipped in the first several years of the academy era then began to rise again as the Navy decided to admit candidates of a slightly higher age. Regardless, the average age remained between fifteen and sixteen years old, with a low standard deviation, indicating that the students' ages clustered

Table 7. Ages by Date of Appointment 1849–60

Years	1849	1850	1851	1852	1853	1854	1855	1856	1857	1858	1859	1860
Average	16.2	15.4	15.1	15.3	15.3	15.2	15.5	16.0	16.4	16.7	16.5	16.4
Minimum	14.8	13.8	13.2	13.8	14.3	14.0	13.8	14.2	14.1	14.2	14.2	14.0
Maximum	16.9	17.0	17.3	16.5	16.1	16.2	17.6	17.0	18.0	18.0	18.1	18.3
Std Dev	0.74	0.98	0.89	0.78	0.52	0.66	1.08	0.73	1.06	1.1	1.01	1.06
Missing	23	2	4	0	5	5	19	9	8	16	8	30
Total	34	46	47	47	27	57	47	62	73	62	83	114

Source: Calculated from Registers of Candidates for Admission to the Academy.

around the average (see table 7). The new students of the academy started at a much younger age than their Naval School counterparts.

Regardless of the reason why young men joined the Navy, they chose it as one possible career and this fact is what is important. The intent of this present work is not a comparison of U.S. Army and Navy officers, their recruitment, social backgrounds, and work experiences. Still, a brief comment on the origins of U.S. Army officers during this same period is beneficial. Entering a military academy gave young people an outlet for their desire for adventure that was compatible with their parents' expectations. William B. Skelton notes, for example, that James S. Thompson, who became a military cadet in 1821, had read about the adventures of military heroes like George Washington and felt compelled to become a soldier. The same was true of Pierre G. T. Beauregard after reading about the exploits of Napoleon. Skelton concludes that young men from commercial, agricultural, and professional sectors of America entered the Army because they were "high in respectability and political influence but in moderate or even straitened economic circumstances." Meanwhile, while more military families might have wished their sons to join the army, restrictions limited the number of appointees to West Point from that group. Still, Skelton asserts that it was hard to "calculate with any precision the actual numbers of officers who selected their careers for economic reasons."[38]

After the War of 1812, Army recruitment was standardized and officers began to enter the Army system from similar social backgrounds. If we look specifically at Skelton's analysis of fathers' occupations for West Point graduates from 1844 to 1860 we see some of the following results: agricultural sector (28.5 percent), commercial/manufacturing (31.4 percent), professional (22.8 percent), government service (14.3 percent). The breakdown of the government service category is particularly revealing: congressmen (0.3 percent); federal civil servant (2.9 percent), Army officer (6.7 percent), Navy/Marine officer (2.4 percent), state/local official (1.8 percent); enlisted soldier (0.2 percent). The parental backgrounds of West Point graduates are similar enough to those of Naval Academy graduates to be a significant point of comparison. What is striking is that relatively few sons of Army and Navy fathers, a total of 9.3 percent, were graduates of West Point; the vast majority were sons of father's with different careers.[39]

The professions were heavily represented in Skelton's statistical analysis, as they are in this present analysis of the Naval Academy. Skelton concludes that the professional group "depended on the fees or salary" to provide for their family, unlike those of a farmer or entrepreneur who had an independent income. If a member of the professional group suffered the death of the head of the household, the family could be in a dire predicament; the farmer or independent businessman could

Table 8. Family Occupational Background USNA 1850–59, West Point 1844–60, Free Male Occupations 1850

Father's Profession	USNA (N)	USNA % of Known	West Point (%)	Free Males (%)
Professional	117	31.5	22.8	2.5
Legal	62	16.7		
Medical	39	10.5		
Religious	8	2.2		
Educational	4	1.1		
Editor	4	1.1		
Commercial	112	30.1	31.4	30.2
Merchant	52	14.0		
Manufacturing	21	5.6		
Financial	11	3.0		
Maritime	10	2.7		
Clerk	5	1.3		
Agent	5	1.3		
Railroad	5	1.3		
Slaver	3	0.8		
Government Service	51	13.7	14.3	0.5
Army/Navy	26	7.0		
Government	25	6.7		
Other	38	10.2		
Agricultural/Farming	54	14.5	28.5	45.2
None			3.0	
Other				21.5
Total Known	372	100.0	100.0	100.0
Total Unknown	179			
Total Cases	551		657	

Source: Data for West Point based on Skelton, *American Profession of Arms*, 159–60, tables 9.4 and 9.5; USNA Calculated from Register of Admissions.

Note: For ease of comparison the author has formatted this table similar to those done by Skelton, and the analysis includes the 372 academy students for which parent's or guardian's occupational data were found. The analysis in this and the following table ends with 1859 to avoid any distortions caused by the growing sectional crisis.

pass along the family business to his heir. Thus, enrollment in either West Point, as Skelton found, or in the Naval Academy, could provide a son with a career and a free education, and it goes far in explaining the dramatically higher numbers of sons of professionals in these institutions than in the general population.[40] Coming from a professional family background, such students were also more likely to accept the style of training for a professional career.

In sum, both institutions drew their students largely from commercial and professional backgrounds (see table 8). Annapolis saw the percentage of students from the commercial realm almost double from 18.0 percent in the school era to 30.1 percent during the academy era, similar to that of the wider free white male population. Another approximately 31.5 percent of Annapolis students were sons of professionals, compared with 23.1 percent during the school era. This was almost a 10 percent larger proportion than at West Point, and was about thirteen times larger than that portion of the general population because the Navy selected students directly from civilian schools where such parents were more likely to first send their children. Meanwhile, Annapolis students were also drawn from a large portion of government families, almost the same at West Point, while both institutes' portions far outpaced that of the general population. At Annapolis, though, there was a dramatic drop from 43.7 percent in the school era to 13.7 percent during the academy era.

Finally, almost 30 percent of West Point cadets came from the agricultural sector, compared with about 15 percent at Annapolis. This undoubtedly partially reflects the land-orientated focus of West Point over Annapolis. This analysis of Annapolis found twenty-six students had a naval or military father or guardian, while academy statistics compiled in 1899 for this period revealed thirty-eight candidates whose fathers were military officers were examined for admission between 1851 and 1860. Of these thirty-eight, eighteen could be clearly identified as being the sons of naval officers, while seven could be identified as being the sons of Army officers; the remainder only specified a rank that could have belonged to either. Of those candidates examined, fifteen were rejected.[41] Despite the presence of some students who tried to follow in their father's footsteps, the vast majority tended to pursue careers different from their father's or guardian's, similar to the dynamic found for students at West Point.

The appointment procedures during the academy era were clarified further in 1852. The naval appropriation legislation passed on 31 August 1852 stipulated that the only pupils allowed to attend a U.S. naval school were those appointed on the recommendation of a member of Congress.[42] Consequently, the geographic backgrounds (see table 9) of the Naval Academy students are significant. The proportion of students from the North and South, relative to the supply of potential students from states that sent appointees to Annapolis was almost equal. Northern students represented 37.9% of the academy's population and 37.0% of potential students, defined as the 15-24 year old white male cohort who could have attended Annapolis from all states that dispatched appointees to the academy. Similarly, Southern students represented about 30.1% of the academy's student body and 24.1% of the potential students. During the school era, these same Northern states represented 30.4% of the student body and about 52% of potential students, while

Table 9. Origins of Appointees 1850–59

States	N	(%)	15–24-Year-Old White Males 1860 (%)
North	209	37.9	37.0
ME, VT, NH, MA, RI, CT	64	11.6	10.9
NY, PA, NJ, DE	145	26.3	26.1
South	166	30.1	24.1
MD, VA	31	5.6	8.0
NC, SC, GA, AL, MS, LA, TN, KY	135	24.5	16.1
Central (IL, IN, OH)	69	12.5	19.8
Other	49	8.9	19.1
Missing Cases	58	10.5	
Total Cases	551		4,067.4 (1860, Thousands)

Source: Calculated from Register of Alumni and Registers of Candidates for Admission (mainly for those who did not graduate). Percentage of white males between fifteen and twenty-four years old based on data in Wattenberg, *The Statistical History of the United States*, Series A 195–209, "Population: Population of States," 24–37.

Note: Birth-state analysis is not included, because the number of missing cases was 302, or 50.8 percent of the data set, which in my opinion renders the analysis meaningless. Geographic breakdown has also been adjusted slightly from the Naval School period to better reflect the nation's increasing sectionalism.

Southerners represented 28.1% of the school's students and 21.5% of the supply of potential candidates. One can speculate on the reasons for the shift from a lessening of political patronage, to fewer job opportunities in the maritime and commercial sectors in the North, or a change in attitude to equalize appointments from North and South to their share of potential students to Annapolis, the 15–24-year-old white male population, as sectional tensions mounted. What is important is that the academy was more representative of the nation's demographic structure.

In the end, statistics can only go so far to describe the academy's students. Examples of individual students provide additional evidence of the change that occurred at the academy: the academy was looking for young, fit, intelligent students who had gone to civilian schools. Some of what the Academic Board expected of the educational backgrounds of candidates for admission to the academy can be gained from one case that came before them just before the outbreak of Civil War. Secretary of the Navy Isaac Toucey wrote Superintendent Blake on 27 February 1861 to discuss the latest batch of boys examined for admission. One lad was "a youth by the name of Hooke," who wanted an "informal examination" to assess whether he was "sufficiently advanced" for appointment. Toucey agreed, and the young man was examined on 4 March 1861.[43] Professors J. H. C. Coffin and H. H. Lockwood reported to the superintendent that he was "wanting in that knowledge of practical skill in the arithmetic of whole numbers, which are required of candidates, and that without much more thorough study of this branch, he would fail in passing the examination for admission in September. He has not been to school for some time and appears to have forgotten what he studied several years ago. In other branches his examination has been satisfactory."[44]

A letter of reference for Marx J. Etting gives some indication of the qualities of the students who gained appointments. John W. Faires, a classics teacher in Philadelphia, wrote to Marx's father, Benjamin, describing the boy; the letter was later forwarded to the superintendent. Faires wrote that Marx was a knowledgeable young man who had succeeded in all the studies he had undertaken at Faires' school. Faires opined that Marx was like most boys and had improved a great deal with the drill he had received at school. Faires believed that the boy was "attentive and diligent" and was of an affectionate disposition. Marx's general character made him well liked by both his teachers and his peers. Faires pointed out that Marx believed in honesty and abhorred lying, but also believed in honor. At one time Marx suffered great ridicule at the hands of a teacher and took the blame for a charge when he was innocent rather than expose "a companion who was guilty." Faires concluded that Marx was "respectful to those who have authority over him" and was ambitious. Marx's teacher believed that "he appears to me to possess those qualities of mind and of heart, which not only are essential to success, but almost invariably ensure it, in the honourable profession of which he has made choice."[45] Marx was the type of young man the Navy hoped might make a good professional naval officer in this new experiment in training. He was appointed to the academy in 1851, although he did not graduate.[46]

While such students might still fail, the academy held out the hope that the more professional selection of recruits would pay off in the end. Younger students just out of school and with knowledge still fresh in their minds had a clear advantage now that naval training was focused on professional academic-style knowledge. The ideal student's educational background may have been like that of Edward Wing, a fifteen year old from an Ohio farm, although he too failed to graduate from Annapolis. His school principal, U. D. Lathrop, wrote the academy on 8 August 1854 and included Wing's grades. He felt that Wing's work was "ordinarily" to the satisfaction of his instructors. He received a 9/10 in Latin and Greek, a 10/10 in arithmetic, and had only been absent from prayers once during his time at Kenyon College.[47]

Furthermore, a candidate also had to be physically fit. Although a student could be rejected on medical grounds, rejections were sometimes appealed. One such case was that of Wesley Williams, whom the academy surgeon rejected because of a physical problem. Williams appealed and a special medical board of the Navy Department was convened in 1850 to review the case. The board ruled in his favor, and Superintendent George P. Upshur was informed that the young man was to be examined by the Academic Board. The special board concluded that "'the want of perfect symmetry in his left arm' will not disqualify him from discharging all the duties of an officer in the navy."[48] The order was passed along to Upshur's successor, Stribling, in October 1850.[49] Williams was eventually appointed to the academy, but he also failed to graduate.[50]

Another gentleman, J. A. Webber, wrote Stribling on 2 October 1851 to discuss the medical rejection of Frank P. Webber. Mr. Webber told Stribling that the boy's "heart had long been fixed" on a naval appointment, and he hoped that his case would be reconsidered. Webber pointed out that in "his time of life," the boy's body is "in a state of rapid change," but he had the assurances of another surgeon that the boy was fit. He concluded that "his deafness," which was evidently the cause of his rejection, "has never been more than slight and temporary." Mr. Webber, who had done military service, told Stribling that the surgeon at his post assured him that the boy would be able to pass the medical examination if given another chance.[51] Meanwhile others, like John Campbell, were admitted to the academy with some strings attached. In Campbell's case, the chief of the Bureau of Medicine and Surgery concluded that he could be admitted, but if his condition took "the form of permanent disease, he will be dropped from the list" of students at the academy.[52] Fifteen-year-old John Campbell of Kentucky was admitted to the academy under these conditions but also failed to graduate.[53]

Even if a candidate failed to gain admission, he could be given a second chance. One such case occurred in January 1853, when the Academic Board examined the son of one Captain Sawyer. The board found that he was "not duly qualified" to join the Navy, but Stribling told Secretary John P. Kennedy that "as the age of young Sawyer is hardly within the limits to authorize his admission into the Navy, and as he appears to be a bright boy," he should try again in September. He added that "in the meantime he can be preparing himself for the examination at some private school."[54] The exact identities of Captain Sawyer and his son are unclear, but a George A. Sawyer was appointed to the academy with the '54 Date. This young Sawyer was fourteen and a half years old, appointed from Vermont, and his father, Horace B. Sawyer, made captain on 12 April 1853. Nevertheless, George failed to graduate from Annapolis.[55]

Admittedly, even some of the students recruited under the new system had to be weeded out, because the profession selected the most suitable officers with the overall acumen—or desire—to continue in the service. The stories of famous Naval Academy graduates who did contribute to the Navy's exploits later in the century reveal backgrounds, and academy entrance experiences, similar to other candidates, but with successful outcomes. Thomas O. Selfridge Jr.'s great-great-grandfather, Edward A. Selfridge, was from Scotland and emigrated to Ireland during the English Civil War. He did not like Ireland, so he moved to America and settled in Worcester County, Massachusetts. Thomas' grandfather had five children, but he died when they were still young. Thomas' uncle, Edward Selfridge, "deprived of a father's care at an early age . . . shipped before the mast and made a voyage to the northwest coast of America." By age nineteen he was in command of a merchant ship sailing from Antwerp to Boston, but the crew mutinied and killed him. His other uncle, Christopher, was a naval constructor, but he died of yellow fever in 1855. His father, Thomas Oliver Selfridge, obtained a midshipman's warrant and joined the Navy in January 1818. After one voyage he returned to the United States, but because it was hard for a midshipman to get a promotion, the senior Selfridge left the Navy and joined the merchant ship *Union* as third mate and made a voyage to China. Later he made voyages to Russia and the West Indies as second and first mates. The owners of the ships offered him the command of his own ship, but the senior Selfridge rejoined the Navy instead.[56]

Thomas O. Selfridge Jr. was thus born into a family with a strong maritime and naval tradition. Thomas Jr. was born on 6 February 1836 in Charlestown, Massachusetts. He recalled that his family inspired him to join the Navy, and their background gave him "an almost instinctive knowledge of rudimentary naval matters." Thomas was well educated, although he changed schools frequently during his father's career. Young Thomas attended the English High School in Boston the year before he joined the academy, and he later reminisced that while reforms to the academy were instituted in 1850, that year's class was sent to sea early because of a shortage of naval officers. Consequently, his '51 Date had "the honor of being the pioneer class under" the full four-year curriculum. Nevertheless, the Navy advanced eleven of the best students to meet the demand for midshipmen. Five of the eleven failed to keep pace with their advancement and returned to their '51 Date grouping. But Selfridge remembered that "I was duly graduated in 1854 at the head of the remaining six, and therefore can justly claim the distinction of being the pioneer graduate of the U.S. Naval Academy." Thereafter, he fought in the Civil War, commanded several warships, and ended his career late in the century after being commander of the European Squadron.[57]

George Dewey, famous from his exploits in the Spanish-American War, became a midshipman in an analogous route. Dewey wrote that his forefathers lived in New England and were "of the old Pilgrim stock whose character has so eminently impressed itself on that of the nation." The first Dewey to America was Thomas Duee, of Huguenot ancestry, who moved from Sandwich, Kent, to Dorchester, Massachusetts, in 1634. George's father was a doctor, Julius Yemans Dewey, who trained at the University of Vermont and established a practice in Montpelier. George was born on 26 December 1837, the youngest of three sons; his mother died when he was five. He attended the district school and lived the life of most boys his age at the time. Dewey wrote, "one of my favorite deeds of bravado was descending the old State-house steps blindfolded, with the on-lookers wondering whether I would slip on the way and take the rest of the flight head first." He also enjoyed swimming in the Onion River near his home, and another time he destroyed his father's cart—the horse survived—when he managed to send it into the river.[58]

Dewey thought he was a bully in his school. He recounted that "some of the boys of my age regarded it as their business to test each new appointee." He was a handful, and his father decided that the young boy needed a more structured life and at fourteen sent him to the Military Academy at Norwich, Vermont. Dewey recounted that "at one time its reputation had been so high that it was considered superior to West Point, and many boys from the South, where the military spirit was more common in those days than in the North, had been among its pupils." The young boys at Norwich lived in dormitories and received military drill, but young Dewey eventually left the school. One night in 1854, he and some other boys broke up a church hymn sing by singing themselves, were arrested, and found guilty. Dewey concluded of the episode that "life in that school provided us with little relaxation. The very insistence of the authorities on continual study in a solemn manner was bound to awaken the spirit of mischief."[59]

He left the school in 1854, seventeen years old, and entered the Naval Academy. Cryptically, Dewey wrote, "at the time that I left Norwich . . . West Point had a great name as a disciplinary institution. There boys had to obey. Annapolis was not then so well known as West Point, being only nine years old." Whether Dewey and his father picked Annapolis for this reason is unclear, but given Dewey's experience at Norwich, it would be a logical conclusion. However, Dewey wrote that he attended Annapolis because there were no spaces for political appointments at West Point. Another boy, George Spaulding of Montpelier, was unable to assume his appointment at the academy, so George's father influenced a senator and obtained the place at the academy for George. Still a teenager, Dewey wrote that once he and his father arrived at Annapolis, they went to see a comedian. Dewey wrote, "I had never seen a real stage comedian before, and I laughed so hard that I fairly lost control of myself, and my father made me leave the theatre."[60] Dewey was still immature, but academy life would force such boys to behave or face expulsion.

Dewey recalled that the entrance exam for the academy was easy, but that the attrition rate once enrolled was high—to be discussed later—because the Navy kept only those who fit the service, despite their background, or the students decided themselves on a different career. Sixty students entered the academy in 1854, but Dewey recalls that only fifteen graduated in 1858; they lost twenty-three students after the first year and another nine after the second, because the Navy kept only

Figure 5. Fencing and Gunnery Practice. *("Battery Practice and Fencing," Frank Leslie's* Illustrated Newspaper, *26 March 1853)*

the best. As at Norwich, Dewey's discipline record hurt him. After the first year, he ranked thirty-three out of thirty-five in his section because of all the demerit points he had accumulated. He had already reached 113; he only needed 200 a year to be dismissed. He also recounted that he was poor in history, geography, tactics, and gunnery and "as for tactics and gunnery, in which I had also been low, I had practice in the Civil War which was far more valuable than any theory."[61]

The role of the facility went beyond pure academics in instilling officer values in the pupils and it made them realize the relationship between the officer and the state. Dewey's description of life at the academy reveals that it brought together students from a variety of locations to serve the country. Dewey felt that the country was "not yet nationalized by the broad community of thought and intelligence of to-day [and] had to be welded by the spirit of corps into a common life and purpose." Dewey concluded of the academy at that time that "when you enter the academy you cease to be a Vermonter or a Georgian or a Californian. You are in the navy; your future, with its sea-service and its frequent changes of assignment, makes you first a man of the country's service and only secondly a man of the world." Dewey felt that the environment helped them bond. The students lived in steam-heated barracks with gas lamps, two students to a room. They made their own beds and swept their rooms, but African-American women "came in at stated intervals [and] did the scrubbing." Dewey also felt that because the numbers of students were low, they grew to know each other well. Still, Dewey found academy life monotonous. Their only breaks were dances, called "stag hops," held in the basement of the recitation hall, and the only respite from the academy came after their second year, when they were allowed a furlough.[62]

Alfred Thayer Mahan, son of Denis Hart Mahan, West Point instructor, entered the Naval Academy in September 1856. When the future captain and naval strategist joined the Navy, the last of the class of "Oldsters" had just graduated, having spent five years at sea and then their sixth at the Naval Academy. Mahan wrote that these midshipmen had been at sea and often had experienced responsibilities away from their superiors. He asked, "how could such be brought under the curb of the narrowly ordered life of the school, for the short eight months to which they knew the ordeal was restricted?" Mahan recounted that, while taking his oral entrance exam, he overheard the exam of another. The other appointee had failed out previously, but from what Mahan gathered from talking with the fellow, he had been reappointed because of political "influence." Nevertheless, Mahan did not see the appointee again. Mahan later wrote that "I suppose from his name, which I remember, and his State, of which I am less sure, that he took, and in any event would have taken, the Confederate side in the coming troubles."[63]

Although he entered the academy after the last of the Oldsters graduated, Mahan believed that they too left behind a certain esprit de corps. One example was the attitude toward hazing, which Mahan wrote was virtually nonexistent at the academy. There was the opinion that such a practice was beneath the sailors. It was the type of activity that the midshipmen expected at West Point, but at the academy they were all officers and gentlemen, and they had to behave as such. He believed that this gentlemanly attitude was the result of the Oldsters: the young students looked up to them with a certain amount of respect that young people accorded those a few years older than themselves. Mahan wrote, "And these men were not merely more advanced in years. They were matured beyond their age by early habits of responsibility and command, and themselves imbued by constant contact with the spirit of the phrase 'an officer and a gentleman,' which constitutes the norm of military conduct." Mahan was unsure how hazing eventually developed at the academy, but he opined that it was just the result of the "school-boy nature" that often arises if left unchecked.[64]

Charles E. Clark's road to the academy was similar to the others. Clark was born in Bradford, Orange Country, in Vermont, on 10 August 1843. His father was James Dayton Clark, cousin of Rear Admiral James Dayton. Charles' father was also born in Bradford and married Mary Sexton of Brookfield, Vermont. His family's roots were in Roxbury, Massachusetts, from where his great-grandparents moved to Bradford. Charles' father was orphaned at two and had few political connections and little wealth, but supported his family with his bookbinding shop. When playing as a young boy, Charles built a small fortification on top of a roof, only to fall off and be saved by a lucky landing. Later he became interested in the new technology of the parachute and decided to try to jump out of his home's second-story window. The endeavor was initially successful until his makeshift parachute—an umbrella—collapsed, sending him straight to the ground. On another occasion he and his brother played with a little cannon, setting it off and nearly striking themselves with its projectile.[65] Charles' childhood interest in military things likely shaped his desire for a bolder and more financially secure career than his father's trade.

Charles started his schooling at the Bradford district school and then went to the Bradford Academy. When he was away from his studies, his father kept him occupied in the bookbindery, perhaps hoping to pass on his trade to his son, "but as he remarked, when there was any real work to do, I suddenly became a great reader." In his father's bookshop the young boy read about the exploits of Marlborough and Napoleon, instilling in him the desire to become a military man with a life of adventure. By the time he was sixteen, Charles convinced his father to write their representative, Justin S. Morrill, Republican, Vermont, to obtain an

appointment at West Point. Several days later Morrill replied that there were currently no vacancies at West Point for any young boys from his district. Charles
had been just a little too late. The appointment to West Point had gone to Doctor
Rockwell's son from Brattleboro. However, Morrill pointed out another option:
the Naval Academy. He told Charles that the vacancy for his district at the Naval
Academy had been offered to a boy from Chelsea, Judge Hibbard's son. Charles'
father and Judge Hibbard were talking one day and, as it turned out, the judge
wanted his son to seek a career somewhere other than at Annapolis, and Morrill
offered Charles the appointment. At first the young man turned it down, saying
he could not stand to see his mother's grief at his impending departure. Morrill
wrote him again and told him of the benefits of going to school at Annapolis and
of receiving an education at the government's expense. Charles then accepted the
appointment and embarked for the academy.[66]

Appointed in the spring of 1860, young Charles would have headed out toward
Annapolis that fall. He traveled from his home to Troy, where he went by boat to
Albany and on to Philadelphia. Eventually making his way to Baltimore, he caught
a train to Annapolis. On the train he saw what he guessed to be a young midshipman dressed in his uniform. He was engaged during the trip in a conversation
with a father and son who asked him all about naval life and the academy. When
Charles arrived in Annapolis, he found it full of other boys like himself being examined. He walked the narrow, "quaint" streets of the town, probably taking in all the
new sights and sounds. Along the streets he overheard some boys asking if Yates
Stirling, from Maryland, had been accepted. Stirling and Thomas Williams—
who turned out to be the midshipman Charles saw on the train—later became his
roommates until the commandant of midshipmen broke up their group. Williams,
from Michigan, was later dropped for academic deficiencies, while Stirling went on
to become a rear admiral and commander of the Asiatic fleet. Clark himself spent
fifty years in the Navy.[67]

Robley D. Evans had the most interesting journey to the academy of the famous
academy alumni. Evans was born 18 August 1846 in Floyd County, Virginia, son of
Samuel Andrew Jackson Evans, a doctor. He grew up in the mountains of Virginia
and recalled that the area was "almost as wild and rough as the partially settled
mountains of the West." Robley's father owned slaves, farmed, and also served in
the state legislature. His region was poor, sparsely settled, and with few slaves, but
people helped their neighbors and were hard working, although "they sometimes
took the law into their own hands to enforce their ideas." The younger Evans, by
age six, had a pony, gun, and his own slave boy. Evans wrote that the young slave
child taught him to smoke, chew tobacco, and "many superstitions and dreadful
ghost stories, some of which I remember to this day." A "black mammy," like many

other white boys in the South, raised the young man. He loved his "mammy," freed during the early days of the Civil War, and even though she had numerous children of her own, "no matter how busy she might be, she could make the time to coddle her young master and comfort him in a way that no other could."[68]

Robley's father died when he was ten, and the family moved to Fairfax Courthouse, Virginia. In 1857 his Uncle Alexander Evans invited him to move in with him at his home in Washington, D.C. Alexander Evans was a lawyer, clerk of the House Committee on Claims, and a newspaperman. Robley started public school but soon found himself in trouble. While sailing a toy boat on a school pond, another boy smashed Robley's boat with a stone. In retaliation Robley did the same to the other boy. Young Robley was expelled and soon started at Gonzaga College, a Roman Catholic preparatory school for Georgetown College. Evans wrote that he spent a great deal of time around the political centers of Washington, but he loved to spend time on the waterfront watching the sailing vessels. According to Evans, this inspired him to join the Navy.[69]

Evans at first decided to run away and enjoy life at sea, but then met Delegate William Hooper, Democrat, Utah territory. Hooper offered Evans an appointment to the academy under one condition: he had to move to Salt Lake City. Evans agreed and was given four days to pack for the long overland trek, leaving in 1859 by the Baltimore and Ohio Railroad. Evans traveled halfway by train, at times stopping along the way. He was still a young boy and enjoyed playing with other children his age. At St. Joseph he met some boys, and they shared a wagon. While at St. Joseph, Robley had a small accident: "I had gone to a gymnasium with some other boys of my own age, when one of them did a trick on the horizontal bar which I was invited to imitate. I tried, but brought up squarely on top of my head on the floor. Slight concussion of the brain was the result, and the doctor had me in hand that night and part of the next day." When Evans felt better, they were ferried across the Missouri River and started their journey across the prairies. During his trip, Evans and his troop met some Native Americans and he lived with Chief Washakie for a period, although at first under duress, but in the end happily. Eventually, he made it to Salt Lake City and stayed with Hooper's family. It is unclear how long Evans stayed in Utah, but he left when he felt that it was long enough to claim residency. Robley then began life at the Naval Academy, to be discussed, during its last year before the outbreak of the Civil War. After the war, he served about forty years, with exploits during the Spanish-American War and as commander of the White Fleet.[70]

Some poorer or disadvantaged students also applied for admission, and the academy was concerned about their fate. James M. Todd's "parent or guardian" was listed as a merchant,[71] but the boy from Massachusetts was actually the orphan son of a U.S. naval officer. Joseph Smith, likely his merchant guardian, looked out for such orphans who came his way and was "instrumental" in sending young Todd to the academy. Smith was also concerned about the young orphan son of a surgeon, Waters Smith, who he hoped would also find a place in the academy.[72] There were several Smiths who attended the academy, but it was impossible to identify the exact Smith in the records, while James M. Todd graduated the academy, only to die in Brooklyn in 1855. Meanwhile, on 12 May 1858, A. H. Wilcox of Albany, New York, wrote the superintendent that his son also longed to join the academy, but he was poor and could ill afford to send his son. He asked the superintendent if "there [was] any chance for him [and] if so on what condition."[73] Still, there is no record of a Wilcox attending the academy between 1858 and the outbreak of the Civil War; whatever his supporters may have thought, the young man failed to fit the mold of a future professional officer, a blend between the traditions of the past and the demands of the future.[74]

Even if a candidate failed to meet the academy's requirements, the superintendent still felt the Navy owed him something if he seemed worthy. One such case was that of J. J. Miller from western Missouri. Superintendent Stribling wrote Secretary Graham that Miller was examined and found "duly qualified," although Stribling doubted he would last long. Stribling reported that Miller had "no advantages of education" and that his friends should have made sure he was better prepared to join the academy before convincing him to try. The superintendent concluded that if Miller were allowed to enroll, he would quickly lag behind the rest of his class. Yet, he felt sorry for him and thought the Navy should pay his expenses "to enable him to return to his home."[75]

The midshipmen reacted in different ways to this reformed environment, but they only resorted to open disobedience if they felt that the academy violated their rights. As the older midshipmen negotiated what a professional officer's treatment was like, they often demanded that the Navy treat them like adults. By 1853 those students still attending the academy, but with prior sea and command experience, were annoyed by the rules under which they had to live, and they struck a committee to approach the superintendent. They concluded that the existing rules "were originally intended to be applied to the Acting Midshipmen and to which we think we should not be subjected." The committee believed that the rules could be changed without any adverse effect on discipline. They felt they had to work too hard at routine chores and believed they were entitled to more servants, especially to make their beds and sweep their rooms. The committee even complained that the lack of help at the academy had forced them "from time to time not only to light our lamps, bring up our wood and make our fires, but also to black our boots and in some cases to bring our water from the pump." They felt their extra workload was not the fault of their one servant, who had to serve thirty midshipmen both in the residences and at the mess hall.[76]

In addition to servants, the midshipmen also felt their activities were unjustly restricted. The acting midshipmen, for instance, were rarely given any time off during Christmas. On 13 December 1858, nineteen midshipmen petitioned the secretary of the Navy for leave over the holidays, commenting that "most of us have not seen our relatives since September 1857, and it may be doubtful whether we will be able to visit them during the next summer."[77] Others believed that the system of being reported for offenses, and having to report offenses even if they were personally unaware they had occurred, was unjust. Despite the fact that they had the right to deny committing the offense, they felt at the whim of the commandant of midshipmen. They also felt they were being treated like children: "We would say that when we request permission to go out in the City to attend church, we expect to go for that especial purpose, and when we do so, we consider that we can conduct ourselves as becomes officers and gentlemen without being put under the charge of any particular individual." They believed that they should be accorded the rights and privileges of their rank as real officers, rather than the limitations imposed on the acting midshipmen.[78] They also protested if they felt they failed to get paid on time. On 1 November 1853, several midshipmen petitioned the superintendent and wrote that "we the undersigned respectfully request permission to draw our allowance of money for this and the last month as we have not yet received that due for the last month."[79]

Finally, they took out their anger on a professor if they believed he had wronged them. On 22 October 1853, the acting midshipmen of the gunnery class decided to report Professor Lockwood for "using threatening language to the Midshipmen while at Great Gun exercise today." The midshipmen reported that he threatened to put some students in the guardhouse "under a sentry's charge" if they disobeyed the orders of the captain of the gun while it was being loaded. The midshipmen questioned "whether any professor has the right to threaten us and the power to punish whenever he may deem it necessary."[80] Lockwood replied that while he was quoted correctly, he had simply wanted to impress upon them his desire that they follow orders so they would not be hurt during the exercise. Lockwood also wished to disavow any right to punish midshipmen on his own authority. In retrospect, he concluded that it would have been more appropriate not to have made any references to the guardhouse or the use of a sentinel.[81] Mahan wrote that some midshipmen also protested over being forced to drill. In the spirit of their youth, they took advantage of their civilian instructor, although a graduate of West Point, who had a stutter. Once during drill while he struggled to say "H-H-H-Halt!" a group of midshipmen continued marching into the nearby water.[82]

If a midshipman felt wronged by a professor, there was another course of action than bad behavior: the midshipman could ask the superintendent to intervene. Midshipman S. A. Smith wrote Superintendent Goldsborough on 18 April 1854 to complain about how Assistant Professor of Mathematics John Van Ness Philip had treated him in class. Smith believed that Philip was giving him lower grades than he deserved and that he "has not allowed *me* [emphasis in original] the privileges allowed by all Professors, due to a protracted absence from the section room." Smith believed that Philip was putting him "lower and lower" in his class and that he had "magnified mistakes whenever they occurred." Smith recounted how on 15 April Philip gave him a problem to solve. Smith went to the board and solved it, then said he checked his book to see if he had done it correctly. Smith then recounted how "Philip then accused me of taking unfair advantage of him and my class-mates," ordered him to his seat, and gave him a zero on the assignment. Smith concluded by stating that "Mr. Philip has also given higher marks for exercises to persons whose exercises were in some cases the same and in others not so correct as mine, the proof of which I have in my possession."[83]

Unsurprisingly, one other aspect of life over which midshipmen could protest was food, but their protest was limited to stating what they believed they had the right to have. On 19 January 1854, twenty-six midshipmen petitioned the secretary of the Navy about the quality of their food. They complained that the coffee was bad and that they were supposed to be provided with hashed or cold meat five days of the week for breakfast, which they rarely got. Instead, they received fried liver three or four times a week, an item "which many of us cannot eat." The oysters and salt fish were also of poor quality. In addition, "no butter is allowed: We find it very inconvenient to do without this necessary. It is an article that the [*sic*] most of us have never dispensed with even at Sea." For supper they were not allowed the meat they believed they needed to enable them to drill every afternoon. Moreover, they asserted that everywhere they had lived—except for the Naval Station in California—they had eaten better for a lower price. Elsewhere they could eat for around $10 a month, while at the academy they found they were spending $11 to $12 a month. The midshipmen could accept the higher price if the food was better, but they reluctantly concluded they would live with the food as it was if the price was lowered.[84]

Acting Master Edward Simpson, inspector of the mess hall, agreed with the midshipmen's assessment of the coffee. As for the hashed meat, Simpson spoke to the mess steward about it earlier and was told that the steward had to discontinue it until the mornings became longer, which would give him more time to prepare it. As for the fried liver, Simpson felt it was "thrown in as an extra." The midshipmen had also complained about the corn bread, although Simpson had no problem with it or the oyster soup. The students had also complained of "tainted articles," but Simpson could only find one instance of some salt pork gone bad. While the butter was scarce in Annapolis in the winter, "this Mess has been supplied with a capital article" and in general the cook's work was above and beyond that called for, especially on Thanksgiving, Christmas, and New Year's Day. Simpson also disagreed with the midshipmen's assessment that better food could be supplied for the same price; he calculated that to increase the quality of the food would run an extra 37.5 to 40 cents a month. Simpson concluded that the midshipmen had "no idea of the expense of ordinary living in the United States, and I conceive that they do injustice to Mr. Swan [the cook] in giving the impression that he supplies bad meats and is an illiberal purveyor."[85]

Superintendent Goldsborough figured that nothing at the academy caused as many complaints as food. He believed the trend would continue "as long as this institution lasts" and that "there are no students, living together at a general table, any where, who, as a general thing, are better fed than those now here." Goldsborough told the secretary that the current high price of goods prohibited any reduction in the price of meals, but the academy had taken steps to regulate price, and every quarter he appointed a board of three officers to assess food prices. As of his writing, however, the board had yet to make a decision, because the mess steward was still readying his data. In addition, an officer ate with the students and monitored the food's quality. If he discovered anything wrong, he was required to report the problem to the superintendent. Goldsborough added that since he became superintendent, the officer at the mess table had never reported any instance of poor food. Despite Goldsborough's opinions—and some questions as to the propriety of how the petition was submitted—he forwarded it to the secretary.[86]

Notwithstanding the changes that had occurred at the academy and the shifting demographics of the students, the Navy and its recruits carried on a discourse over the concept of professionalism, and the best type of recruit, as new requirements and old expectations met at Annapolis. On 14 October 1859, twenty-three midshipmen presented a petition to the commandant of midshipmen, Commander Thomas T. Craven, about "the scholastic routine of this institution." They believed that the amount of time spent on the "Professional Department" at the academy was too little and would leave them unprepared for their futures as "graduates of the Naval Academy." The midshipmen believed that the one weekly recitation in gunnery was insufficient, "while for the ensuing term no time whatever has been allowed for this branch." In the amount of time allotted, they were expected to become proficient in the lessons of Lieutenant Edward Simpson's course on ordnance, Lieutenant John A. Dahlgren's course on boat howitzers, gunnery theory, and four hundred pages of written material. They believed this was too much material and that the situation was similar with seamanship. The midshipmen judged that the small fraction of time spent on "this important study cannot fail to produce an undesirable deficiency in our nautical information"; so much so that they were willing to "sacrifice our knowledge in some department of a less practical character, rather than fail to avail ourselves of the base advantages now offered us for improvement in our profession." The midshipmen believed that their three recitations a week in chemistry were also of little professional value. They did not want time off; they wanted the extra time devoted to seamanship and gunnery.[87] In this way they would meet the purpose of the traditional naval officer but would not receive the broader education the Navy now intended for its professional officers.

Despite the growing pains, by June 1859, Superintendent Blake believed that the institution was holding its own with West Point. With a further eye toward professionalization, he thought that "if the earliest age, and the standard of qualifications for admission are a little advanced, the number of graduates, I am quite sure, would be equal to the growing wants of the service."[88] But sometime in late 1860 the superintendent read a newspaper editorial on the academy by an "Old Salt." While disagreeing on several aspects of education at the academy, "Old Salt" asserted that Blake had "lost sight of the fact that the institution was created to benefit the navy, and not to injure it," and that personal politics had come into the fray. The "Old Salt" advocated a more professional way to train young officers, yet he contended that the school was not letting them grow up into men. Nevertheless, he believed that supporters would "be glad to see instead of the pale faced youths, who graduate, a set of men who have more Physique, and who would be better qualified to lead the boarders, and stand the wear and tear incident to naval life."[89] Blake, naturally, disagreed with some of editorial and concluded that the academy graduated more students than West Point, disciplinary problems were falling, and the number of graduates would actually increase yearly.[90]

The academy had undergone major transformations from 1849 to 1859, and despite criticisms, the four-year program emphasized seamanship and the importance of other areas, as it taught young acting midshipmen entering the Navy direct often from civil school how to be officers. The first class of academy acting midshipmen graduated on 10 June 1854 at a simple ceremony in the academy's chapel, where they received their graduation certificates and subsequently their midshipmen's warrants. The chaplain said a prayer and Superintendent Goldsborough spoke to the class. Subsequent graduation ceremonies were similar, with the Board of Examiners and Academic Board also present, and included guest speakers. The academy also began presenting awards to top students at graduation. During the 1857 ceremonies, for instance, New York midshipman Allen V. Reed, an advanced student from the '54 Date, received a sword for being first in his class. Reed spent forty-two years in the Navy and died as a rear admiral. The last graduation ceremony before the Civil War, on 13 June 1860, awarded Midshipman Moses Stuyvesant, from Indiana, '56 Date, the first-place sword. Stuyvesant spent twelve years in the Navy, but died in 1868, a lieutenant commander.[91]

CHAPTER 4

Discipline and Law in the School Era

T
he Naval School did not act in a lawless vacuum but provided a transitional area for socializing new midshipmen into the behavioral expectations of a professional naval officer. Therefore, Annapolis regulations taught students to "conduct themselves upon every occasion with the propriety and decorum which characterize the society of gentlemen."[1] The disciplinary methods employed reflected not only the general philosophy of American military management, but also the reformist attitudes toward maritime life in this period. But military law was also meant to ensure discipline rather personal rights or freedoms and to rid the services of unwanted individuals.[2] Those who remained were those the Navy believed best suited the needs of its client, the country, and would follow orders. As a profession, Annapolis administrators tracked and recorded midshipman discipline. Still, the application of naval law at Annapolis considered the midshipman's inexperience. At first authorities treated students leniently and according to the offense's seriousness, but if their misbehavior persisted or worsened, the authorities responded in kind and weeded out those unsuited to the service. Through naval law and discipline at Annapolis, young midshipmen deciphered the behavioral expectations of officers, responded to authorities, and bonded as comrades.

Harold D. Langley believes that the national reform spirit stirred from 1812 to the Civil War, characterized by the elimination of flogging and the grog ration, and from concern for the welfare of younger sailors. Some men and women believed they had to be "their brother's keepers," and this desire spread into maritime life through the American Seamen's Friend Society. Civil groups wanted to improve the "dignity" of naval men but also maintain proper discipline.[3] The society called for the better treatment of sailors in maritime industries and the Navy and the abolition of corporal punishment. In 1842 a pamphlet was published entitled *An Inquiry into the Necessity and General Principles of Reorganization in the United States Navy, with an Examination of True Sources of Subordination*. The anonymous "Observer," John Murphy, criticized that, despite calls for naval reorganization, none had occurred.

In some cases, he agreed with the use of the cat-o'-nine-tails, but he opined that this punishment should increase in severity with rank. He said that he felt the Navy's duty was to elevate the men's character rather than sink to the lowest level. In 1843 "Tiphys Aegyptus" wrote *The Navy's Friend*, covering his thirty-nine months in the Navy. He criticized the men's disobedience of rules and condemned commanding officers who allowed midshipmen a free hand in disciplining the lower deck—perhaps an allusion to the *Somers* mutiny.[4] But naval reform faced a conservative officer corps, and it was also virtually impossible to eliminate flogging because of its association with disciplining slaves; any discussions soon opened the schism between North and South. Consequently, until congressional momentum built in the late 1840s, to be discussed in chapter 5, all reform supporters like Secretary of the Navy Levi Woodbury, from New Hampshire, could accomplish was to advise officers in 1831 to show restraint and use alternatives to flogging. But few showed any such initiative.[5]

The U.S. Navy worked by authority and dominance over subordinates, but Annapolis reveals that it shifted from brutal discipline to measured responses. The laws governing the U.S. Navy originated with the Royal Navy, and the Continental Congress tasked John Adams to draw up the Articles of War of 1775, based on Royal Navy and ancient Roman regulations. Adams believed the American Navy should be kinder than its British parent and that sailors breaking American law should be made to wear badges of shame or collars rather than be flogged for every violation, something he felt was un-American. Still, U.S. naval discipline followed a tradition set by influential officers like Thomas Truxtun and Edward Preble. Truxtun ran his ship like a miniature kingdom. Officers only gave their opinion if asked and followed his orders without question. He banned drinking, decreed that no one was to sleep on shore without his permission first, and maintained distance between officers and men. Edward Preble was a similar commander, who believed "bad characters" composed a ship's crew and his job was to expunge them. One midshipman, Thomas Baldwin, for instance, gave Preble trouble and was caught shoplifting. Preble's goal was to rid the service of the troublemaker; someone who failed to live up to professional expectations. Preble knew that a court martial would likely just give the man a slap on the wrist and send him back to sea. Instead, by convincing him to resign, rather than humiliate his family with a court martial, Preble rid the service of an undesirable.[6]

The regulation that governed the Navy, and its relationship with society, was the "Act for the Better Government of the United States Navy" passed on 23 April 1800.[7] The statute reveals that the government expected its sailors to be of good moral standing, loyal to the Navy, and act as a cohesive group. Commanders were to be examples to their men and exhibit honor, patriotism, and subordination to duty—all fundamental characteristics of the profession. Importantly, they were to regulate the actions of their subordinates, inspect their behavior, and keep immoral practices suppressed. If anyone was found guilty of such activities, the commander was to rectify the situation. The Navy strictly forbid any number of activities, like drunkenness, "scandalous conduct," cruelty, and fraud. If an officer was found guilty, he could be cashiered or suffer a court martial.[8] Fundamentally, Congress forged naval law to ensure that officers knew their duties to the state. In war, they fought the enemy and during both peace and war protected the nation's growing commerce.

The professional officer, and his men, were to remain at their posts and prepare for battle when ordered. Failure to comply meant death or other court-martial punishment. In battle, an officer was to do his "utmost to take or destroy every vessel" and "do his utmost endeavour to afford relief to ships belonging to the United States." The nation expected all shipboard personnel to do their duty and help their fellows when called upon, no matter the cost. Desertion was punishable by death, and naval personnel were to report deserters from other naval vessels. Mutiny and disobedience of orders were intolerable. Anyone who attempted to form a mutinous party, would, if convicted by a court martial, "suffer death." Moreover, anyone who simply uttered seditious words, tried to cover up such talk, or failed to do their best to stop a mutiny, was at a court martial's mercy. Officers and men were required to obey the lawful orders of superiors and were forbidden to strike or draw a weapon on a superior. Punishment was death or any other sentence a court martial deemed appropriate. The Navy even officially forbade quarreling between people in the Navy, even with words.[9]

If a sailor was a naval private—an enlisted rank at that time—the captain could order up to twelve lashes, or put him in irons. A court martial had to sanction any stronger punishments. Murder was, of course, forbidden, and could be punished by death. Their duties toward merchant vessels were clear: carry out orders and convoy the merchantmen. Naval men were forbidden to demand any extra fee for this service and were to treat the officers and crew of the merchantmen respectfully. If they failed to carry out their duties, or mistreated the merchantmen and their crews, the officers and men were subject to "making such reparation as a court of admiralty may award, and of suffering such further punishment as a court martial shall adjudge." The Navy could punish anyone who neglected his duty with a court martial. Such neglect included grounding the ship, sleeping on duty, neglecting assignments, or leaving their station before the end of watch.[10]

The Navy had several levels of military hearings to dole out punishments to officers and men, enforce the profession's ethos, and eliminate those who failed to meet the demands of their career. The general court martial was at the top, followed by a court of inquiry and a summary court martial. The president of the United States, the secretary of the Navy—who was also the judge advocate general—a ship's captain or squadron commander convened a general court martial on land, at sea, or at the Naval School. A panel of five-to-thirteen officers composed it and could try both officers and enlisted men for offenses graver than those handled by twelve lashes, suspension, or confinement. A president presided over the court martial and acted like a civilian judge. The prosecutor was generally another officer, or a civilian lawyer, and was known as the judge advocate. The accused could defend himself or be represented by an officer or a civilian lawyer. He could also "object to members of the court and have them removed if he believed they were prejudice[d] against him." Evidence was submitted, testimony was given under oath, and the proceedings were recorded.

The first part of a court martial was public, both sides presented opening statements and evidence and could cross-examine witnesses. The second part was a closed affair, where the board met secretly to deliberate on the accused's fate. A simple majority was needed to convict in all cases except those punishable by death or dismissal. In the latter case, a guilty verdict required a two-thirds majority. In either case no one on the board was allowed to discuss in public the proceedings or deliberations. The secretary of the Navy reviewed the results of each case, except if the court martial was carried out on a foreign station, and he or the president of the United States could overrule the verdict.[11]

In contrast, a court of inquiry was an investigative body used mostly to look into cases of neglect of duty. It could be convened by a ship's captain or squadron commander, the secretary of the Navy or the president of the United States. The court of inquiry consisted of a judge advocate and three commissioned officers. They could call witnesses and question them in the same manner as the court martial but could only report facts. The board gave their report to the secretary of the Navy, who decided the next course of action, possibly a court martial. But officers on the court of inquiry could not serve on the court-martial board. Finally, the records of the proceedings could remain secret or be published, depending on the Navy's mood. The other two forms of naval disciplinary hearings were quicker, less formal, and dealt with minor shipboard problems. A hearing at the captain's mast, the "deck court," occurred aboard ship and was used against enlisted men. A commissioned officer presented the charges, and the captain decided the man's punishment, if any, and entered the details in the ship's log. The summary court martial, introduced in 1855, largely formalized the "deck courts" proceedings.[12]

Naval law ensured that officers were a band of brothers who assessed their own, but a higher authority appointed them, and it was to this higher authority that these professionals were answerable. The regulations ensured that everyone knew their duties and their relationship with each other and with the public. These ideals of brotherhood, honorable duty, and service carried the Navy through the nineteenth century. The new Naval School at Annapolis therefore operated in the context of existing naval law and discipline, but students rarely saw its full force as they would if they were at sea, unless their disobedience struck at core officer values, such as respect and following orders.

Secretary of the Navy Bancroft believed that putting midshipmen in a naval school would help uphold the ideals of the naval officer when they later commanded a ship and represented the nation. He concluded that Annapolis would show the midshipmen "that a warrant in the navy, far from being an excuse for licentious freedom, is to be held a pledge for subordination, industry, and regularity—for sobriety, and assiduous attention to duty." Therefore, he believed that the Naval School should have a higher standard than civilian colleges. He concluded "the President expects such supervision and management as shall make of them [the midshipmen] an exemplary body, of which the country may be proud." Consequently, Bancroft gave Franklin Buchanan, the school's first superintendent, "all the powers for discipline conferred by the laws of the United States, and the certainty that the Department will recommend no one for promotion who is proved unworthy of it from idleness or ill conduct, or continuing ignorance, and who cannot bear the test of a rigid examination."[13]

Buchanan enunciated these expectations on 10 October 1845. He told the students and staff that naval regulations required the students to undergo a thorough examination of their abilities and moral character before being promoted to lieutenant. Because of this, he expected students to take every opportunity to learn about their profession and to remember that "a good moral character is essential to your promotion and high standing in the navy." Buchanan urged them to avoid intemperance and remember their country's expectations. Meanwhile, he told the officers and instructors that they had to enforce the law, "however painful" it might be, and that they had no room to overlook anything. Buchanan believed they had no discretionary powers, even though commanders were given some leeway. The superintendent felt that any officer who failed to enforce the law was committing a dereliction of duty.[14]

Naval School regulations regulated all aspects of life at Fort Severn, and a conduct roll recorded any student infractions. These included "neglect of duty, disobedience of orders, inattention to studies, tardiness at recitations, breaking liberty, incorrect deportment at recitation, indecorous conduct at the mess-table, or elsewhere, irregularity at meal hours."[15] The regulations banned the importation of liquor onto the school grounds, and midshipmen were forbidden from cooking food in their rooms without the superintendent's permission first and could only eat there if they were sick and the surgeon recommended "room service."[16] Regulations also banned smoking and chewing tobacco virtually everywhere inside Fort Severn, and "no Acting Midshipman will be permitted to chew or smoke tobacco" at all.[17] The midshipmen were also required to spend almost all their time within school grounds and could only go into Annapolis if, by 4:00 PM, they recorded their names in a liberty book. The officer-of-the-day then took it to the superintendent, or his substitute, to approve the request. The amount of time the midshipmen were allowed outside the grounds was limited: "permission to be absent will be granted only after the regular hours appropriated to recitations and study during the day, and extend only until 10 o'clock P.M., unless [given] special permission to exceed that hour." Upon returning, the midshipmen were required to report to the officer of the day, who recorded their return in the liberty book, which was inspected by the superintendent at 9:00 each morning.[18] Finally, the regulations added, "the students are cautioned and enjoined not to mark, cut, or in any manner deface or injure the public buildings or property of any kind."[19]

Beyond discipline, the regulations gave the administration a method to assess the future naval officer's suitability to the service. The rules stated that one of the school's goals was "to ascertain whether their [the students'] qualifications and deportment are calculated to reflect credit upon the Navy if retained in it." Consequently, Buchanan would send the most serious infractions to the secretary of the Navy to decide the student's fate.[20] Superintendent Buchanan took Bancroft's instructions to heart probably because they supported his own belief in naval discipline and because most Naval School students were officers with prior sea experience, rather than boys just taken from the civilian world. For example, on 4 December 1846, he discovered a drunken midshipman and judged that only a court martial could handle it; naval law left him no choice.[21] He concluded that "the laws of the navy do not grant to a commander discretionary power to overlook such an offence as drunkenness or any offence against those laws: they point out the punishment for certain offences. And my experience as Superintendent of this School since its organization convinces me of the propriety and necessity of adhering strictly to them."[22] Buchanan believed it would be a "dangerous precedent" to be lenient in this case, for if the law was not strictly enforced, everyone would expect leniency.[23]

The rules that Buchanan submitted to George Bancroft in August 1845 governed the school until the reorganization began in 1849. They reflected the spirit—if not the precise words—of those who governed the Navy as a whole and told all officers "to observe towards each other a courteous deportment, and to conduct themselves, on all occasions, with propriety and decorum."[24] The midshipmen generally responded well to this philosophy and even began to form miniature bands of brothers in unofficial societies, albeit a source of trouble for Annapolis authorities. With Midshipman Edward Simpson as their leader, for instance, the later-famous naval officer and the "Spirits Club" stole oil lamps from the city and put on an offending play in an old Annapolis theater. The midshipmen also held a dance in an old barracks and served a dinner in the mess hall. Later groups like the "Owls" and the "Crickets" were formed and often combed Annapolis committing pranks. Park Benjamin reported that these students drank into the night, left liquor bottles and cigar butts around, and came to breakfast in their "dressing-gowns." The Owls were a particularly bad society and drank at Rosenthal's saloon, which they made their clubhouse. The Owls saw themselves as kindred spirits with their colleagues at West Point. One of the Owls' drinking songs was a variation on "Benny Havens Oh," sung at West Point, substituting Rosenthal—or Rosy-gosy— for Benny: "Oh! We'll sigh our reminisces of Rosy-gosy, Oh!"[25]

Perhaps because of such behavior, the historiography of the Naval School era sometimes assumes that the midshipmen, in particular the "Oldsters," were harder to control than academy-era students because many had sea experience and considered themselves real officers already.[26] Moreover, Benjamin concluded that the Naval School midshipmen found studies and drills problematic. Nevertheless, he asserted that the older students from the '40 Date accepted their new studies and drill, although the younger students of the '41 Date hated both. He wrote "whether the midshipmen of the date of '40 were inherently any better behaved than their comrades of '41, or whether it was because they were cramming for their examination for promotion, it is hardly possible to decide." However, Benjamin surmised that "it is fairly certain that they [the Date of '40] comported themselves on the whole much better than the '41 date, and controlled their younger brethren at least sufficiently to permit the School to be well and fairly started."[27]

Extrapolated for the entire school era, Benjamin's speculation is essentially correct, and it is possible to test Benjamin's assertions with statistical analysis of conduct rolls. For the Naval School era, disciplinary records exist for the period from 1846 to 1850 as the school recorded, almost scientifically, the qualities of the young midshipmen. That Annapolis assessed its students from the outset also reveals that the Navy was cognizant of the need for a professional organization to ensure that its initiates were monitored as they were indoctrinated into the demands of their career. While not all midshipmen attending the school in this period committed offenses that were deemed serious enough to be recorded, the records illuminate the types of activities that the midshipmen undertook that authorities deemed improper. It also allows us to generalize about the character of midshipmen. For the period 1846 to 1850, a 20-percent random sample was taken of the records of 202 midshipmen who were recorded as committing offenses. Unfortunately, the punishments inflicted, and the individual who reported the infraction, were not recorded; the 40 records extracted yielded a total of 111 infractions (see appendix A). The records reveal that, overall, the midshipmen had a greater tendency toward order in this period than previously assumed.[28]

The most common infraction was breaking liberty: 50 out of the 111 infractions, or 45 percent, were so categorized by the authorities.[29] Of those who overstayed the time they were permitted to be gone from the school grounds, seven of the offenders were less than one hour late in returning, while forty-three were for an undefined period during a specific date—based on the vagueness, it could have been anywhere from twelve minutes to twenty-four hours. The next most common infraction was being tardy to a recitation or class—twenty-six infractions, or 23 percent. A subsequent breakdown of these numbers is telling if we conclude that being late for class was a function of how much one either enjoyed the topic or felt it was applicable to one's career. For example, learning different languages would better allow them to represent the United States abroad, while learning more scientific skills would better equip them for the changing role of technology in naval affairs. Nevertheless, there was a tendency among the first lot of midshipmen to be late for French: fifteen of the twenty-six tardy infractions involved that course, while seven were for English. Meanwhile, three tardiness infractions involved math, while only one was for being late for mechanics. The practical side of naval education was still winning supporters, at least among the students, as they and authorities negotiated what was important for a professional naval officer.

While 24 of the 111 infractions listed were for neglect of duty, 23 were in connection with liberty rules. Eleven of the infractions were for remaining outside the grounds beyond the time set by the superintendent; three more were for neglecting to report when they returned from leave; and nine were for neglecting to report their return from liberty and overstaying their time off the grounds. One midshipman was guilty of being in bed at noon when the superintendent went to inspect his room; he was charged with neglect of duty. "Disobedience of Orders" infractions also show that these midshipmen were relatively orderly: three of the seven infractions were for leaving the yard without permission; another midshipman lost his temper and slammed a window shutter; another failed to carry out orders properly in a small boat; and another incurred debts in Annapolis contrary to orders.[30] This offense is ironic given that Buchanan's family quickly accumulated debts in Annapolis and Baltimore while trying to live up to the social expectations of his new post.[31] Only 2 of 111 infractions were for behavior unbecoming of an officer. One infraction—for indecorous conduct—was for breaking a barn door and chasing a horse; the other was awarded to Midshipman Frederick A. Boardman, almost seventeen at appointment, Date of '49, for attacking Midshipman William

Harrison Cheever, about seventeen when appointed, Date of '48, and using reproachful language while doing it! Boardman failed to graduate and resigned from the Navy on 19 June 1856, while Cheever graduated Annapolis and died as a lieutenant in 1857.[32]

The conduct rolls alone cannot prove with certainty how well the midshipmen responded to regulations and school life during this period. Benjamin concluded that discipline before 1846, when Congress formally recognized the school in a 13 August law, was also lenient; officials wanted to make a good impression on Congress that the institution was running smoothly.[33] It is conceivable that there was underreporting of discipline problems on the official conduct rolls, especially after the disciplinary Buchanan was replaced. Furthermore, the school era had fewer regulations than those that followed, and the midshipmen also had limited time at Annapolis to commit a large numbers of infractions. Nevertheless, further breakdown of the school era offenses by the offender's date of appointment reveals that members of the Date of '41 committed 74.9 percent of the 111 infractions, but those offenders only represented 3 percent of the large Date of '41. Combined with the mild nature of the infractions committed, we can conclude that these older midshipmen were reasonably well behaved. In response, the school handled matters internally rather than subjecting students to the full force of naval law. Still, several problematic episodes likely gave the impression that midshipmen from this era were difficult to manage. Sometimes discipline was handed down at a court martial, or court of inquiry investigation, if offenses struck at the core values of officership.

In 1847 George P. Upshur became superintendent and had a more lenient view of discipline because of the age of the students. Consequently, Benjamin concluded that discipline declined because Upshur was an "amiable, gentle, quiet man, of the type that inspires affection rather than fear."[34] Upshur showed restraint, for instance, on the night of 1 May 1847, when the watchman reported unknown people—most likely midshipmen—returning to the school after 2:00 AM by jumping over the walls. Lieutenant Ward investigated and found that Midshipman John T. Walker, age unknown, Date of '41, and another midshipman were recorded in the liberty book as having returned at 9:40 PM, but in reality had returned much later by jumping over the wall near the lower gate.[35] Ward reported the matter to Upshur, who decided to investigate and handle the matter himself rather than bother the secretary of the Navy. Upshur concluded that only two officers were involved in the incident and the offense was forgivable.[36] Consequently, Walker graduated but died as a lieutenant in 1856.[37]

The next step up the disciplinary ladder was suspension, and the inexperience of the offender could play a mitigating role in his punishment. During the night of 28 May 1847, Midshipman Henry C. Hunter, age unknown, Date of '41, was discovered to have broken into the kitchen and taken some food. Hunter was suspended from duty and told to remain within the school grounds but was allowed to attend recitations. Lieutenant Ward, then acting superintendent, reported the matter to the secretary of the Navy. Further investigation revealed that it was common practice—"as old nearly as the School"—for midshipmen to enter the kitchen without permission and take food. Ward believed that because of Hunter's "extreme youth" and "frankness in making the acknowledgment" of his crime, his suspension from duties and privileges would be sufficient punishment for him and a warning to others.[38] Hunter graduated Annapolis but resigned as a passed midshipman in 1854.[39]

On 19 June 1847, Superintendent Upshur wrote Secretary John Y. Mason to remind him of the case. Hunter had been under suspension for twenty days, and Upshur thought that because Mason had been absent when Ward originally reported the affair, it may have slipped the secretary's mind. Upshur found that Hunter was truly sorry for what he did and reported that he "has evidently experienced considerable mental suffering in consequence of his present position." Upshur recommended that the department restore Hunter to his duties and privileges. The superintendent suggested that the secretary send Hunter a letter of admonishment, which, with his punishment, would be sufficient "in the case of one so young and so sensitive as Mid[shipman] Hunter."[40]

One of the clearest examples of Upshur's disciplinary philosophy occurred in October 1849. On 27 October, the superintendent permitted seven midshipmen—only six actually decided to go—to visit Annapolis between 5:00 and 8:00 PM. Before they left, Upshur reviewed the regulations that governed their conduct outside the school and reminded them that they were forbidden from visiting a tavern, hotel, or "other house of public entertainment." But when they returned later that evening, one of their number was drunk: Midshipman Robert T. Chapman, aged about twenty-three, Date of '47.[41] He admitted that he visited an apartment in one of the local hotels and drank champagne. Upshur was disappointed in the young man, but he told the secretary of the Navy that Chapman was a smart person and would eventually prove to be a "valuable officer." Despite his age, the superintendent concluded the department would grant him clemency, because "these young gentlemen have been only a few days at the School and have had very little time to make themselves acquainted with its rules and have as yet no knowledge of the naval laws."[42] Chapman graduated, but as he was from Alabama, he went South and joined the Confederate States Navy during the Civil War.[43]

A student's willingness to cooperate could also play a part in convincing the superintendent to show clemency. If offending midshipmen accepted the restrictions placed on them as punishments, they were given the lesser punishments. On

23 July 1849, for instance, Midshipmen Alexander Simmons, age unknown, Date of '41, and William Van Wyck, age unknown, Date of '41, got into a fight. Several punches were thrown before they could be separated. Upshur called both gentlemen into his office—separately—and asked them to pledge to refrain from solving their disputes in future by fighting. Both were given time to consider their fates: Simmons declined to pledge not to fight, while Van Wyck accepted the pledge under the condition that he would be allowed to defend himself if attacked. Van Wyck was not suspended, while Upshur suspended Simmons mainly for his unwillingness to pledge never to fight again while under his command.[44] Simmons failed to graduate, but Van Wyck succeeded, only to die a passed midshipman in 1854 after *Porpoise* disappeared off China.[45]

Finally, if the students failed to respond to moderate forms of discipline, the authorities retaliated in kind. In 1848 Midshipman James B. Yates, age unknown, Date of '41, failed to respond to the subtle pressures of lenient discipline. Upshur found that Yates consistently neglected his studies and for three weeks before his suspension—and his second report to the secretary—had failed to show up to half a dozen recitations. When Upshur asked why, the young man replied that he had been unprepared. Upshur failed to accept this and concluded that "counsel, advice, argument, lectures, rebuke, orders, are of no avail—all are utterly wasted on him." Upshur believed that Yates was hopeless. On 24 January 1848, for example, he left the yard without permission, and no one could find him when Upshur called him to his office. Upshur ordered the officer of the day to keep an eye out for him and at 10:30 PM a light appeared in Yates' room; he had returned clandestinely. Upshur called him to his office and asked him when he had left and returned to the yard. Yates declined to respond but failed to deny his absence.[46]

In response, Upshur suspended Yates from everything but his academic pursuits and forwarded the case to the secretary. Upshur was sad that he had to report Yates for the second time but felt that he was "learning nothing, literally nothing valuable at this School," and he expected the Board of Examiners to reject him at the next round of examinations. In the end Upshur considered Yates "altogether unfit for the navy."[47] A similar incident involved Midshipman Henry Key, who also left the grounds without permission. When Upshur failed to find him, he sent a sergeant into Annapolis to look for him. The sergeant returned with Key and reported that he found him in a hotel playing billiards. Upshur concluded that Yates and Key were alike, always breaking rules, and that "they are also uselessly occupying quarters to the exclusion of men greatly their superiors in every respect."[48] It is with little surprise that neither Yates nor Key graduated from Annapolis. Key and Yates resigned from the Navy on 2 May and 11 May, respectively, soon after this episode.[49] By February 1848 Upshur was exasperated over the number of midshipmen leaving the yard without permission. He reported Midshipman J. M. Ford to the secretary for leaving without permission and suspended him from everything except his academic duties. In Upshur's mind the situation was out of control. Ford was the third midshipman now under suspension for leaving the grounds without permission. Upshur was at a loss as to what to do. His belief was that prompt dismissal from the Navy was the only cure for the epidemic of leaving the yard without permission.[50] Ultimately, Ford too never graduated and resigned on 17 April 1848.[51]

Despite Upshur's style of discipline, the Navy Department reminded him that if his efforts to discipline the midshipmen leniently failed, it might be necessary to resort to greater force. Secretary of the Navy Mason told Upshur that he believed the midshipmen's actions were those of misguided young officers. Mason ordered the offenders confined to the grounds and that the entire class was to be lectured about the offender's fates. Mason concluded that if anyone committed such an offense again, then they would be tried by court martial for disobedience of orders.[52] Another case occurred with Midshipman Edward Pasteur, Date of '41, age unknown, on 24 February. At 10:00 PM surgeon and chemistry instructor John A. Lockwood found Pasteur drunk on the streets of Annapolis and trying to enter a house where he knew some women. Eventually, he was convinced to return to his room. Upshur thought Pasteur was a bad seed, frequently leaving the grounds and getting drunk, but until then was unable to prove it. Upshur thought that Pasteur possessed "none of the acquirements essential to an officer and makes no perceptible progress in his studies." The superintendent thought that the school would be better off without his "example." When Upshur questioned him on the matter, Pasteur refused to answer. Upshur decided to suspend him from his privileges and forwarded his case on to the secretary.[53] Pasteur, like the others, also failed to graduate and resigned on 2 May 1848.[54] The resignations of all these midshipmen came soon after Annapolis authorities voiced their displeasure over their behavior. Rather than dismiss them from service, it seems likely they were given the opportunity to resign, or did so on their own accord.

Drinking, however, combined with any other offense led to immediate trouble with the superintendent. On 17 February 1846, Midshipman Augustus McLaughlin, age unknown, Date of '40, requested permission to go to Baltimore to visit his sick mother. Superintendent Buchanan gave him permission and was under the impression the midshipman was in Baltimore when he ran into him the next day when Buchanan decided to visit Annapolis to meet a visiting friend at a local hotel. When Buchanan arrived at the establishment, he checked its billiard room to see if his friend was there; instead he found McLaughlin playing billiards; he appeared to have been drinking. McLaughlin explained that the servants had somehow delayed his departure for Baltimore and he missed his carriage. Buchanan was upset that McLaughlin had been drinking after he had pledged to abstain. The young man exclaimed that this was the first time he had broken his pledge, but Buchanan was unsatisfied and ordered him to return to the school. The two departed the hotel and walked back to the school, where Buchanan ordered McLaughlin to his room. He refused, and in front of Buchanan, Professor Lockwood, and the officer of the day, proceeded to leave the school grounds. Buchanan ordered him to stop; again he refused. Buchanan then ordered the officer of the day to go after him and order him to return; again McLaughlin refused to obey. That was the last that Buchanan saw of the young man. Rumor had it that he had left Annapolis by carriage, and Buchanan requested that the Navy hold a court martial to deal with him.[55]

Instances of student misbehavior, such as McLaughlin's, also show the camaraderie of the corps of midshipmen. Faced with naval discipline, they exhibited almost professional-style corporateness when their comrades were in trouble. Sometimes when a fellow student was dismissed, the others would petition for his reinstatement. For example, after Midshipman McLaughlin was dismissed, some of his friends petitioned the Navy on his behalf. Buchanan forwarded the petition to the secretary, because it was prompted by "the kind feelings of the mid[shipmen] for their companion," but the superintendent could see little justification in reinstating someone who had so violated naval law.[56] It seems that his friends helped save McLaughlin's career. He graduated, but from Maryland and appointed from Arkansas, held Southern sympathies and served with the Confederate States Navy during the Civil War.[57] Meanwhile, the school authorities also found that when they investigated an incident involving students, the midshipmen subscribed to a code of silence. The students often failed to offer information to aid in a fellow's punishment; they would not snitch on another student.

One such case during the school era occurred in November 1847. The residents of Annapolis were sometimes subject to the pranks and noise of the midshipmen, as they were subject to those of students from nearby St. John's College. On 19 November 1847, some midshipmen were in Annapolis misbehaving and by 10:00 PM, Capa Crabb and Goodman McBlair, a visitor to Annapolis, came to Upshur's residence to report a disturbance. About ten or fifteen minutes earlier, Crabb and his family were bothered by a noise outside their residence. When Crabb went to investigate, he found that the enclosure around his and neighboring homes, and some nearby trees, were damaged. He discovered the culprits to be "navy officers" and politely told them to stop what they were doing. They did, apparently, and he followed them back to the school and then returned to fetch McBlair to visit Upshur's residence.[58]

Upshur called the officer of the day and the gate watchman, and they reviewed the liberty book. It showed that at 9:35 PM, shortly after the incident occurred, Midshipman William West, age unknown, Date of '41, returned. The officer of the day also noted that someone came back with West, but it was not recorded in the book because the officer of the day and the watchman were busy at other tasks. The next day Upshur visited the scene of the crime and found it as Crabb had described. In response, Upshur sent a carpenter and workers from the school to repair the damage, but the tree was not replaced because it was rare and Upshur was unable to find a replacement. Meanwhile, that afternoon, Upshur questioned the midshipmen who returned before and after West, but all denied participating in the disturbance and claimed ignorance. Furthermore, West refused to say whether he was involved. Upshur demanded answers, and West replied that someone had entered the yard with him, but he declined to reveal his name. Upshur repeated his order with the same results. The superintendent then asked West if the other man was an officer; again West refused to say, but he added that the gentleman was not attached to the school.[59]

Upshur knew of one captain and two passed midshipmen in Annapolis who were not attached to the school who might be the culprits. The superintendent believed the captain innocent and concluded he had "neither the right nor the disposition to believe that it was either of the others." While Upshur still wanted the truth, he failed to see the need to punish West if he really were innocent. Upshur believed "it possible that a false idea of honor or friendship might [have] induce[d] him even if innocent to suffer reproach, rather than incur the risk of involving a guilty companion, I offered him the only alternative I could." Upshur told West that the evidence before him made him look guilty and explained that while he could not force West to admit his guilt, he was honor bound to acquit himself if he was innocent. West asked one half hour to consider his fate, and when his thirty minutes expired, Upshur again asked him about his involvement, but West still declined comment. Upshur then told him that he had no choice but to conclude that he was guilty and to forward the facts to the Navy Department. The superintendent then suspended West from duties and privileges but ordered him to continue attending classes.[60] West, from New York, graduated Annapolis and retired in 1866 a commander after twenty-five years service.[61]

Valle asserts that the school's demerit system "kept the midshipmen out of the toils of the regular naval justice system except for the most aggravated cases, usually involving fights or duels." Thus, Annapolis authorities threatened or used a court martial, or court of inquiry, only as the ultimate way to assess if a midshipman was suitable as a future officer. Still, the numbers of courts martial fell after

1845, when discipline began to be administered at Annapolis. Courts martial now only dealt with extremely serious offenses like gross misconduct.[62]

The most infamous outbreak of disciplinary problems at the Naval School involved the Professor Henry Lockwood effigy affair.[63] The incident is important because it illustrates the type of behavior that the Navy was especially wary of when its future naval officers showed signs of mass disrespect toward their superiors, which at sea could be deemed mutinous conduct. The affair shows how the Navy and the midshipmen defined and negotiated the qualities of a professional officer. The incident shows how far the students had to go before turning a court-martial threat into reality and reveals that midshipmen would sacrifice themselves rather than see all their classmates punished.

The affair began on 21 March 1848, when a number of midshipmen gathered in the lower part of the school yard and began to chant "Down with Gunnery" and "Text Book, Text Book" in dissatisfaction with their gunnery course. The executive officer, in the superintendent's absence, restored order, and the students returned to their duties and recitations. But the next morning an effigy of Professor Lockwood, the gunnery instructor, appeared hanging from the school's flagstaff with a model gun attached to it, stolen from a storage space. Upshur concluded that the incident was premeditated and an "unparalleled assault upon law and discipline." Eventually, the effigy was removed and the midshipmen assembled to discover who, in the dead of night when all should have been asleep, had committed the offense. Upshur threatened to punish the whole class if the culprits failed to present themselves, whereupon Midshipmen John McLeod Murphy, Edward Scovell, and John Gale, all from the Date of '41, came forward. Upshur suspended them immediately but exclaimed that more midshipmen must have been involved.[64]

Upshur was disappointed that the midshipmen's behavior had degenerated to such a degree, and he blamed himself. As superintendent, he hoped to impose as few restrictions as possible and govern by "moral rather than by legal force." Therefore, he tried to "maintain good order and obedience at as small a cost of personal feeling as practicable" and was as lenient and understanding as "the nature of the institution under my charge would admit of." Still, he speculated that he may have "carried the system too far." Previously, he had "counseled, advised, persuaded, lectured, rebuked, suspended and reported, and you [the secretary] have reprimanded and finally ordered offenders to sea" if they continued to misbehave. Upshur believed the latter policy impressed upon the others the seriousness of the offense, and he felt that prompt dismissal from the Navy would have an even greater impact.[65] As for the effigy incident, it went to a court martial, one of the few held at Annapolis from 1845 to 1861, despite threats to hold them on other occasions.

On 17 April 1848, a general court martial convened at the school to deal with the charges against Murphy, Scovell, and Gale. Captains Charles Morris, Charles W. Morgan, and Charles J. McCauley, and four commanders, David G. Farragut, Robert Ritchie, Franklin Buchanan, and Samuel Barron sat in judgment. The judge advocate was Pinkney Whyte, of Baltimore.[66] Murphy was charged with treating his superior, Lockwood, with contempt, behaving in a riotous and disorderly manner, and violating article 3 of the school's regulations, which instructed everyone to treat each other with proper decorum.[67] Murphy felt that the charges were invalid because they failed to state whom he had supposedly aided in hanging the effigy and whom it represented. Moreover, the charges never suggested how Murphy prevented Lockwood from carrying out his duties. Murphy also believed that it was unjust to charge him with violating the school's proper decorum regulations because the charges failed to state which officer he had offended, or how it had breached Murphy's duty. Besides, Murphy argued, the regulation was just a "rule of politeness" rather than a law. But Murphy's strongest argument against the charges was that they violated his rights as an officer. Specifically, he objected to being charged with treating his superior with disrespect, since Lockwood was not a superior under naval law. The professor, Murphy argued, did not hold a commission, and his appointment as an instructor was neither confirmed by the Senate nor signed by the president. Under existing law, Lockwood could only be deemed to hold the equivalent rank of petty officer. It therefore went against naval tradition and law to charge Murphy with contempt for a superior. Murphy believed that if the court found the charge valid, it would have ramifications for the whole Navy: a port captain, commander, or captain might be placed in charge of the police department of the school and find himself outranked by a hypothetical civilian superintendent.[68]

The judge advocate responded to Midshipman Murphy's statement. Whyte asserted that while it was desirable for the charges to contain the utmost precision, it was not incumbent on the framer to "use the technical strictness with which indictments are drawn." Whyte quoted Lord Hale, who had declared that the technical strictness demanded by an accused for the charges was growing to such an extent that it was becoming easy for the "grossest crimes" to go unpunished.[69] Whyte also believed that the charges sufficiently indicated that Professor Lockwood was the injured party and that no greater description was required. But Whyte agreed, somewhat, with Murphy's contention that a professor was not an officer and elements of the charges were too vague to allow the accused to defend himself. Murphy was not given a description of the offense he was accused of committing, nor was he provided with information upon whom he committed the offense against. Whyte noted that he had not seen the charge before it was written and concluded that he could not defend it before the court.[70]

After hearing both sides' arguments, the court deliberated and found Murphy not guilty on all counts. While Murphy had acted poorly, the naval officer's professional power with respect to civilian employees was at stake because of how the prosecution framed the charges. The court concluded that under the present law, Professor Lockwood's rank only equaled that of a petty officer and therefore he was not Murphy's superior. The court also agreed that other elements of the charges were too vague, as the defendant contended.[71] Still, the wider importance of instilling a proper officer ethos in the midshipmen was important, and when the court martial of Midshipman Gale convened on 25 April 1848, the secretary of the Navy did not leave himself open to the same procedural attacks as Midshipman Murphy had initiated. Consequently, Gale was charged with disobedience of orders in connection with the hanging of the effigy and failing to show a courteous deportment toward Professor Lockwood, thus "disobeying the first clause of the third Article of the Rules and Regulations for the government of" the school. Gale had also disobeyed the second clause of the third article of the school's regulations and had failed to conduct himself with proper decorum.[72]

While the judge advocate constructed a case against Gale for hanging the effigy, the defense laid the groundwork to claim that the midshipman's rights had been violated because he was not informed that offenses at the school would be handled by a court martial and that his confession was made under duress. Previously, the superintendent had handled discipline himself and in a more lenient manner than would a court martial. Moreover, under the law, a confession, Gale argued, was involuntary if made after threats by the superintendent, and it ought to be inadmissible. Gale averred that the standard here ought to be higher where the individual in authority was the accused's superior.[73] Nevertheless, Gale conceded that discipline and subordination to authority were essential to the efficient running of a military organization. His argument also reveals that he was conscious of his status as a student learning the profession's ethos at the hands of older officers. Gale told the court that "obedience to orders—subordination to authority, are the first precepts taught by the older officer to the younger—the first lessons learned on the entrance upon his novitiate by the young aspirant for the duties and honors of a proud and itemly [*sic*] disciplined service. Thus taught him almost from his very childhood these principles grow with his growth and strengthen with each succeeding year. They are at once his pride and his duty, and become as apart of his being."[74] Therefore, when a superior orders an officer to do something, the officer carries out that order without hesitation. Thus, the accused argued, his admission of guilt was the result of being ordered to admit his part in the affair by the superintendent. Gale, by carrying out his duty, was forced into self-incrimination, and his admission was involuntary.[75] However, the court disagreed and admitted Gale's confession into the records.[76]

After the prosecutor questioned several officers in charge at the school, he called Midshipman Arthur H. Otis, Date of '41, who provided vague testimony about his recollection of events. He told the court that during the period of the effigy incident, he lived in room 17 with Gale, a Mr. West, and a Mr. Hunter. Under the judge advocate's questioning, Otis confirmed that a copy of the rules of the school, as entered into evidence, was put in their room; he could not say whether the regulations were in the room on 21 and 22 March. When cross-examined, Otis told the court that he was uncertain if the rules had been in the room since Gale had come to live there, but that when they were, they were kept near the fireplace. Otis was then excused, and the judge advocate informed Gale that if he had any evidence to present to the court, he was now permitted to do so.[77]

Gale called Midshipman John V. Philip, Date of '41, who also supported the claim that the confessions were given under duress. Then Gale called Midshipman Francis G. Clarke, Date of '41, who testified that Upshur had declared that he would rule with a strong arm from that point forward and that there had been some discussion among those assembled about reporting to the superintendent to declare that they were all involved. Under questioning Clarke also told the court that he saw nothing about the effigy to indicate that it was intended to represent Professor Lockwood. To the contrary, Clarke told the court, there had been some talk that the effigy was a "stuffed paddy" connected with St. Patrick's Day. Still, under cross-examination, Clarke admitted that when he saw the cannon on the effigy, he assumed it referred to Professor Lockwood.[78]

Gale next called Midshipman Joseph B. Smith, Date of '41, who also vouched for Upshur's temper and recounted that he told the assembled midshipmen that while he had tried indulgence and persuasion in the past, henceforth he would use force. Smith also told the court that he too heard some others mention that they believed the effigy to be a "stuffed Paddy" rather than a representation of Professor Lockwood.[79] In closing Gale argued that the prosecution had failed to show a disobedience of orders. Like Murphy, Gale tried to play a game of semantics and argued that the school's regulations were not in themselves orders but laws. Thus, he challenged the third article of the school's regulations, which governed proper decorum, because it was not "expressed in terms of sufficient directness and simplicity of subject meaning, to constitute orders." Like Murphy, Gale added that the charges were flawed, because it was impossible to tell what "proper decorum" and "deportment" meant. Finally, Gale told the court that the charge of improper deportment against another officer was invalid, because Professor Lockwood was not an officer and reiterated his argument that he gave his confession under duress.[80]

The court found that Gale's involvement in hanging the effigy was unproven, but it did accept that he had failed to show proper decorum toward Professor Lockwood. The verdict ordered that Gale was to be publicly reprimanded in front of all the school and dismissed until he present himself at the start of the next year for an entrance examination.[81] The sentence was not only meant to punish Gale, but also to serve as a warning to others. Still, the testimony of the witnesses Gale called substantiates other observances of midshipmen behavior. They failed to provide any testimony that would harm their fellow midshipmen, but when asked a direct question by the court—in this case whether they thought the effigy reminded them of Professor Lockwood—many witnesses, like Clarke, grudgingly did their duty and answered the question truthfully.

On 29 April 1848, Midshipman Edward H. Scovell faced the charge of disobedience of orders. Specifically, he was accused of hanging or aiding in the hanging of an effigy, thus disobeying the regulations that said fellow officers should be treated with a courteous deportment and of violating the second clause of the third article of the school's regulations for not conducting himself with "propriety and decorum."[82] Scovell also pleaded not guilty.[83] After the prosecution outlined its case, the first witness for the defense was Midshipman Law, who recounted how Upshur had assembled the midshipmen the morning of the hanging of the effigy. Law thought that Upshur was excited but that he said nothing Law deemed to be threatening. Law told the court, as others had, that Upshur said there would be consequences if the guilty failed to come forward. The midshipman was uncertain of Upshur's precise words, but when Murphy, Gale, and Scovell came forward, Law "thought they had saved the rest of the School from the probability of a punishment." Law also told the court that he had formed no opinion at the time of the effigy incident as to whom the effigy was meant to depict, but neither did he recall anyone comparing the effigy to a "stuffed Paddy." Nor did Law have any recollection of the assembled midshipmen desiring to go to the superintendent's office to claim they had all been involved in the incident.[84]

The next day Midshipman Charles McGary, Date of '41, appeared for the defense. When the judge advocate later asked McGary, "Do you not know that the actors in the disturbance of the day previous were known to the Commander or that Lieut. [Sidney] Lee [the executive officer] had informed him who they were?" "I do not know," McGary replied. Unsatisfied, the judge advocate meandered in his questioning until he asked McGary about prior discussions of the event to weaken McGary's credibility. Specifically, Whyte was curious to know how often since 22 March McGary had discussed the assembly with other midshipmen. McGary replied that he was uncertain, but that "the conversation has been repeatedly spoken of by myself with others of the midshipmen." Scovell then tried a redirect and asked McGary if, when Upshur called for the guilty parties to come forward, he told them to what offense they were answering. McGary replied that Upshur had not been clear on this point. When the court then asked McGary if the midshipmen had been told what the assembly was about when they were called, he tried his best not to let his fellow midshipman down, replied vaguely, and simply stated that they had been assembled to discuss the "act" that had occurred. Unimpressed, the judge advocate stepped in and pressed McGary for more information. "In what act?" questioned Whyte. "In hanging up the image or in the manner in which their disapprobation had been expressed," McGary admitted. Under further questioning by the defendant, McGary explained that some midshipmen had expressed a desire to go to the superintendent but only to admit to "feeling" for the act rather than participating in it.[85]

The defense then called Midshipman John K. Wilson, Date of '41, who offered little new. The final witness Scovell called was Midshipman William Law. Previously Law had claimed that there was no later attempt by the other midshipmen to admit involvement. Scovell asked Law if upon further reflection he wished to amend his previous statements. Law replied that "I have not a distinct recollection that there was a proposition made in precisely those words [used by the accused in court]— but there was one, something to that effect."[86] Law did not want to stretch his actual recollection of events to support his fellow midshipmen any more than reality would allow. He was caught between his loyalty and duty.

In his defense, Scovell told the court that the charges and the evidence were virtually identical to the Gale case; Scovell stated that "I may almost be said to have been tried already." As Gale had argued, Scovell judged that he could not be charged with disobedience of orders because the third article of the school's rules was not an order. Scovell told the court that "a violation of said article therefore does not constitute the military crime of disobedience of orders." In the case of the first specification, the first clause of the third article governed relations between officers and, as had already been proven, Professor Lockwood was not an officer. As for the second specification, Scovell argued that charging a midshipman with breaching propriety and decorum for suspending an effigy, without showing any motive for the suspension, was unacceptable. By this definition, Scovell argued, the suspension of anything could be taken as a breach. As had Gale, Scovell also argued that his "confession" had been made under duress—he was following orders to confess under pain of punishment for the entire school.[87]

Scovell argued that in the excitement the superintendent and the students misunderstood which charges they were answering; therefore the confessions could not be entered into evidence. Scovell told the court that in the heat of the moment, Upshur may have been focused solely on the effigy incident, been unclear in his speech, and erroneously assumed that they knew to what he was referring. Scovell explained that in the confusion he answered to what he thought were the charges and assumed that he must have been implicated in some misconduct other than just the hanging of the effigy. Scovell also contested the assumption that some kind of guilt was present among all the midshipmen: "Here we see a number—many of whom *must* have been innocent, seriously proposing to acknowledge themselves guilty [emphasis in original]." Scovell then asked the court, "what then is more probable than that those who *did go over only carried into effect what others proposed?* [emphasis in original]." Scovell explained that evidence could not be based on acts motivated by feelings no one could prove. And besides, the prosecution had failed to present any physical evidence that the accused—or any other specific person— had committed the crime. Scovell asserted that he had only admitted guilt on the assumption that, as a typical student, he must have been guilty of something.[88] Scovell's defense that he was unaware that he was answering to the charge of hanging the effigy shows that he felt he had been wronged, but that he felt this wrong could be corrected.

The court dismissed all charges against Scovell except disobedience of orders and sentenced him to be publicly reprimanded, dismissed from the Naval School, "and not allowed to return to it until required to present himself there at the next examination."[89] Scovell's case reveals the ideal of midshipmen solidarity—in their desire to accept responsibility for the effigy incident as a group—and the level of discomfort the witnesses felt when they had to be slowly pressed into admitting that the evidence against the accused was correct. The midshipmen stuck together when battling the authorities, but their unity became fractured when they struggled with their professional obligations and especially when they fought among themselves. Meanwhile, the incident reveals that the Navy took seriously any midshipman activity that looked like mass disrespect for authority. In the end, the Navy retained Midshipman John McLeod Murphy, although his later career was spotty. Murphy, from New York, resigned once in 1852 but became an acting lieutenant during the Civil War, only to resign again in 1864. Meanwhile, neither Gale nor Scovell graduated from Annapolis. Scovell remained in Annapolis, and Upshur reported that he seemed aware of the gravity of his offense and should be readmitted. Consequently, Upshur recommended that the department readmit Scovell, and he lasted until 1850, when he was finally dismissed, likely in accordance with the new Naval Academy rules.[90] Gale, however, continued to be a nuisance, as discussed below, and was finally dismissed from the Navy on 9 September 1848.[91]

Midshipmen solidarity, however, often disintegrated over matters of personal honor, and fights between them at the school at least twice took the form of duels. Joyce Appleby concludes that, originating among European army officers, dueling "found a second life in the United States" for "men struggling to find a civil way to disagree on matters of interest and principle." Moreover, she asserts, it boiled down to "masculine ideals of honor."[92] Still, Christopher McKee asserts that the number of duels in the Navy before 1815 was low, resulting in eighteen "statistically insignificant" deaths. Nevertheless, its violence gained notoriety, such as the duel between James Barron and Stephen Decatur in 1820. Meanwhile, the eighteen deaths were largely young officers; twelve were young midshipmen. Consequently, McKee concludes that two factors caused the phenomena in young officers: "One is dealing with men whose defined role was as fighters who must have the courage to face death, and with *young* men still in the process of establishing personal identities." Place young men together in a confined space, and McKee believes that minor issues spiraled quickly out of control in a profession where "one who had never established his bravery through combat, could in that society [not] have his courage challenged and still remain a member in good standing of his peer group."[93] When the young Uriah Levy waited to assume command of *Vandalia* in 1838, for example, and a Pensacola innkeeper accused Levy of lying about his belongings being stolen from the inn, Levy refused to strike the man dead over a matter of honor. But Levy's reaction ran counter to the philosophy of many of his fellow officers, in particular those from the South who took slights to personal honor as a grave trespass. Thus, Levy's refusal to fight the innkeeper made him an outsider in the eyes of his comrades.[94]

In a confined area of young men in their late teens or early twenties, it is no wonder that similar duels occurred at Annapolis as the young officers established their professional identity. Robert J. Schneller concludes that "honor placed the individual above the group. Dueling was the ritualistic expression of honor, the code of gentlemen."[95] On 4 May 1848, Midshipmen Byrd W. Stevenson, from Virginia, and Walter W. Queen, from D.C., and both of the '41 Date, fought one of the infamous Annapolis duels.[96] But duels were not how Annapolis wanted scandal-free future professionals to settle their disputes, even if the students had the notion that this was how it was done.

Superintendent Upshur was aware of the role of dueling among men, but he was also aware of the history that the school was trying to make. When Upshur reported the duel to the secretary of the Navy, he argued that it must be punished, or other people attached to the school would duel on the grounds because "they feel secure against the civil laws of Maryland." Upshur also noted that "duelling [*sic*] however reprehensible in itself has hitherto been sanctioned by precedent and practice among military men as a necessary evil. Without expressing an opinion on that point, I would respectfully remark that a grave aspect is imparted to this act by the time and place in which it was perpetrated."[97] Because Upshur wanted the school's name to remain unsullied, the incident led to a court of inquiry to ascertain the facts.

The inquiry convened at the school on 29 May 1848.[98] Most students called to testify denied actually witnessing the duel, but details emerged over what caused the dispute. There had been a fracture in the group corporateness, and the students felt a duel was the best way to solve their disagreement. According to Midshipman Robert Stuart, Date of '41, Stevenson told Queen that he had failed to vote for him as a member of a school club because he did not like Queen and felt that other students would make better members. Queen then apparently uttered some remark that Stevenson said proved Queen was a coward.[99] Midshipman J. C. P. DeKrafft, Date of '41, told the court that on 1 May, around 11:00 PM in Annapolis, he heard Stevenson call Queen a coward and then Queen called Stevenson an "infamous liar." In response, Stevenson tried to hit Queen, but one of his friends restrained him. As they both returned to the school yard by different routes, they met again at the gate and Stevenson demanded an apology, but Queen told him that he had started the affair.[100]

The court found that Queen apologized to Stevenson at the gate, but he withdrew it the next day by a note. This led to a "challenge" from Queen that caused the duel on 4 May at the Tenpin alley within the school grounds, where James Johnston, Date of '41, acted as Stevenson's second, an unknown citizen as Queen's second, and Stevenson shot Queen in the hip at a distance of fifteen paces. The court made no recommendations for punishment, as the duty of a court of inquiry was simply to provide the Navy Department with the facts.[101] In the end, the court of inquiry into the duel was different from the courts martial into the hanging of the effigy of Professor Lockwood. In the Lockwood case the midshipmen called to testify seemed much less willing to present evidence against their fellow midshipmen, since it was the midshipmen against the establishment. In the Queen-Stevenson dueling case, however, it was a matter of personal honor between two midshipmen, and the students were more than willing to tell the court how the dispute started.

On 7 June 1848, there was yet another duel between members of the '41 Date. At 8:00 PM Midshipman Francis G. Dallas, from Massachusetts, was carried into the school yard in a carriage with a bullet wound to his right shoulder, the result of a duel with Midshipman John Gale, from Maryland, who the court martial over the Lockwood incident had ordered dismissed from the school.[102] While at the school, Dallas became embroiled in a dispute over honor between himself and some other midshipmen. On 24 May, Dallas wrote Midshipmen Gustavus Harrison, Date of '41, and George M. Dibble complaining that his reputation had been insulted and asserting that he was ready to fight for his honor. The dispute seemed to center around Dallas' spotty service record, in defense of which Dallas produced letters from Surgeon Barrington detailing his ill health. In early June, Midshipman Gale wrote Dallas that the charges against him arose long before coming to the Naval School and that he was prepared to prove it, even if he were "compelled to resort to measures as disagreeable to me as they ought to be to you." Things came to a head on 6 June, when Dallas and Gale finally settled matters with a duel outside school grounds at Bladensburg. Midshipman Charles C. Hunter, from Vermont, Date of '42, acted as Gale's second, while a civilian was Dallas' second.[103] Dr. W. Gray Palmer reported on 7 June that Dallas received a shot to his shoulder and was left unable to raise his right arm. But Palmer reported that both sides were eager for another round: "I mean that Mr. Dallas demanded it and the other party was willing to oblige him; they were, as I said before, prevented by my intervention."[104]

As the case was being reviewed by the secretary of the Navy, Dallas was informed on 4 July 1848, that he had passed his lieutenant's examination. Shortly thereafter, the secretary informed him that the president had decided to dismiss him from the service. Dallas retorted that the president had committed "a *gross* act of *injustice* [emphasis in original]." Secretary Mason, sounding somewhat sympathetic to the young man, informed him that Gale and Hunter had also been dismissed. Mason also returned Dallas' letter containing his comments about the president, adding that his chances of being reinstated "will not probably be promoted by such language as you employ in this letter."[105] Dallas was finally kicked out of the Navy; the Navy would not have its young men dueling and behaving badly combined with their poor commitment to the service to begin with. Midshipmen Queen, Stevenson, and Johnston were all initially dismissed in June for participating in the first duel.[106] Johnston's dismissal stood, while Stevenson continued in the Navy until he was "dropped" in 1854, likely in accordance with the final ultimatum to the Oldsters when Annapolis became the academy. Queen, however, graduated from the Naval School and retired at the rank of rear admiral after forty-five years; being born in and appointed from D.C. likely gave the young midshipman the connections needed to remain in the service.[107] Dismissal was the ultimate form of punishment for misbehavior and often—but not always—ended the midshipman's career.

In the 1840s, the Naval School provided an environment where future officers learned about their profession and the Navy kept them under control. At Annapolis, the Navy monitored student behavior with conduct rolls, in the increasingly sustained manner of a professional organization. In response, the midshipmen were generally well behaved. Daily infractions included tardiness and overstaying leave, while examples of gross insubordination were virtually nonexistent. Midshipman behavior also reveals that the young men were bonding as a group, learning to interpret the values and rights associated with a professional officer: honor, loyalty, and integrity. In response, school authorities handled most infractions internally and disciplined when necessary. But the Navy took seriously any infractions that struck at core officer values: respect for authority and each other and carrying out orders. If the midshipmen violated such regulations and officials feared it was a group response, a court martial tried the accused and served as an example to others. This dynamic continued in the academy era. The Naval School and Academy students largely accepted the Navy's style of discipline, as they fitted into the expectations of their profession, and the Navy refrained from enforcing the full extent of the law against the students unless necessary.

CHAPTER 5

Discipline and Law in the Academy Era

As the political crisis in the country deepened over slavery, naval discipline became wrapped up in the debate. Southerners wanted flogging maintained in the Navy, while Northerners claimed that Southerners supported "tyranny" at sea and at home. Embroiled in the era's political debates, the House nonetheless passed a bill outlawing flogging on 23 September 1850 by 131 to 29. In the Senate, however, the margin of victory was much closer, where it passed twenty-six to twenty-four. The president signed it the same day.[1] Officers generally felt that corporal punishment gave them power over lower-ranking officers and especially over the enlisted men. Discipline, and the ability of officers to inflict it, helped separate them from their men and solidify their professional identity as being in command.[2] With flogging now removed as a disciplinary option, the problem arose of devising new punishments. Still, some reform-minded officers, often Northerners, provided examples for how the Navy could manage discipline without resorting to violence.

Uriah Levy was one captain who advocated civilized punishment methods. Levy, from a Philadelphia Jewish merchant family, started his maritime career in the civilian world, going to sea at age ten as a ship's boy in 1802. By 1811 he was a schooner master. With the outbreak of the War of 1812, Levy requested an appointment in the U.S. Navy as a sailing master, in charge of ship operations and navigation.[3] It was exceptional for someone to progress from sailing master to the next higher officer rank of lieutenant, typically reserved for those who entered the officer profession by first becoming a midshipman. Regardless, Levy obtained a rare lieutenant's appointment in 1817, after obtaining letters of support from his shipmates and captains. Still, Levy soon faced ridicule from his fellow officers, possibly because of anti-Semitism, Levy's outspokenness and boastful reputation, and jealousy of his affluence from his merchant career and real estate investments.[4]

Levy's experience in the civilian world, combined with his Northern upbringing, likely created a reform-leaning officer. He saw no need for violence to uphold his personal honor, and as captain of *Vandalia* in the late 1830s, he was one of the few commanders to follow Secretary Woodbury's 1831 orders to limit flogging. Instead, Levy developed alternate punishments, like a "black list" of offenders, separated from the rest of the crew. Moreover, Levy also treated younger sailors leniently. Boys, for instance, were never flogged; they were paddled instead if severe punishment was required. Still, in one instance, Levy ordered a boy tarred for misbehavior, an act that nearly got Levy dismissed, because his critics seized on the opportunity to humiliate him. Saved, Levy obtained captain's rank in 1844, but his unpopularity and ill health left him without a command, even through the Mexican-American War. Levy, nonetheless, saw himself as "the sailor's friend" and his nonviolent punishments received press attention among advocates of naval reform.[5]

By the late 1840s, debate about flogging in the Navy reemerged, as the gag rule against discussions of slavery expired. John P. Hale, Democratic representative from New Hampshire, adopted the Navy's use of flogging as an analogous cause. By 1849 Hale, then New York senator, obtained a detailed report to Congress, from the secretary of the Navy, about naval punishments. It linked disciplinary problems and flogging to the grog ration, and Hale convinced the Senate to outlaw flogging in 1850.[6] But it was a struggle. Senator Stephen R. Mallory, Democrat from Florida, for instance, told the Senate that the Navy had a long tradition of training men under the lash. Moreover, he objected to the implication that sailors were treated as poorly as slaves. Instead, Mallory believed that the Navy was composed of a variety of men from all the depths of society, and an effective means of discipline should not be removed just because the North thought it was as degrading as slavery. Furthermore, Mallory exclaimed that sailors entering the profession knew what the life was like and supported the lash.[7]

While Hale campaigned in Congress, Levy worked behind the scenes, met with lawmakers, and published opinions in newspapers. As flogging's abolition looked to be overturned, Ira Dye concludes that prominent reform naval officers, like Commodore Robert F. Stockton, Democratic senator from New Jersey, rose to support its demise, and "the fight to eliminate flogging was over."[8] Nevertheless, it took until 1862 before the grog ration was eliminated. In the meantime, naval officers like Levy and Robert Stockton showed that the Navy could manage ships and men without resorting to brute force. Consequently, in this reformed atmosphere, the Navy prepared a code of discipline comprising forty-six chapters, called the "System of Orders and Instructions," proclaimed by the president on 15 February 1853. By 5 April, the attorney general, Caleb Cushing, found that the regulations had taken away from Congress the right to make regulations in this area and that therefore the regulations were illegal. Consequently, new regulations passed on 2 March 1855, called "An Act to Provide a More Efficient Discipline for the Navy," laid out various punishments ranging from discharge to demotion or loss of liberty for various infractions.[9]

When a vessel of the United States returned to port, the commanding officer was now required to submit to the secretary of the Navy a list of those enlisted crew members who had served for three years. If the crew member had carried out their duties and the captain believed that he was suitable for honorable discharge, he was to be issued a certificate confirming his "fidelity and obedience." The dishonorably discharged could reenlist within three months, while the captain was to give preference to the "faithful and obedient" when he issued temporary shore leave.[10] This act was only a supplement to the regulations of 1800, which had been guiding the Navy to this time.[11] Still, it provided new measures to help the Navy deal with the vacuum that had been created with the abolition of flogging.

With flogging removed as the symbol of an officer's power, the summary court martial replaced floggings of petty officers and other inferior ratings.[12] The summary court martial was intended to be for "the trial of offences which he [the commander] may deem deserving of greater punishment than the commander of a vessel himself is by law authorized to inflict of his own authority, but not sufficient to require trial by general court-martial."[13] Summary courts martial were presided over by three officers and could be called at the behest of the ship or shore-station commander. Evidence and the proceedings were recorded and forwarded to the Navy Department, and the ship's medical officer was to ensure that the punishment inflicted would not adversely affect the health of the accused.[14]

The new punishments were aimed at those privileges sailors disliked losing. The panel was permitted to hand out sentences ranging from discharge with bad conduct; solitary confinement for no more than thirty days, optionally in irons and with diminished rations; confinement for no more than two months; reduction in rank; loss of liberty; or an increase in duties or loss of pay.[15] A general court marital could also issue such punishments, which opened up the punishment scheme to infliction upon the officers.[16] Finally, after the outbreak of the Civil War, a new set of regulations was passed on 17 July 1862, entitled an "Act for the Better Government of the Navy of the United States." The new act again outlawed flogging at sea or by court martial and restated the disciplinary actions that could be taken under the 1855 act.[17] It also declared that all punishments must be noted in the ship's log.[18]

After the new regulations of 1855, a gradual set of punishments governed wider naval discipline rather than brute force. The U.S. Navy, especially after 1855, was only a violent, oppressive place when needed. Naval law and discipline at the academy introduced new midshipmen to what was expected of them under naval regulations. The 1840s had witnessed the extreme example of punishment meted out during the *Somers* mutiny, and as Ira Dye explains, there was a movement to recruit more American-born sailors into the Navy, but "American youths were perceived to be avoiding" the service because of "its image of Jack the drunken sailor, and the ever-present brutality of flogging."[19] Consequently, the reforms that created the Naval Academy brought little change to the disciplinary philosophy already in place at Annapolis. But as a professional entity, the discipline became more quantified with the more rigorous program and matched the wider reform attitude growing in the Navy. Philosophically, the academy continued to handle its discipline internally, and only on a few occasions did it reach the court martial or court of inquiry level. By disciplining the students in such a manner, the academy hoped to instill in them the values of a naval officer and the behavior that the Navy expected of them when they graduated.

The laws of the Navy still applied to the academy, and the superintendent had the right to make additional rules. The superintendent and the commandant of midshipmen also had the right to inspect every part of the academy. Under the new academy discipline regulations, everyone was confined to the academy grounds by default and could only leave with the superintendent's permission. The new academy regulations also banned "combinations," likely to curtail the activities of school-era groups like the Owls.[20] Midshipmen were only allowed out on Saturday afternoons and had to be back by 8:00 PM, while only half were allowed to leave the grounds at any one time. Sickness had to be proven, and no one was allowed in another's room (or out of their own) during study hours. Fighting—with deadly weapons or otherwise—was formally forbidden, although, as we have seen, it was unacceptable even in the school era, as were cards and other games, alcohol, and visiting local hotels or taverns. Students also had to use proper language and only were allowed to carry firearms with the superintendent's permission. The pupils were also again told not to mark, cut, or deface "public buildings or property of any kind." And they all had to attend chapel.[21]

During this period the academy feared that bad behavior would spread like a disease that would eat away at the ethos authorities tried to instill in the young men. Hence, a breach of the moral norms was a serious offense. On 12 October 1852, six acting midshipmen were reported to the secretary of the Navy for a "breach of morals and discipline," which Secretary John P. Kennedy said had caused him "much mortification." He believed that "grave offences against discipline and morals cannot fail to injure the Institution." Kennedy hesitated to dismiss the midshipmen, because they had only recently enrolled. But he told Superintendent Stribling to assemble all the midshipmen and read his correspondence "as a warning to all." As for the "delinquents," he proclaimed that they were to remain within the academy grounds for the next three months and to abstain from any misconduct under pain of being disqualified for naval service. Kennedy told Stribling to tell the midshipmen to "resist all temptations, however seductive, to a vice which will degrade and disqualify any officer for his duty, and, if habitual, must separate him from the service." Nowhere in the correspondence did Kennedy refer to the nature of this ghastly "vice."[22]

In the end, academy authorities were often lenient toward the students because of their inexperience, but they were willing to resort to greater force if the offender was older and should by then know the professional expectations of an officer. In late April 1850, Midshipmen George F. Morrison, Frederick A. Boardman, and Henry A. Adams, all about seventeen, committed acts of insubordination. The matter was serious enough that it was reported to Secretary of the Navy William Preston, who concluded that it had impaired the standing of the "young officers themselves" as well as the academy, but he believed these acts were the fault of the midshipmen's "youth and indiscretion." The secretary told George P. Upshur that he was to express the department's "unqualified disapprobation" of the midshipmen's "violation of discipline and morals." Nevertheless, the secretary decided that the midshipmen were worthy of the department's leniency, because they promised that their behavior would be good in the future. The secretary ordered that Morrison and Boardman, whom he believed were the "principal offenders," be denied all privileges beyond the academy and were to remain within the school grounds for one month. As for the others involved, the secretary hoped that the example made of the two midshipmen would be "properly appreciated by all their associates and brother officers." And he ordered that their punishments be read publicly to the professors and students.[23]

Despite the scale of justice at the academy, sometimes authorities resorted to dismissal to get their point across. Even when dismissal was considered, the student's newness to the Navy still was a factor. For example, it played a role in the discipline of Acting Midshipman Edward C. Stockton, Date of '49, almost fifteen when he was appointed, and another midshipman.[24] On 27 July 1850, Stockton and the other boy left the academy grounds without permission. Stribling admitted that under normal circumstances such a violation of regulations would not be tolerated and they would be dismissed from the Navy. But Stribling believed that there were mitigating circumstances that he felt warranted leniency. That day a group of students from Baltimore visited Annapolis and paraded in front of the government house. The midshipmen, Stribling asserted, were curious and wanted to see the visitors, so, "with the usual thoughtlessness of boys [they] left the premises to see them." Stribling decided to report the incident to the secretary but told him that the boys were "both very young, and were not at the moment perhaps, aware of the very grave offence they committed." Stribling surmised that he would be able to fashion some other punishment for them, other than dismissal, which would impress on them and the other students "the necessity of strict obedience of orders, at all times and under all circumstances."[25]

For the lesser offenses the academy sometimes used money as leverage. In 1852, for example, the academy withheld the pocket money of sixteen of forty-four midshipmen listed on a disciplinary report. Four were punished for smoking, while the others were chastised for unspecified infractions.[26] Meanwhile, inexperience mitigated an offense that might otherwise have been dealt with harshly: disobedience of orders. An incident with the boats occurred in October 1852 involving seven midshipmen. Orders to remain away from land or other boats were clearly known to the midshipmen, but they landed at a wharf in Annapolis anyway. Even worse, they then loaded liquor on board, which was grounds for dismissal. Regardless, Stribling asserted that "they are to be sure mere boys, and allowance must be made accordingly."[27]

On 21 May 1853, inexperience once again was a factor in the students' fate. The new secretary of the Navy, James C. Dobbin, ruled on the fate of Acting Midshipmen George A. Bigelow (about fifteen), Charles J. McDougal (about fifteen), Henry L. Ingraham (about sixteen), Charles E. Cushman (slightly over fourteen), Francis P. Vultee (about fifteen), and two other midshipmen.[28] They were charged with violating academy regulations, but "in pursuance of your recommendation [Stribling's] of the delinquents on account of their youth, the Department is inclined to extend forbearance, and permit them to remain at the Academy." Still, the secretary informed Stribling that he was to reprimand them and "warn them of the consequences of a similar offense hereafter."[29] In contrast, the academy dealt more harshly with older students because the authorities feared their influence on the professional development of younger midshipmen.

The older students, including the "Oldsters," represented older brothers to the younger students (figure 6). The Oldsters often had facial hair, kept together, and largely ignored the "Youngsters." Yet, the Oldsters looked out for the new members of the academy, and eventually third-class students selected a new student, or fourth-class man, as his "plebe" and "defended [him] against all comers." Furthermore, Oldsters wore uniforms, while the acting midshipmen wore a cap and jacket like the midshipman's, but without the gold-laced cap band and buttons on their pocket and cuffs. In 1855 the uniform was modified with a silver anchor on the cap, gold anchor on each collar, and a double-breasted jacket, to further differentiate older and younger students, and full-fledged naval officers. The uniform then remained virtually static until 1865. Authorities also appointed an Oldster as a senior cadet officer, and by the late 1850s, Commandant of Midshipmen Lieutenant C. R. P. Rodgers allowed the first-class men to discipline the younger students. Further distinctions were enacted by the close of Superintendent George S. Blake's

Passed Midshipman.   Midshipman.

Figure 6. Midshipmen, 1852. *(Midshipmen in full dress, 1852, Special Collections & Archives Department, Nimitz Library, U.S. Naval Academy, Annapolis, Maryland)*

era to give the first-class men slightly different privileges than the younger students. In all, over the academy era, younger students could expect to be slowly treated more like officers than students, while becoming a role model for those new students below them.[30] Separated from their real families, the younger midshipmen looked to the older midshipmen to see, both physically and professionally, how they should look and behave.

The academy believed that the discipline of older midshipmen had an important effect on the younger students. One such case involved Acting Midshipman John Adams Howell, who was appointed in 1854 and was approximately seventeen in 1857.[31] Lieutenant J. Taylor Wood, a professor's assistant, reported Howell for leaving the mess hall without permission. Wood concluded that Howell "thus allowing in himself a disregard & contempt of the Regulations" had set "a bad example to the junior class."[32] The authorities seemed concerned that disciplinary problems with one student would spread to others like a malignancy. Lieutenant R. H. Wyman, another professor's assistant, wrote on 31 October 1859, that Midshipman Samuel Hiatt (about fifteen) had been on "every report of delinquency and generally for two or three different offences against the regulations of the 'Academy.'"[33] Wyman concluded that "I consider his whole bearing and conduct as tending to contaminate the young gentleman with whom he is associated."[34] In the end, Hiatt would never graduate.[35] Hiatt was the type of potential officer unbecoming to the professional ethos of the U.S. Navy. Howell evidently learned his lesson, graduated Annapolis, and retired as a rear admiral after forty-eight years.[36]

Later in life, Alfred Thayer Mahan reflected on the cat-and-mouse game the midshipmen played with the authorities in the 1850s while he was at the academy. The discipline that Mahan suffered at the academy often caused the boys to rebel. The sometimes "uproarious" larking while officially condemned, was secretly tolerated by the staff. An overseer patrolled the midshipmen's residences wearing rubber soles to avoid detection. In reprisal, Mahan wrote, the students often tapped on the gas pipes from room to room to warn colleagues of the inspector's approach. Mahan believed that but for the advance warnings, many students would have been reported for violations of regulations.[37]

Mahan also reported there was once a lieutenant who liked to play detective. He often made surprise visits to the rooms when the midshipmen were supposed to be asleep. On one occasion some of the students were out of their rooms cooking oysters, a process that took a considerable amount of time because the frying pan they used was small. As the covert culinary operation neared completion, their enemy sprung forth and tossed the whole dinner out the window. None of the midshipmen were reported for their nighttime gastronomic foray. On another occasion a midshipman was visiting another's room when the warning came along the gas pipes that an inspection was imminent. The visiting midshipman hid under his friend's bed but accidentally left his hand exposed. The lieutenant came in the room with his lantern, saw the exposed hand, and stepped on it. The midshipman let out a yelp of pain and surprise, but the lieutenant left that as his punishment.[38] Such officials had many violations to watch for as the academy further regulated and quantified midshipmen behavior.

The Naval Academy regulations contained provisions for demerit rolls compiled by the Academic Board in June and October each year. Similar to West Point, the delinquencies were put in various classes and the highest-class offense would carry a demerit of ten points. In essence, the Navy now tracked in a professional and scientific manner the level of midshipman conformity to naval norms. First-class offenses received ten points and were meant for willful neglect of duty, orders, or use of profanity; being in a club or house of public entertainment in Annapolis; publishing without permission; or using firearms or fireworks without authorization. Second-class offenses won a pupil eight points for doing such things as bringing strangers into the mess hall or having one's light on after taps. Absenteeism, a third-class offense, received six points, as did dress uniform violations; loud talking, abusing servants, or being unkempt were fourth-class violations and received four points. Fifth-class offenses were for lateness or anything else an officer deemed worthy, while they could also issue one to ten points for "disrespectful, ungentlemanly, disorderly, insubordinate, or unmilitary conduct." Any delinquency above the fourth-class was to be multiplied by one-sixth for the third class, one-third for the second class, and one-half for the first-class offense. If a midshipman received more than 200 demerit points annually, he was deemed "deficient in conduct" and subject to dismissal.[39]

Again the academy applied naval law, but it took into consideration that the students were new to the Navy while quantifying their progress toward professional norms of behavior. The students responded in kind and again only misbehaved as a group if they felt their rights were violated. However, at a certain point, the authorities expected the midshipmen to start acting more like professionals. The Bureau of Ordnance and Hydrography outlined the importance of the conduct rolls. The bureau believed that "as at West Point, the object of a separate roll being to give prominence to conduct."[40] Even if midshipmen went over the allowed number of demerit points, the authorities gave them some leeway. Midshipmen Robert H. Offley (about fifteen) and George P. Dodge (about fifteen) in May 1851, had exceeded the demerit limit and were "liable to the penalty of" dismissal, but on Stribling's recommendation, they were saved. Instead, Secretary William A. Graham told Stribling to warn them that while they would be permitted to be examined in June, they had to show improvement in the interim, because "the Department will forbear no longer."[41] The students' June exam, however, was the final straw for the department. Dodge was dismissed on 12 June, while Offley is recorded only as never graduating Annapolis.[42]

Yet the behavior of the midshipmen from 1850 to the outbreak of the Civil War was generally good, showing that most students accepted the behavioral expectations of their future career. As for the Naval School era, a 20-percent random sample of the conduct rolls was analyzed. In general, offenses that could be characterized as riotous, mutinous, or otherwise challenging to military authority were almost so rare as to be hardly worth noting. Offenses that warranted demerit points generally dealt with absences without permission, room order and cleanliness, visiting during forbidden periods, tardiness, general noise, and skylarking. The academic years 1853–54 and 1854–55 were typical. Absenteeism topped the list of infractions in these years, composing 22.7 percent of the offenses, followed by having a messy room (9.7 percent), military exercise offenses (poor marching, etc., 9.1 percent), and comparable offenses in the classroom (8.6 percent). Meanwhile, lateness composed 5.6 percent of the offenses. In contrast, disobedience of orders made up only 1.5 percent of the offenses, while disrespect to a superior and insubordination each accounted for 0.4 percent of the violations.

The remaining offenses were miscellaneous infractions each composing between 0.2 percent and 4.6 percent of the total (see appendix A). About 76 percent of the absences involved military functions, while the failure to turn up for academic functions only composed 16.4 percent of the violations. Similar results were found for the specific breakdowns for lateness: military, 54.1 percent; academic, 31.1 percent; mess (breakfast, dinner, supper), 13.1 percent; and joint military and academic offenses (an offense the authorities happened to list and count together), 1.6 percent. Generally the midshipmen offered no excuses for their violations, and midshipmen themselves made up 39.5 percent of the reporting personnel. This figure appears to fly in the face of the "band of brothers" argument, but all the other academic years sampled show that officers of the academy composed the highest percentage of reporting personnel by a 16.2 percent margin over the midshipmen (see appendix A). The percentage of midshipmen reporting their fellow students was also likely a function of the disciplinary duties that older midshipmen eventually had over their younger colleagues.

Even for those who received demerits, half of the demerits issued were accounted for by 20 to 30 percent of the midshipmen. The demerits also show that the authorities were generally lenient on the students, or authorities considered the infractions mild. The average demerit points issued ranged between four and five, out of a possible high of ten points, with a low standard deviation, indicating perhaps leniency even in the issuance of demerit points, or that the students' behavior warranted no more than a small number of points. Virtually the same pattern of midshipmen misbehavior ashore was found for each of the academic years analyzed, with little variation (see appendix A). And even the guilty got a reprieve under the academy system. On 17 May 1854, for example, the superintendent forwarded a request from the midshipmen that their demerit points for forgivable offenses be reduced and the secretary of the Navy, J. C. Dobbin, approved a scheme.[43] The conduct rolls are also full of instances where the superintendent reduced a midshipman's total number of demerit points, probably for subsequent good behavior as the future officer realized what the Navy expected of him.

Some academy staff members also questioned the effectiveness of demerit points and advocated a greater level of standardization. In June 1853 Superintendent Stribling, for instance, felt that some better method of disciplining the students had to be found because of their youth. Stribling suggested the creation of a guardhouse, where offenders could be confined for a period until they learned proper behavior. He believed that "there are many boys, who require some more stringent mode of punishment, than we can now adopt, to produce the desired effect; for such boys, moral suasion will not answer." Stribling suggested to Commodore C. S. McCauley, president of the Board of Examiners, that confinement might be the solution.[44] When the pupil's behavior warranted, the academy punished. The authorities gave the students second chances, but the authorities remained concerned with instilling in the students an appreciation of discipline and preventing them from getting out of control.

When all hope was lost, the academy dismissed the student—the ultimate form of sanction by the profession—or held a court of inquiry or court martial into their behavior. Josiah G. Beckwith Jr., for example, was one student with demerit problems, but only because he was a bad student. Beck, fifteen when he joined the academy in 1853, was the son of a doctor and politician. He thought that demerits should only be given for serious offenses and that discipline at the academy was too harsh. He felt that demerits were given for "little trifling omissions, such as being late or absent from roll call when perhaps you did not hear the drum beat; or for stepping into a neighboring room for a book to find out how a lesson is in study hours." Beckwith also found the academy had numerous "internal regulations" issued by various superintendents, not specially stated in the official regulations, which could also receive demerits. It is likely Beckwith found discipline hard because he was simply unwilling to accept it. Nevertheless, although his demerits were high, he stated he would not disappoint his parents through dismissal or resignation. His letters give the reader the impression that the young man knew he was in trouble from the outset. But in the end he resigned after being caught drinking—another unacceptable recruit expunged from the Navy before becoming a professional disappointment.[45]

One case that prompted a court of inquiry concerned Midshipmen C. L. O. Hammond and Charles S. Haralson, Date of '47, caught drinking in their rooms in December 1852. Stribling noted that "I have reason to fear that they have been in the habit of thus violating the regulations" and he knew of only one way that remained to handle their case: dismissal.[46] On 4 December 1852, Stribling reported another midshipman, Clarence Barrett, who was only fifteen, for smuggling alcohol into the academy.[47] Stribling was becoming extremely concerned about the effect of alcohol on the institution and decided enough was enough; an example should be made of those students involved in alcohol-related offenses. He told Secretary John Kennedy that "unless a speedy example is made of those detected in committing this demoralizing offence, I fear very serious injury will be done to the Youth at the Academy, and to the usefulness of the Institution."[48]

On 9 December 1852, under instructions from Kennedy, the academy convened a Board of Inquiry to investigate Hammond, Haralson, William H. Smith, and Barrett, although no detailed record of the inquiry seems to have survived, and Smith's offense is unknown.[49] Secretary Kennedy then wrote to Stribling that four other midshipmen investigated by the Board of Inquiry should be given the "right to resign" over the incidents. Hammond's father wrote the secretary that he was disturbed about his son; in response, Kennedy told Stribling to let those charged in the four cases investigated by the Board of Inquiry resign.[50] As with other midshipmen who had been found committing serious offenses, the secretary was mortified by Midshipmen Smith, Hammond, Haralson, and Barrett. He concluded that their offenses went "against the moral propriety which should characterise the conduct of gentlemen in every relation of life." He hoped that their actions were the result of the "thoughtlessness of youth rather than to any fixed habit of delinquency," and he hoped they would take their punishments as a warning against the vices that "invariably destroys the character of all who allow it to obtain the master of habit." Midshipmen Smith and Barrett were allowed to resign, while Hammond and Haralson were turned back one year in their class and went to sea until school resumed on 1 October 1853, but both resigned in 1854.[51]

Despite the lenient options available, such boards were also required to investigate more serious charges. On 8 December 1852, Superintendent Stribling; Lieutenant Thomas T. Craven, commandant of midshipmen; and Acting Master L. R. Carter convened a Board of Inquiry to investigate complaints against Acting Midshipmen George E. Law (about sixteen), James C. Erwin (about sixteen), and Joseph Jay (age unknown).[52] The case is significant, because, like in the school era, it reveals the solidarity of the midshipmen. More important, it reveals the secretary of the Navy's desire to remind the midshipmen they were becoming men and professional naval officers. The first case investigated was against Law for being drunk on 9 November 1852. That Sunday morning, after inspection, Lieutenant Marcy—formerly Passed Midshipman Marcy, and now a professor's assistant—was walking toward the executive office when a Mr. Armstrong (possibly Lieutenant J. Armstrong, another professor's assistant) told him that he had found Midshipman Law so drunk that he was unable to take care of himself. Eventually, Marcy found Law under a bed in one of the rooms. Law had also taken off his outer garments, and some of the other occupants had lent him some clothes. Law's clothes, cap and jacket, were dirty, and it looked as though he had fallen on the ground. While walking to his room, Marcy noticed that Law was unsteady and offered assistance, but it was declined. Marcy then confined Law to quarters. The academy doctor visited Law to see whether he was sick or drunk and ascertained it was the latter. After he sobered up, Law was called before the board and asked if he had any statement to make, to which he replied that "he had nothing to say." The board then told him that he would be unaffected by revealing who gave him the liquor, but Law "declined to say where he got it." Law was then permitted to leave and the board turned to Acting Midshipman Erwin's case.[53]

Erwin was charged for the same offense, as well for using improper language to the superintendent and Lieutenant Marcy. On 9 November Stribling, Marcy, and Erwin were in Erwin's room assembling a trunk. Marcy recounted that Erwin was "much excited" and on several occasions made uncalled-for remarks. At one point Erwin commented that if the trunk were his, "no Negro should search it." Marcy noted that he had little strong evidence that Erwin was drunk but felt that given his excited state, he must have imbibed. Acting Midshipman Thomas Selfridge was called before the board and asked if he had seen Mr. Erwin "in a state of intoxication." Selfridge replied, "No sir—I did not." When asked if he had seen Erwin drinking, Selfridge again replied that he had not seen Erwin drinking that day. Captain Stribling then stated that when he was in Erwin and Jay's room working on the trunk, he thought that Erwin's behavior was improper, insubordinate, and that he was very excited. Stribling concluded that he believed Erwin was "under the influence of liquor." Erwin denied that he was drunk but admitted that he indeed had been excited that day. When asked where he obtained the liquor, Erwin declined to answer but denied that he had been "over the walls" to get it. He also declined to answer whether he had been drinking in the previous twenty-four-hour period. Finished with Erwin, the board then moved on to his roommate, Acting Midshipman Jay.[54]

Jay was charged with disgraceful and insubordinate conduct because he was intoxicated, smoked, and used insubordinate language toward the superintendent and Lieutenant Marcy. He was also charged with bringing liquor into the academy. After church on Sunday, Marcy went to Erwin and Jay's room and asked who owned a trunk. He was told it was Jay's, and he sent for the midshipman. When Jay finally arrived, Marcy found that he was "excited." He told Marcy that the trunk was his private property and no one had a right to search it. Jay refused to answer any questions, and Marcy took Jay to Stribling to discuss the matter. Marcy smelled liquor on Jay's breath, and when they all returned to Jay's room, the midshipman was uncooperative and Stribling opened the trunk over Jay's objections. The contents were acceptable, except for the discovery of a piece of tobacco, but Marcy asserted that Jay had been drinking.[55]

Earlier, Marcy had rocked the trunk back and forth, heard something solid moving around, and "inferred from this there was a bottle either full or empty, inside the trunk" now mysteriously missing. Stribling corroborated Marcy's account of events, and the board asked Jay if he had anything to say; Jay declined. The board then asked Midshipmen Alfred W. Broadhead (sixteen), Joseph P. Fyffe (an Oldster and about twenty-five), and Eldred B. Ragland (almost sixteen) if they saw, or knew, how Erwin, Jay, and Law obtained the liquor they used on Saturday or Sunday. But like a good band of brothers, all three midshipmen denied any knowledge of the affair.[56] Professionally, the situation was disappointing to the secretary of the Navy. He warned Law, for instance, that his conduct was "altogether inadmissable [*sic*] in a pupil of the Academy. He has forgotten the high character of the duty and responsibility that belong to an officer of the U.S. Navy. He must henceforth learn to distinguish between the conduct expected from that position and that of a mere schoolboy. A repetition of such an offence will incur a more severe comment from the Department."[57] By 17 January 1853, the secretary dismissed Law, while Erwin and Jay had their yard privileges suspended for three months. Kennedy told Stribling that if he could think of anything else to do, he would consider approving it.[58]

The Office of the Secretary of the Navy was keenly interested in monitoring qualities of midshipmen at Annapolis, and Stribling forwarded any findings to the secretary. Stribling concluded that for the sake of the younger midshipmen, offenders had to be disciplined. He told the secretary that "the younger Students unfortunately look up to the Midshipmen, & are easily led by them; their influence has already had an injurious effect, and nothing will in my opinion, stop the evil habits exhibited in these cases & others heretofore reported, but a rigid enforcement of the Laws & regulations." In the end, the midshipmen pledged never to use alcohol again while they were at the academy. Since Stribling believed that their pledge would be good for both the students, the academy, and by extension the Navy, he recommended leniency. The pledge saved the Navy from "the necessity of dismissing from the Navy, many who might otherwise become ornaments to the Service."[59] The decision was something of a compromise that allowed the Navy to keep those recruits it felt would make good professional officers, while reminding them and all the students of the deportment expected of them.

The midshipmen then present at the academy proved a special case. Despite the reforms that had taken place in 1849 and 1850, there were still some older midshipmen. Despite advocating some degree of leniency, Superintendent Louis M. Goldsborough felt that the older midshipmen had to take greater responsibility for their actions. He wrote, "nearly every one of the Midshipmen now here has attained the age of manhood, & been several years at sea, & therefore cannot plead either ignorance of Naval customs, laws, or regulations, or extreme youth, in extenuation of any really bad conduct." Just as important, they were to be role models for the younger acting midshipmen: "they [the midshipmen] are all old enough to know & feel the full force of their example, good or bad, upon the minds of all the Acting Midshipmen who are so much younger, & possess so much less experience, than themselves." Sending offenders to sea, or dismissing them from the navy after their second offense, would "at once produce a wholesome moral influence."[60]

Goldsborough's concerns came to a boil when on Saturday, 26 November 1853, Midshipmen Hudson M. Garland ('49 Date) and James G. Maxwell ('49 Date) were found drunk. The superintendent believed that "drunkenness is bad under any circumstances; but in an establishment like this composed mainly of unsophisticated youths," where social and military values were to be instilled and discipline maintained, it was unacceptable. Goldsborough believed it had been a problem since the academy was founded and was a source of most of the disciplinary problems. Still, he admitted that at present the vice seemed to be restricted to a few midshipmen. Goldsborough exclaimed that at West Point, which had fifty years of experience dealing with the problem, the rule was that "'Any Cadet found drunk, or under the influence of wine, porter, or any spirituous or intoxicating liquor, shall be dismissed [from] the service.'" Goldsborough submitted that the Navy should be more lenient toward the students and at least provide them with a second chance "to afford the offender an opportunity of reformation," thereafter the Navy should expunge them.[61] Garland graduated but died a lieutenant in February 1861. Maxwell also likely reformed and also graduated Annapolis but died in February 1867, a lieutenant commander.[62]

On 13 March 1854, Superintendent Goldsborough reviewed the types of punishments that were allowed at the academy. Although there was a demerit system, Goldsborough discerned that it was meant as a "numerical register" of violations rather than as punishments and only had repercussions at the final examination. While this was useful for the long-run demand of naval officer professionalization, he felt that the academy needed an immediate form of punishment that would have a greater effect on the students in the short run. The regulations needed specific punishments for varying classes and needed to affirm the superintendent's right to punish. As it stood, the lack of any specificity in the regulations made for inconsistent discipline and forced the superintendent constantly to refer matters to Washington.[63]

The present regulations, he felt, left him merely as a "medium of complaints" rather than an enforcer of order and discipline. While he admired West Point, Goldsborough still conceived of the Naval Academy as having a different purpose. But the institutions were similar in one regard: they were designed to educate.[64] He confided to a fellow officer that "they are both schools—military schools—one for the benefit of the land, & the other for the benefit of the sea, forces; & as discipline, in its comprehensive sense, means the same things in either service, the general rules to enforce it there, cannot, in reality, be inapplicable here; & hence, if those in vogue do afford, confessedly, good results, we could not, it would seem, go materially astray by imitating them [West Point] ourselves as closely as circumstances will permit."[65] The more Goldsborough thought about the regulations at West Point the more he felt they were designed out of need.[66] Discipline was another method of naval indoctrination and professionalization.

A few weeks later Goldsborough believed that the academy should further its goal of handling matters internally, as a professional institution would demand. To those ends, he wanted the right to call a general court martial and suspend students from privileges and duty, reprimand them, and confine them to quarters and the academy grounds. If the student disobeyed, the superintendent could then confine them in a darkened cell; alternatively, a general court martial could sentence a midshipman to the same fate. He also hoped to subject miscreants to confinement in a darkened prison or dismiss them unilaterally from the academy and hence the Navy, or put them back one year or be dismissed from the Navy after finishing their final exam. He also felt the superintendent could give the student the option to resign. But in the end, midshipmen could only be dismissed from the service—in any manner—by the president of the United States or by the sentence of a general court martial.[67]

Nevertheless, as things stood it was naval justice in miniature, and only Congress could grant him greater autonomy from the secretary of the Navy. In the meantime, he told the chief of the Bureau of Ordnance and Hydrography, Commodore Charles Morris, that "I have purposely varied the punishments [in his proposal] in order to meet different shades of offences." Nevertheless, he sounded like he would be happy if disciplinary procedures were clearly laid out for both the students and officers of the academy.[68] The Navy Department heeded some of Goldsborough's suggestions, and the academy regulations were revised again in 1855 and put the superintendent more firmly in charge of discipline. Furthermore, the new regulations defined punishments more clearly into three classes. The first-class punishments could confine midshipmen to the academy or their rooms, give them reprimands, and suspend them from a variety of privileges or even from class. Second-class punishments were more severe and could land the midshipmen in the guardroom, while the third-class punishment was dismissal, unless he was granted the option to resign.[69]

The 1855 regulations gave the academy more professional autonomy to discipline students without first consulting the secretary of the Navy. The superintendent or officer in command could issue first- or second-class offenses, while the loss of recreation rights could only last up to twenty days, and suspension from drills, exercises, and recitations could only last two weeks. Meanwhile, the superintendent could only confine a student to the guardroom for a week without further authorization from the secretary of the Navy. Moreover, the academy was only to use confinement, the regulations proclaimed, "upon those who, in the judgement of the Superintendent or commanding officer, shall be guilty of highly insubordinate, riotous, or mutinous conduct," or who refused to obey more lenient punishments. Following orders, even to be punished, had to be instilled in the professional future officer and if a pupil hesitated, the Navy could use the ultimate punishment: dismissal.[70]

A 50-percent sample taken of the "Orders for the Suspensions of Acting Midshipmen, 1856–62" for the period before the outbreak of Civil War contained sixty orders concerning ninety-five students; often groups of students were suspended for committing offenses together. One such group included Acting Midshipmen Robert Boggs (age unknown), James P. Robertson (about seventeen), Herbert B. Tyson (about fifteen), and Moran L. Ogden (age unknown), who were caught playing cards on 5 October 1858.[71] They were suspended and deprived of their right to recitation until 15 November, which was the longest duration suspension in the sample, forty-one days. The average suspension, eight days, was much shorter, and the smallest duration was for two days.[72] Despite the view of some superintendents, the Navy believed in graduated punishment for its officer recruits and the rules remained to the outbreak of the Civil War.

As in other disciplinary cases, inexperience also played a factor in the outcome of a suspension as the academy tried to remind the students of their responsibilities. On 9 February 1857, Acting Midshipmen Edward G. Furber (almost eighteen), Henry L. Howison (about eighteen), Henry M. Herman (about seventeen), Robert L. Meade (about sixteen), and Roderick Prentiss (slightly over fifteen) were suspended for leaving the grounds without permission. They were deprived of recreation privileges and had to remain within the academy, but "Meade & Prentiss,

in consequence of their being very young, were released Feb 21st/57 & the rest
. . . Feb 24th/57." Furthermore, an apology sometimes mitigated the effects of the
suspension. On 3 March 1859, Acting Midshipman Sullivan D. Ames,[73] '56 Date,
about nineteen, was suspended for being disrespectful toward a professor. He was
released on 6 March, because he wrote an apology and pledged that another incident of that sort would never happen.

Finally, academy authorities also took into consideration a student's level of
guilt compared to other students involved in an offense. Students John C. Dowling
(about sixteen) and another student were suspended on 2 May 1857 for being
drunk.[74] Dowling resigned, but his comrade was released from his suspension on 18
May, probably because he was found to be less inebriated than Dowling. Similarly,
on 25 March 1861, Acting Midshipmen Morton W. Sanders (about seventeen),
Daniel Trigg (about seventeen), and Al Johnson (age unknown) were suspended for
making a noise on *Constitution*, the school ship to be discussed in the next chapter.
Sanders was released on 27 March because he was found less guilty, while the others were released on 6 April.[75]

When midshipmen felt they were not respected as officers, however, their discipline degenerated. For example, Acting Midshipman George M. Bache, about seventeen, felt humiliated over how he was treated one day in class when, on 22 April
1858, he told Passed Midshipman Joseph N. Miller, professor's assistant, that he
was unprepared for the recitation. As punishment, Miller ordered him to go to the
blackboard and "there tell him that I was unprepared," which Bache felt was treatment "unbecoming an officer, and for the purpose of humiliating me before the
section."[76] Miller recounted that Bache told him that "I do not wish you to speak to
me in that manner in the sect[ion] room."[77] When Bache discussed the matter with
Captain Thomas T. Craven, the commandant of midshipmen, he found "it was
impossible for me to control my feelings, and speak to him as I would have done
in cooler moments."[78] Bache felt that Craven treated him like a child, rather than
a fellow officer. As the situation worsened, Craven ordered him to Superintendent
George S. Blake's office three times, Bache refused until the last command and
then only slowly started to move in the right direction. Craven found that Bache's
"manner and bearing through out were highly disrespectful and insubordinate."[79]
Bache, in turn, felt indignant about being treated as anything but an adult officer.[80]

While the students protested when they felt their rights were violated, they also
protected their fellows, like a band of brothers, and showed a level of corporateness. On 17 January 1853, for instance, 107 midshipmen signed a pledge not to
drink.[81] Secretary Kennedy believed that it was meant to persuade the department
to be more lenient on Erwin, Law, and Jay. Still, he respected the pupils' act and
was sure that they would uphold their pledge. Consequently, Kennedy agreed with

their proposal, and Kennedy told Stribling to impose any punishment he deemed fit on Erwin, Jay, and Law, short of dismissal. Neither Erwin nor Jay graduated, but Law finished Annapolis, resigned from the Navy in December 1860, but resumed duties as a lieutenant in April 1861, only to be dismissed from the service by November.[82] There were similar such cases. In 1857, for instance, when Acting Midshipman Joshua Bishop (about eighteen) was reported for intoxication, sixty-six students signed a pledge to refrain from drinking "anxious to place his [Bishop's] case in as favorable light as possible with the Department." Their solidarity worked: Bishop eventually graduated and served in the Navy for forty-two years.[83]

Midshipmen also refused to implicate their friends when the authorities caught them misbehaving. On the evening of 14 January 1858, gunpowder exploded on the third floor of Building Number 3 of the midshipmen quarters, and Commander Joseph F. Green, the commandant of midshipmen, questioned thirty-four of the building's occupants. Green reported that everyone except Acting Midshipman Christopher Orth denied knowledge of the explosion's origins. Orth admitted to trying to explode gunpowder, but after initial failure, he declined to partake in any further experiments. Orth refused to name the others present. In the end, Green found no damage and could not discover how much gunpowder was used, and only Orth was reported for the incident. Still, Orth never completed his studies at Annapolis.[84]

Midshipmen were especially aghast if authorities accused them of behaving unprofessionally. On Christmas day 1854, for example, between 10:00 PM and midnight, Acting Master W. K. Mayo, returning to his room in Building Number 3, saw a number of people enter. He followed and heard the sound of moving feet on the second floor. As Mayo climbed the steps to the floor, he yielded the stairs to an oncoming person so that they could have the rail in the darkness. But the man grabbed Mayo by the neck and started to strangle him. Mayo figured that person was excited by the holiday, so he demanded his name, but there was no reply. Two other men appeared and tried to wrestle the assailant from Mayo, who now realized that his assailant was drunk. As with Mayo's assailant, the other men refused to give their names in the darkness, whereupon, probably fearing for his life, Mayo called out to Midshipman William Cheever, Date of '49, whose room was nearby.[85]

At that point the men identified themselves as Midshipmen John G. Walker, Charles Cushman,[86] and Benjamin P. Loyall; Walker was Mayo's assailant. Mayo believed that Cushman and Loyall were as guilty as Walker, because they had refused to give their names when ordered. By this time, Commander Craven had arrived, and Mayo asked Loyall why he failed to give his name. Loyall replied that there was "a struggle between his association and his duty."[87] Mayo believed that the officer's duty was clear: "I am pained to think that this officer who came to this Academy with every recommendation that high-tone and integrity could give deemed the calls of 'association,' more potent than the demands of that duty and of that reverence for the laws which require him to bring to punishment all offenders; and, being witness to any mutiny or sedition, to do his utmost to suppress it."[88]

However, Acting Midshipman Loyall was shocked by Mayo's recollection of the incident. Loyall believed that Mayo was accusing him of an act of mutiny for allegedly participating in the affair and then keeping his name, and the names of the other midshipmen, a secret. Loyall said that he neglected to tell Mayo his name because he failed to hear the request and because he was occupied "in the *strict* performance of my duty [emphasis in original]." Loyall believed that the accusation of mutiny was simply the result of a misunderstanding between himself and Mayo. Loyall explained that his "struggle between duty and association" meant that "if possible it was my desire that an affair so unfortunate for Mr. Walker should not be made public."[89] Loyall concluded that "If there is any thing at all connected with any act of mine on that evening, that can be construed, or even tortured into an unwillingness to suppress insubordinate or mutinous conduct, it is beyond my humble power to comprehend the virtual meaning of a strict construction of the rules and regulations of the United States Navy. And I think that a little more reflection would be sufficient to persuade my accuser, that he is giving a latitude to the bearing of a clause in those articles, which the occasion cannot in any [way] warrant."[90] It appears that Loyall interceded as best he could to do his duty but also to maintain his loyalty to a fellow midshipman. For Loyall, it was a professional dilemma that officers might also face in the real naval world. Despite the incident, Walker, from New Hampshire, graduated the academy and retired in 1897 at the rank of rear admiral. Loyall also graduated, but was dismissed in October 1861.[91]

As in the school era, the ultimate way for the academy to investigate the behavioral qualities of the midshipmen was through a court of inquiry or court martial. However, the secretary of the Navy, J. C. Dobbin, noted that only if authorities could narrow their focus to specific individuals would a court of inquiry be the proper course of action.[92] Consequently, when Secretary Dobbin called a court of inquiry on 6 March 1857, it investigated the suitability of Acting Midshipmen Norman H. Farquhar (age unknown, but of the '55 Date) and William Welch (about seventeen) for continued naval service after accusations of behavior unsuitable for a naval officer. The academy authorities alleged that on 15 February, Farquhar and Welch entered the offices of the superintendent and clandestinely searched through papers and official reports. Captain Jean M. Powell acted as the president of the inquiry, while Commander William W. Hunter and Lieutenant George F. Emmons acted as members, with James R. Howison as the judge advocate.[93]

The first witness was Commander Green, the commandant of midshipmen. Green told the court that on 15 February, between 4:00 and 5:00 PM, he saw Welch and Farquhar enter the academy, pass the guardhouse, and enter the superintendent's office, possibly after returning from church in Annapolis. Green, then in his quarters and observing events from a window, expected the midshipmen to emerge quickly from the office when they discovered that because it was a Sunday, neither the superintendent nor his secretary was there. When the midshipmen failed to emerge, Green went to investigate. When he reached the superintendent's office, Green saw Welch leave, and as Green entered, he met Farquhar coming out and asked him what he was doing there. Farquhar replied that he went to the office to get his passbook, or bankbook, and had only been there two minutes, but Green told the court that Farquhar had actually been there about fifteen minutes.[94]

Superintendent Goldsborough told the court that the day after the incident he called Midshipman Welch into his office and asked for an explanation. Welch repeated that he and Farquhar were looking for their passbooks, but finding the passbook box locked, they entered Goldsborough's office to look for the key; when they could not find it, they left. Goldsborough then sent for Farquhar, who corroborated Welch's story and added that they had also examined some books in the secretary's office, but not the class reports. Goldsborough lectured Farquhar about his behavior, as he had done with Welch, and dismissed him.[95] On 9 March the inquiry found that Welch was less than forthcoming in his explanation to the superintendent when questioned, but that Farquhar promptly admitted his and Welch's actions. A note of unknown authorship at the end of the case file added, "Mid[shipmen] Farquhar and Welch. Let them be dismissed."[96] In the end Farquhar remained in the Navy, spent forty-seven years in the service, and retired in 1902 with the rank of rear admiral. But Welch, the less-forthcoming officer, although from a seafaring background from New York, failed to graduate from the academy. It seems likely that he was dismissed because of this case.[97]

Under the ethical training of moral science, and the disciplinary guidance of academy authorities, the midshipmen came to accept that fellow professional naval officers had to treat each other with respect and honor. Still, this could have unintended consequences. One such case occurred between Midshipmen Moffitt and Lynch on 27 April 1851. In response, an inquiry opened on 6 May with Lieutenant Thomas T. Craven as president, Passed Midshipman Samuel Marcy as a member, and Passed Midshipman Samuel Carter as a secretary and member.[98] On 10 May, the court found that Moffitt told one Mr. Davidson that Lynch was showing people, inside and outside the academy grounds, letters between Lynch and Davidson "prejudicial to the character of Mr. Davidson." By 27 April Davidson went to the academy to see Lynch. They talked, but Davidson refused to give up his informant. Then Lynch told the midshipmen assembled before mess that someone was circulating rumors about him defaming Davidson. Lynch exclaimed that person was a "liar, a coward, and no gentleman," but the court concluded that Moffitt was elsewhere at the time. The inquiry surmised that at the mess table, Moffitt was informed of Lynch's speech, so he came forward to claim responsibly for telling Davidson of the rumor. Finally, the situation degenerated into the fight outside the mess hall.[99]

The court found that Lynch's course of action was "most unusual." They concluded that his actions were "demoralising in its tendency, and calculated to effect [*sic*] most injuriously the discipline of the school." The inquiry asserted that such behavior had to be dealt with and recommended a minimum punishment of being "put back one year in date of his warrant." Meanwhile, it decided that Moffitt was involved in the fight because of the circumstances with which he was faced and recommended that he only be publicly reprimanded.[100] Later, another student, Alexander J. Dallas, Date of '46, came to Moffitt's defense and asked the secretary of the Navy to transfer some of Moffitt's punishment to him for his role in the affair, although he denied that he helped spread the rumors to get Lynch and Moffitt at each other's throats.[101] The whole affair was thus thrown into some confusion, and the inquiry, finished with its fact-finding mission, forwarded its report to the secretary of the Navy to sort out.

On 6 June, Secretary Graham concluded that the difficulties between the two midshipmen "seems to have been mainly occasioned by the instrumentality of Midshipman Dallas." Three years earlier there had been a disagreement between Lynch and Davidson, which would have faded into the past except that Davidson asked one Mr. McGunnegle if Lynch had been heard making any derogatory remarks about Davidson. McGunnegle replied he had not heard anything of that nature from Lynch, whereupon Midshipman Dallas was told that if he ever heard Lynch speaking in a disrespectful manner about Davidson, he "would consider it his duty to inform him." Moffitt became involved in the affair, and somehow he and Dallas thought that Lynch had been speaking unkindly of Davidson. However Moffitt became involved, the secretary concluded that Dallas "is advised to be less meddlesome in the affairs of others for the future." The secretary concluded that the language and behavior of Lynch on the parade ground, and Lynch and Moffitt at the supper table, was a "gross violation of the regulations of the Academy." Lynch was suspended on furlough pay for two months, while Moffitt was suspended with furlough pay for one month. Graham concluded that the decision was to be "read in the presence of the several classes."[102] Dallas seems to have gotten off with just the warning, but was dismissed in June, likely after poor results in his examinations.[103]

In the end, the midshipmen also directed their misbehavior against their comrades who went outside the norms expected of their group. Taking regulations too seriously often landed midshipmen in trouble with their peers, as happened to Alfred Thayer Mahan.[104] While at the academy, Mahan reported his class for an offense. Some of his friends stood by him, but in retaliation most of the class ignored him. Mahan's father told him about similar problems at West Point if someone reported one of their fellows. The results were the same, and students stopped speaking to the tattler, but they eventually realized their mistake and apologized to him. Mahan told his friend, and former roommate, Sam Ashe, that "I hardly give the present first class credit for so much manliness as to make that reparation, even should they find that their course should be a wrong one." Mahan was pleased that his father supported his reporting his classmates and was happy that his friends Billy, Cenas, and Borchert still supported him. As for the rest, they "may go to hell."[105]

The academy even had its share of bullies. On 11 March 1858, Acting Midshipman William Anderson Hicks, about sixteen, reported that Midshipman Andrew Jefferson Clark, seventeen and from Alabama, was constantly after him to fight.[106] A week earlier Hicks was standing in the doorway of a building, saw Clark coming, and tried to get out of his way, but Clark lunged at Hicks and tried to hit him. Hicks tried to defend himself, returned to his room, but Clark followed with a rock, although a fight failed to materialize. The next day, Sunday, Hicks returned from breakfast, and Clark struck him twice in the head with a stick. After a further confrontation, Clark finally agreed to meet in Hicks' room on Monday, and they "had it out." Hicks felt forced into the fight because Clark "was determined that I should have no peace at all. He has had difficulties with nearly every student in our building. And he had been trying to get up the name of a bully which I don't think he will ever succeed in doing."[107]

Clark agreed with the basic narrative of events but interpreted them differently. He acknowledged running into Hicks when he tried to pass through a door, but asserted that it was an accident. In return Clark said that Hicks struck him before Clark tried to hit him with a brick and twice with a stick. Then Hicks challenged him to a "fair fight," to which Clark agreed, but then "after I accepted the challenge he carried a stick for me."[108] Commander Green investigated the affair, reported both midshipmen for the fight, but concluded that Clark was more in the wrong because he assaulted Hicks with a stone to the head and then a stick.[109] Clark eventually left without graduating, weeded out as a potential officer that neither his fellows nor the Navy wanted. Hicks, from Mississippi, resigned with the Civil War and served in the Confederate States Navy until his death.[110]

Sometimes the student body's displeasure with a comrade went so far as to punish him themselves if they felt that the authorities had failed to handle things properly. Midshipman Henry Foot, for instance, was a terror and a disgrace to his comrades over 1858 and 1859. Foot joined the academy in 1856 and was put in charge of the money used to pay the cook but often kept the money himself. Furthermore, while on the practice ship the previous summer, he took other midshipmen's provisions and then denied it. Instead, he attacked one of the ship's company who reported his action, but eventually, "at the demand of a mid[shipman]," he confessed to the crime.[111] Foot failed to bond with his fellow midshipmen, who were developing a sense of duty, loyalty, and honor.

After the students reported him to the superintendent, Foot dishonored them again by assaulting the slave girl who worked in Professor Lockwood's house. Foot returned to the academy drunk and beat her when she refused to gratify "his passion." Although the witnesses were unable to "fully prove" the facts of the case, Foot admitted culpability. The midshipmen finally had enough with the troublemaker; the attack on the slave girl was the last straw. After repeated attempts to get him to reform, the students finally committed an "outrage" against him in retribution.[112] Furthermore, 116 midshipmen petitioned the secretary of the Navy in defense of the reprisal. The petitioners complained that "for two years we have been forced to behold wearing the uniform of the Navy, an individual, who would not have been admitted in respectable society—one, so degraded by his vices that to be seen in his company was considered a disgrace—Sir, we feel deeply for the honor of the service" and that was why some of their members took action against Foot. In a show of group solidarity, they petitioned the secretary so that a few would not take the fall for an action which all supported.[113]

The administration finally decided to do something about Foot, and a court of inquiry was ordered for 11 April.[114] Foot was dismissed from the service, and on 27 April the secretary dismissed seven midshipmen for what they did to Foot in retribution. Fourteen other midshipmen were allowed to stay in the Navy for their part in the affair, but the "Department further directs that you [Superintendent Blake] will have them transferred at the earliest moment to the Practice Ship, and, from your receipt of this communication until the termination of the cruise, withhold from them the usual indulgences extended to the Acting Midshipmen."[115] Six of the midshipmen who were originally dismissed—Bruce Lambert, James F. Fuller, James P. Robertson, Thomas D. Fister, Morgan L. Ogden, and Stephen A. McCarty—were then reinstated on 20 May and ordered to join the practice cruise under the same restrictions that had been imposed on the other midshipmen.[116]

The midshipmen's behavior, relations with each other and the naval hierarchy, were important elements in their introduction to the naval officer's world. From the

Navy's perspective, it had a professional organization's outlook and tracked carefully student behavior and took it into consideration when deciding who made a suitable officer. Discipline at the school and academy operated along a continuum from lenient to severe. Lenient punishments used conduct rolls and demerit points, while students were punished more severely with suspension, confinement, courts martial, and dismissal. Older students were expected to be well behaved and be role models for the younger ones; older students were expected to be fully aware of what the Navy expected. For their part, the midshipmen responded in kind and were generally good. When they acted up it was often with minor offenses: smoking, being late, or losing their temper. The institution accepted this level of misbehavior as part of the process of socializing the young recruits into their profession. Still, some midshipmen wanted to be treated like adults before they had acquired the acumen of mature officers. At other times the students tried to protect their own and hesitated helping an investigation.[117] Finally, when midshipmen felt that justice acted too slowly, they acted themselves if a colleague behaved outside expected norms. There was a delicate balancing act between duty to the service and one's band of brothers. The outbreak of Civil War in 1861 tested the academy and its students.

CHAPTER 6

Summer Cruises, School Ships, and the
Outbreak of Civil War

By 1850 the Navy renamed the school the Naval Academy, and its goals were clear: some liberal education, but an emphasis on utilitarian goals and professional indoctrination. The academy would rid itself of those midshipmen just there to study for their lieutenant's exam and start a four-year program with summers spent at sea in a fashion analogous to West Point's summer encampments.[1] Henceforth, at-sea training supplemented a midshipman's introduction to naval life on land. At sea, the philosophy of indoctrinating youths into a naval officer's life continued. The academy's summer practice ships represent what sociologists and maritime historians call a "Total Institution," isolated from the rest of society for a specific purpose. Erving Goffman defines a total institution as "a place of residence and work where a large number of like-situated individuals, cut off from the wider society for an appreciable period of time, together lead an enclosed, formerly administered round of life." Donald Chisholm concludes that the U.S. Navy was an "artificial system" constructed to "achieve some stated ends," and Heide Gerstenberger warns that how the ship is used, or the purpose of the total institution, is a major component in analyzing the total institution. Consequently, an analysis of the U.S. Naval Academy's summer cruises must be placed within this unified paradigm.[2]

By the 1850s, the academy employed summer practice ships as total institutions to provide a regulated life to embark young midshipmen safely into the naval world and the demands of their profession. The academy and its summer cruises highlight that the U.S. Armed Forces had a professional culture well before the emergence of scientific management practices. At sea, young midshipmen incorporated the knowledge they first acquired on shore, and the academy taught them the expectations of naval officers in command of men. The establishment of summer training cruises, along with the four-year, shore-based, training program, marked a true break from the old system of naval education. Henceforth youths, often in their mid-teenage years, without sea experience, went straight into an academy that introduced them gradually to life at sea in a supervised environment with appropriate role models. Eventually, the academy concluded that the combined shore- and sea-based training was a success and created professional officers.[3]

On these cruises, students learned practical seamanship and visited naval yards and other countries they would visit later as part of their duties as officers. By 1859 the summer-cruise system was fully integrated with the shore-based system, and a school ship was also attached to the academy during the academic year to initially teach new appointees without even leaving shore. This integration proved successful and led to better student performance at sea. The only true problem the administration faced was finding a large enough vessel to accommodate the growing numbers of students. In turn, although the academy did not tolerate misbehavior among the students, for their part, they were generally well behaved and took to applying their shore-acquired knowledge. But when the country began to disintegrate with Lincoln's election in 1860, it tested the professional ethic that the Navy instilled in its future officers. Despite spending much time at sea and on land devoted to the national Navy, many Southern midshipmen resigned as their home states seceded. For many, the professional ethic meant that they had to resign if they disagreed with Washington or felt they would be unable to fire on their friends.

When George Bancroft founded the Naval School at Annapolis, Superintendent Buchanan recommended that the Navy attach a sloop of war or brig to the school to teach gunnery, seamanship, and naval evolutions, but it took until 1851 before a vessel was attached to the academy, although the regulations required a third-class sloop since 1849.[4] However, by 1851 the academy needed a vessel, because its new midshipmen were just young men, without any sea experience, taken directly from the civilian world. Therefore, during the academy era, the midshipmen spent most of the year at Annapolis, but after their June exams, the institution sent them to sea to incorporate their shore experience with real-life scenarios. There, academy administrators concluded that the system helped prepare the young men for professional roles. The summer cruises were comparable to summer encampments at West Point, but Alfred Thayer Mahan wrote that "at West Point it was accompanied by a degree of social entertainment impossible to ship conditions."[5]

Officials conceptualized the practice ships as an important aspect of student professionalization. The academy's Board of Examiners, often composed of senior officers, articulated this philosophy after the first summer cruise of 1851. They concluded that the cruises were "an excellent feature in the arrangements made by the Navy Department for forwarding the professional knowledge of the youths committed" to the academy's care.[6] On 15 June 1853, the board wrote James C. Dobbin, secretary of the Navy, and supported Superintendent Stribling's demand that the academy train midshipmen at sea for the "active duties of their profession" on at

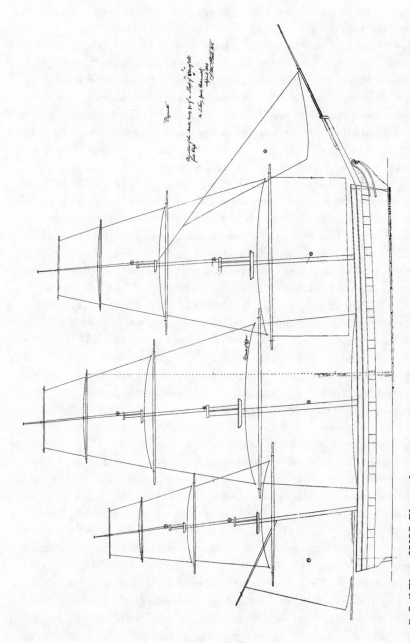

Figure 7. Sail Plan of USS *Plymouth*. ("*Plymouth*," *Sail Plan, Dash Flat 107-14-9a, Records of the Bureau of Ships, 1940–66, Ship Design and Construction Drawings, compiled 1862–1909, N4, RG 19*) Note: The plan has been edited for clarity.

least a frigate-class vessel.[7] Meanwhile, Lieutenant Robert H. Wyman, who studied the issue in November 1854, wrote that the practice ship was where midshipmen first learned the "ideas of the Naval Service afloat," which "influence[d] their
whole future career, sowing the seeds for either an active or a careless officer."[8]

The summer cruises were isolated from society, and their purpose was to give
the students "their earliest impressions of the discipline, & etiquette of a ship of
war." Accordingly, Superintendent George S. Blake asserted that "it is most essential that these impressions should be correct in every particular."[9] Consequently,
from 1851 to 1860, the Naval Academy employed two vessels as summer practice ships: *Preble* and, occasionally, the larger *Plymouth*. The Navy built *Preble* at the
Portsmouth Naval Yard and completed it in 1839. She was a 16-gun, third-class
sloop, about 117 feet long, 32 feet wide, with a depth of 15 feet. The Navy started
building the third-class sloops in 1838 and probably designed them to meet the
needs of a Navy focused on its peacetime roles of commerce protection and service
on "distant stations." The vessel academy officials preferred was *Plymouth* (see figures 7 and 8). This sloop was a first-class ship that carried twenty guns. Launched
in the early 1840s, the Navy constructed her at the Boston Naval Yard. *Plymouth*,
approximately 147 feet long, 38 feet wide, and 17 feet deep, resembled a packet,
handled well, and was fast in a wide range of sailing conditions.[10]

The role of the ship as a training vessel was paramount, and the academy tried
to configure it as closely as possible to an active warship. The practice ships were
important physical textbooks for the students, regulated their lives, and conditioned
them for their adult roles. On these ships, the Navy reinforced the "ethical codes"
specific to the profession and confronted the students "with the need to develop
an occupational personality" and with the "language and behavior that sets them
apart from the layman."[11] The ship's rules declared that "all else is to be considered
subservient to this object except the cleanliness and safety of the ship." The Navy
intended the practice ship to instruct the acting midshipmen in practical seamanship, vessel management, and the rigors of naval life. Therefore, they subjected students to all aspects of naval routine and operations, even when in port. Meal hours
were regular; the commandant divided students into two messes and required them
to live on Navy rations. The cruise also permitted students only one shore visit at
each port of call, they had to return by sunset, and they had to be well behaved.[12]

In early 1855 Superintendent Louis M. Goldsborough implied that the vessel's
size was a function of its utility as a physical textbook. The number of students he
wished to embark on the practice ship was large. He discerned that "it would, in
many particulars, work badly for the Students themselves, as well as for the pro-
gramme and arrangements of this Academy, if the whole number of 90 were not
to go to sea." Undoubtedly, if all were unable to go to sea, it would interrupt their

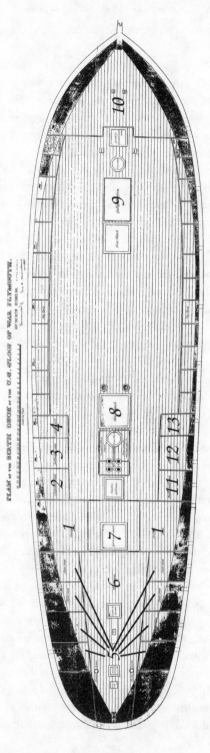

Figure 8. Berth Deck of USS *Plymouth*. 1. Steerage 2. Carpenter's Room 3. Sailmaker's Room 4. Captain's Store 5. State Rooms 6. Ward Room 7. Spirit Room 8. Main Hatch 9. Galley Platform 10. Sick Bay 11. Boatswain's Room 12. Gunner's Room 13. Dispensary. (*"Plan of the Birth* [sic] *Deck of the U.S. Sloop of War Plymouth," Dash Flat 134-2-2, Records of the Bureau of Ships, 1940–66, Ship Design and Construction Drawings, compiled 1862–1909, NA RG 19*) Note: Plan has been edited for clarity.

professional progress through the landward and seaward side of training, and he demanded a larger vessel.[13] By April 1856 Goldsborough reflected on the results of the cruise. As he feared, the ship proved too small, and the students were too crowded to be educated effectively; it was especially hard for the fourth-class midshipmen without any prior sea experience.[14] With evidence in hand, Goldsborough convinced the Navy to provide them *Plymouth* for the 1856 cruise. Rather than substantially modify the warship, the Navy kept *Plymouth*'s original spars. Goldsborough opined that they should operate *Plymouth* like a full-fledged warship so that the students would become fully familiar with naval life.[15]

The summer practice ships were the physical representations of the ideals the academy strived toward. Equally important were the cruises and where they went. The first summer cruise of 1851 was short and lasted only six weeks, but subsequent cruises went farther afield. On the cruises, the students visited ports and naval facilities in the United States and across the Atlantic in places like Spain, Britain, and France. Visits to these ports are revealing, because they came during heightened tension between Britain and France and the increased naval activity of the nations.[16] Fundamentally, the geography of the summer cruises is significant, because it showed the initiates, as a group, the "societal roles played by the occupation" as it fulfilled its tasks for the benefit of their collective client, society.[17] When in port, the pupils observed naval operations at shipyards and interacted with the officials they might encounter later as adult officers.

Perhaps wary of the first endeavor, the academy's Academic Board told the 1851 practice ship to stick close to home and cruise the coast from Maine to Chesapeake Bay.[18] The midshipmen embarked on *Preble* on 5 August after traveling from Annapolis to New York on the steamer *John Hancock*.[19] Commander Thomas T. Craven, commandant of midshipmen, was in charge, and he feared that the Navy would cancel the cruise because of the nation's other needs. The government, for example, might call *Preble* to active duty to police the activities of Narciso Lopez and the Cuban filibusters who attempted a Cuban revolt on several occasions.[20] Nevertheless, *Preble* docked at Eastport, Portland, Boston, New London, and Norfolk, and the students visited the associated dockyards. However, Craven was disappointed that the cruise was only six weeks instead of two months.[21]

The initial summer cruise a success, the 1852 cruise took the students farther from home along routes that active warships often took in the Atlantic. The students embarked on *Preble* on 14 June and sailed six days later. On the outward passage, they visited Hampton Roads, and Craven took the students to the Norfolk Naval Yard. They observed the dry docks, machine shops, and the gigantic *Pennsylvania*, where they could watch, firsthand, various elements of naval operations. After leaving the American coast, the ship visited western Madeira and the

Canary Islands, locations the American West African squadron often visited while ostensibly suppressing the slave trade and, more important, stopping the Royal Navy from interfering with U.S.-flagged vessels they suspected of involvement in the practice. Finally, the Navy Department ordered her to return via St. Thomas for arrival back at Annapolis by the end of September. After the cruise, Craven thought that it proved the importance of an approximately four-month practice cruise in the system of naval education.[22]

Craven believed that observing the activities of foreign navies was important for the students' development. Upon their arrival in Spain on 27 August, after seven days sailing from Fayal, the Spanish captain general and the military and civil governors of Galicia visited *Preble* and were impressed. They invited the Americans to visit the nearby naval arsenal, and Craven decided to bend his instructions to avail the students of the offer. He believed that it would be a useful instructional opportunity despite the department's restrictions on the ship's movements. Then, true to his orders, *Preble* arrived back on America's East Coast by September.[23] Similarly, the 1854 cruise visited the ports of the traditional naval powers, this time with the expressed permission of the secretary of the Navy, J. C. Dobbin, who ordered them to visit ports like Plymouth, Portsmouth, Brest, and Cherbourg. On the return voyage, the students could visit Madeira and one port in the West Indies, if there was time. Evidently, the secretary of the Navy heard, to a degree, Craven's wish for more latitude on where to travel. By 10 June the secretary amended his orders and allowed him to visit the "Western Islands" and the "Dock Yards and Naval Establishments at the ports mentioned" in his previous dispatch. After the cruise, Craven reported that in every locale, commanders of foreign stations were "very kind and polite in their attentions to us, and afforded us every facility for viewing and examining every part of their docks."[24]

The 1855 and 1856 cruises continued in a similar fashion under the charge of Commander Joseph Green, in *Preble* and *Plymouth*, along the U.S. coast.[25] Meanwhile, the 1857 cruise of *Preble*, also under Green, again went deeper into the Atlantic, as did the ship's 1858 cruise under Craven. The 1858 cruise carried students of the first, second, third, and fourth classes; left the United States on 24 June; and arrived at Cherbourg on 18 July 1858. From there they visited Cadiz and Madeira and departed for Norfolk on 14 August, where they arrived on 12 September ready for the coming academic year.[26] Craven had looked forward to conducting several evolutions in the bay, but on 15 September, the Navy ordered *Preble* back to Annapolis immediately and then to Norfolk to be refitted for an expedition to Paraguay.[27] In the end the academy's needs were subservient to the wider needs of the nation and its small Navy.

The final two summer cruises of the antebellum U.S. Naval Academy employed *Plymouth* and again sailed across the Atlantic. The 1859 cruise (figure 9) carried 107 acting midshipmen, left port on 22 June, visited naval facilities in Europe, and returned to Annapolis that fall. Then the Navy used it as a school ship, tied up alongside the academy during the academic year, a feature to be discussed further below. In 1860 the last cruise of *Plymouth* embarked members of the first, second, third, and fourth classes, although some of the students were already aboard when it set sail in June 1860 to again visit ports across the Atlantic.[28] The cruise completed, *Plymouth* arrived at Hampton Roads on 3 September after a twenty-two-day sail from Santa Cruz.[29] For the administration and the students, the practice ships functioned as living textbooks, but where the students visited was as important in their professional development as what they learned on the ship.

The vessels and where they took the students were significant aspects of the students' education, but, ultimately, the midshipmen were on the ships to learn practical seamanship and warship operations—skills that set them apart from the rest of society (see figure 10). Therefore, the instructors used all available time, such as waiting to return to Annapolis at the end of the cruise, to drill the students in seamanship, navigation, and gunnery. They trained the midshipmen with navigation textbooks and instruments, taught them how to manage a ship, and divided them into groups to take turns running the vessel. Meanwhile, to assist in their training, the ship embarked other members of the academic staff, like Lieutenant Samuel Marcy, who had assessed West Point's system, and in 1854, Professor William

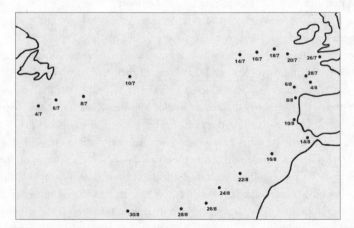

Figure 9. 1859 Summer Cruise, USS *Plymouth*. *(Calculated from logbook, "'Journal' of a Summer's Cruise Aboard USS Plymouth June–Aug 1859," E 176, Records of the United States Naval Academy, NA, RG 405. Locations originally plotted using ArcExplorer, Java Edition for Education, v 2.0.1, Environmental Systems Research Institute, Inc., 2003. Map by the author; locations approximate)*

Figure 10. Midshipmen Receiving Onboard Instruction, c. 1853. *("Middies Learning the Ropes . . . ," Frank Leslie's* Illustrated Newspaper, *26 March 1853)* Note: The source title states that the students trained on *Constitution*, but this vessel was not used at Annapolis until 1860.

Chauvenet, head of the Department of Astronomy.[30] The latter man probably helped teach the students the art of celestial navigation and brought to the cruise his experience from the old system of naval education at the Philadelphia School. The practice ship was, essentially, a little academy that systematically continued and assessed the pupils' professional development that they began on shore.

In terms of practical seamanship, during the 1851 cruise on *Preble,* Marcy did his best to instruct the boys despite an inadequate supply of navigation texts and instruments.[31] On the 1854 summer cruise, the second-class midshipmen learned methods for finding the ship's position as described in Bowditch's work on the subject. Meanwhile, the cruise taught the pupils of the first class the use of the sextant and how to find the ship's position by dead reckoning, latitude by the sun, and other more advanced methods.[32] Furthermore, during the 1858 summer cruise, as soon as the students sailed, Craven divided them into two groups: one at the guns and another for making sail and getting under way as if they were running an active warship. The ship instituted a day-and-night quarter-watch and—despite no evidence that the Navy outfitted *Preble* with any steam equipment—Craven drilled the students as firemen and reported good progress. Finally, he occupied the third-class midshipmen with the sextant and chronometer to fix the ship's position.[33]

The summer cruise program was a well-planned affair to teach the midshipmen the officer's role on a warship. On the 1853 cruise, for instance, during the day, the first class—the oldest students—took command of the deck "so that every evolution of tacking or wearing, boxhauling and chapelling, making and taking" were "performed under their own directions." Craven concluded that the exercise "added much to their practical [professional] experience." Furthermore, to fix their training in their minds, as well as the special symbols and language of their career, the academy required that the students make and explain drawings of the yards, masts, and sails, and then the commandant of midshipmen conducted oral examinations on the subjects.[34] Finally, starting with the 1859 cruise, the academy ordered the pupils to keep journals while at sea, and the instructors evaluated their quality. Craven, for example, reported that "their journals have been examined by me and many of them show a very creditable degree of observation on the parts of those who have written them."[35]

The midshipmen's training was practical, but formal, and was meant to teach them seamanship and the skills an officer needed to maintain efficient operation of the warship. However, the Navy believed that shipboard discipline was also important in this endeavor. On land, the academy had gradually introduced the midshipmen to the rigors of naval discipline and used it to teach them professional deportment. At sea, the instructors maintained this philosophy; the academy's goal was twofold: reinforce an officer's expected character and instill in the students the discipline and respect for the orders needed to maintain the efficiency of a warship. Charles P. Kindleberger concludes that "whether worker-management is efficient or not on dry land, decisive orders smartly obeyed are needed in the many crises produced by nature on the sea."[36] Naval officers were at the pinnacle of the structure that maintained ship operations, and the Navy wanted the summer cruises to develop a disciplined cadre of professionals that could effectively follow orders.

Superintendent Stribling's instructions to Commander Craven in 1853 illustrate best the academy's summer cruise disciplinary philosophy. On 21 June 1853, Stribling stressed to Craven that he must maintain the midshipmen's proper decorum when in port. Stribling wrote that "the character of the Officers & Gentlemen should never be forgotten; you cannot impress this too strongly upon their minds."[37] Superintendent Goldsborough echoed a similar philosophy to Commandant Green in 1856.[38] The instructors were to hold the students to the same standard on ship as on shore and mold the midshipmen into proper officers. The vessel was a total institution that controlled all aspects of their existence. The superintendent forbade the pupils to draw any of their pay or articles from the purser without the commandant's permission. Furthermore, the instructors were to keep the students "accustomed to the exercise of self-denial" and to the proper care needed for their belongings and themselves. Moreover, the academy banned tobacco, alcohol, and profane language, and Commandant Green, for example, was to deal with infractions quickly and with due punishment. Additionally, Goldsborough gave Green the discretion to use other forms of discipline and punishment he required.[39]

Structurally, the academy believed that maintaining the physical integrity of the ship was important to indoctrinate the students into the demands of their profession. For example, in mid-July 1851, Superintendent Stribling surmised that the students should embark on *Preble* as quickly as possible because classes were over and discipline began to suffer under the lack of structure. Consequently, he wanted the steamer *John Hancock* dispatched to Annapolis to bring the students to New York, where they would join *Preble* immediately. Although she was still being prepared for the summer cruise, Stribling thought that it would give the students a good opportunity to gain knowledge of the ship and at least there they would be "under proper discipline."[40]

The most serious disciplinary breakdown during the antebellum summer cruises occurred in September 1856 and highlights the academy's disciplinary philosophy at sea. On 25 September, while somewhere in Chesapeake Bay near Annapolis, Lieutenant William Wilcox ordered the acting midshipman in charge, as part of his command training, to summon disobedient students on deck. He returned to report that Acting Midshipman Samuel Greene (about sixteen) said he was sick and that the rest, with the exception of Acting Midshipman Jefferson Slam (age unknown), refused orders. The first lieutenant then took two of the older first-class midshipmen below deck to repeat the order. The wayward students obeyed after about thirty minutes, but in a "mutinous manner," and Wilcox had to separate them like children. The pupils had disobeyed direct orders that would normally have seriously jeopardized the operations of an active warship, and academy officials used the incident to teach them a lesson.[41]

The students admitted that their action was wrong, but they said that it was in protest because they thought that the Navy had violated their rights.[42] In Annapolis, however, the incident raised concerns for Superintendent Goldsborough. He concluded that if the academy failed to drill the students to obey orders, they would be "useless for the Naval Service." Therefore, he suspended them and felt that the academy should make examples of them for the other students.[43] Consequently, the Navy dismissed the pupils for their "insubordinate and mutinous conduct," but Acting Secretary Charles Welsh reviewed their cases upon receiving requests from them for reinstatement. He reinstated Midshipmen James L. Taylor (about fifteen), and Samuel H. Hacket (age unknown), and Walter R. Butt (about sixteen), but the academy had also found Midshipmen Samuel L. French (age unknown) and Henry F. Condict (about eighteen) deficient at their recent examinations. Combined with their misbehavior on the summer cruise, the department could "perceive no grounds for their claim to its further indulgence," and their dismissals stood.[44] Such recruits had failed to develop, and the Navy had no use for them.

Shipboard discipline was, therefore, another way to regulate the midshipmen and acclimatize them to the duties and the responsibilities of a naval officer. It also showed them the level of organization that was required to efficiently run a warship from the perspective of both officers and men. Accordingly, the academy recorded and monitored student discipline with almost scientific precision. In response, despite occasional problems, the students generally behaved themselves at sea. Because of the unique separation of *Plymouth* from the rest of the academy for the 1859–60 academic year, to be discussed below, it was possible to extract and analyze a 20-percent random sample of the conduct roll for the school ship for that year (see appendix A). For demerit points given, the students tended to commit offenses related to only their study periods: study hours or study room offenses composed 34 percent of the sampled offenses; the next highest was absenteeism, which was far behind at 9 percent of the sampled offenses.

In the military realm, the students were more compliant. Offenses such as disobedience of orders were low: 0.5 percent of the sampled offenses. Generally, the pupils tended to be absent more from military functions, like drills, than academic ones, but lateness was almost completely absent, with only two cases found in the sample. Meanwhile, the total number of dereliction of duty offenses was only ten. It makes any wider conclusion speculative, but it perhaps shows a level of camaraderie: 40 percent of these offenses were for failing to report other midshipmen, while fellow students reported 39.4 percent of the offenses. Student behavior, in the close confines of the ship, was good and compares favorably with their behavior on land. In terms of discipline, the pupils accepted well their indoctrination into the behavioral expectations of a naval officer. Moreover, they exhibited some group solidarity as they became a band of brothers.

From a professional perspective, academy authorities were equally interested in measuring the students' progress as they gained sea and command experience. Summer cruise instructors therefore assessed the students' levels of professional development through their daily progress in activities such as managing the ship, gunnery, and practical seamanship. The academy's measurement of student progress revealed that sea-based training complemented the skills they had learned first on shore. Again, the academy had established criteria by which it measured how far the students had come in meeting the standards of their profession—the academy used more than just a "rule-of-thumb" approach.

From the outset, in 1851, Commandant Craven concluded that the Annapolis shore-based system had shown immediate success in the level of student development. All the students had acquired knowledge of tacking, weaving, steering, making knots, splicing ropes, and other elements of practical seamanship. In the naval dimension, *Preble* had fired 175 single 4-pound shots to drill the students in gunnery. Craven exclaimed that the students were already proficient in gunnery from their instruction on shore under Professor Henry Lockwood's supervision. Craven noted that "the oldest seamen express[ed] great surprise that boys so young should so far excel themselves in the practice of this highly important branch of the naval profession." Craven reported similar findings for the 1852 cruise and believed that the pupils were more than capable of taking command of the deck and carrying out basic naval evolutions.[45]

During the 1854 summer cruise on *Preble*, Craven made a point of favorably comparing the progress of the midshipmen, who the academy had first trained on shore, with members of the crew who were only familiar with the ship since they left port. On the ship's return to Chesapeake Bay, Craven divided the crew into two groups—the regular crew and the students—for gun exercises with the broadsides.[46] Afterward, Craven surmised that the structured, shore-based education affected the quality of the young men and the running of the ship. He wrote that "the results were in each case that the firing of the young gentlemen who had had the benefit of instruction at the Academy was vastly superior to that of the crew who had only been exercised at the guns for the time the ship had been at sea, and a majority of whom were, as far as acquaintance with the routine and exercises of a man of war are concerned, very much the kind of men we should have to depend on for manning our ships in case of war."[47] Craven believed that the summer cruises benefited both the students and the Navy. Furthermore, as he measured their progress, it revealed that as each class advanced through their training, they became more proficient at sea.

For the 1859 summer cruise, *Plymouth* was once more the practice ship. Moreover, by that fall, there was something of a housing crisis at the academy, so the administration housed the newer class of students on *Plymouth*, docked alongside the institution.[48] That fall twenty-one pupils from the last year's fourth class were repeating a year, and Superintendent Blake recommended that they be trained ashore and kept separate from the new fourth class.[49] The latter's placement on *Plymouth* during the academic year is significant, because it provided the final link between shore- and sea-based educations. After the students' training over the winter, the academy sent them to sea on the same ship and measured their progress quantitatively and qualitatively to assess their development and the academy's program.

Craven attributed the success of the 1860 summer cruise to housing the youngest pupils on *Plymouth* over the winter. Craven noted that during previous summer cruises, he had to instruct the younger midshipmen in using the marline spike, used to splice rope, but on the 1860 cruise, it was unnecessary because they were sufficiently drilled on the procedure over the winter on the ship.[50] Lieutenant Edward Simpson, head of ordnance and gunnery, was also impressed with how well the students handled themselves aloft during the summer cruise, in particular the fourth-class midshipmen, the youngest who had been housed on *Plymouth*. He believed that abandoning the school-ship system would henceforth be a backward step.[51] Having the ship tied up along shore during the academic year merged elements of their academic and practical training and resulted in better progress when the students put to sea.

To adequately grasp the students' level of progress, the commandant of midshipmen measured their progress in a quasi-scientific manner. His procedure is significant because it reveals that the academy used a structured approach to develop their young officers, symbolic of a profession. Measuring their progress at sea allowed the institution to judge the abilities of the students and the level of the academy's success in officer development and to adjust their program in an almost scientific manner. Quantitatively, the average rank of the first and third classes fell between good and very good, while the second and fourth classes averaged between fair and good. When it came to attention to duty alone, the second class

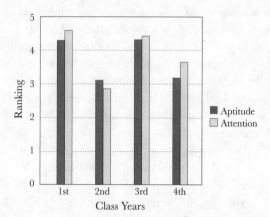

Figure 11. 1860 Summer Cruise, Student Progress Report. *(Craven's Report in Craven to Blake, 30 September 1860, letters received by the superintendent of the U.S. Naval Academy, 1845–87, Records of the U.S. Naval Academy, NA, RG 405. Hereafter, letters received)* Note: Craven's 1860 report ranked the students from poor to excellent. I assigned each grade a number from 0 to 6 and then conducted statistical analysis. Excellent = 6; Very Good = 5; Good = 4; Fair = 3; Tolerable = 2; Indifferent = 1; poor/none/very little = 0.

only averaged between tolerable and fair. The fourth-class midshipmen, housed on the school ship, averaged lower than the first and third classes, but ahead of their older comrades in the second class (see figure 11 and table 10).[52] Statistically, the full integration of the shore- and sea-based training system, using the school ship during the academic year, undoubtedly provided some benefits.

Table 10. Summer Cruise 1860, Descriptive Statistics

		Aptitude		Attention	
	No. Students	Standard Dev.	Missing Cases	Standard Dev.	Missing Cases
1st Class	27	1.12	1	1.19	0
2nd Class	8	1.27	0	1.62	0
3rd Class	54	0.9	0	0.87	0
4th Class	26	1.47	0	1.07	0

Source: Calculated from Craven Report in Craven to Blake, 30 September 1860, letters received. For a further discussion, see appendix B.

Note: It is unclear why the population size of the second class was only 8.

Qualitatively, Craven surmised that the students' training during the academic year allowed them to spend more time on other topics during the practice cruise. Furthermore, the benefit of having one class trained first on a ship attached to the institution, translated to all the students. For example, at sea it allowed Craven to devote more time to the older classes and "at an earlier period of the cruise to place the young gentlemen of the 1st class in charge of the deck, requiring them when so occupied to perform all the duties of Lieutenant in charge of the watch." He avowed that "the experiment of putting the 4th class on board ship for the first year of the academic course, had proved eminently successful."[53] The Navy unified the education system for the midshipmen, and academy authorities believed that this was demonstrated at sea with acting midshipmen better able to meet the demands of their profession. The movement for a more professional U.S. Navy began before the Civil War; the outbreak of the conflict just interrupted this process during the 1860–61 academic year. The 1860 summer cruise was the last before the outbreak of the Civil War. That fall Annapolis embarked new students on the school ship *Constitution*, docked near the academy, while other classes continued instruction ashore.

Classes resumed in October 1860, and administrative routine was normal. In September, William Harwar Parker reported to the academy as seamanship and naval tactics instructor. Because the academy used his book on naval light artillery, he also taught that subject. As a former Naval School student, pre-Annapolis

Figure 12. Old Gate House, 1861. *(U.S. Naval Academy Gate House, 1861, Special Collections & Archives Department, Nimitz Library, U.S. Naval Academy, Annapolis, Maryland)*

appointee, and now instructor, Parker was in a unique position to observe the institution's developments since his graduation in 1848. While the academy had operated under its reformed organization and curriculum for several years, Parker asserted that it lacked the requirements for instruction purely in "the strictly professional branches" like artillery. But he based his contention on the academy having had "no books on seamanship or naval tactics exactly adopted to the wants of the midshipmen" and instructors having made do with "compiling and translating" other works. For example, Parker wrote *Seamanship* for the "senior class" and "translated Chopart's *Naval Tactics* for them also."[54]

The Navy listened to the opinion of officers like Parker, and others, as they fine-tuned the academy's program. As enrollment increased—the Date of '60 equaled 114 midshipmen, the largest since 1841—professors demanded more help. French Professor Arsene Girault, for instance, complained that the third class would consist of ninety pupils, while forty-seven would be in the second class. Girault wanted an assistant because he believed he and his present staff would be unable to instruct that number adequately.[55] Joseph Winlock, professor of mathematics, had the same concerns and wanted four assistants.[56] Professor H. E. Nourse, who taught ethics and English, also desired more help and suggested the appointment of Master E. P. Lull, who was willing to help.[57] By 6 September Secretary Isaac Toucey responded and appointed Lieutenant Parker and Master Lull assistant professors of mathematics and Lieutenant Thomas Selfridge assistant professor of ethics.[58] Still, instructors feared the ramifications on the younger midshipmen's development. Professor Winlock wanted the classes divided into smaller numbers so that each student would receive some individual attention as they entered naval life.[59] Winlock concluded that "in the fourth class, particularly, so much is dependent upon an early and correct knowledge of the acquirements and mental aptitudes and the consequent correct classification of this large number of youths of very unequal ability and education, that any want of sufficient attention to them in the beginning of the term, must, inevitably serve to increase the number of failures at the February examination."[60] He also argued that the officers assigned to teaching should be knowledgeable and have the time to carry out their tasks properly.[61] By 12 December 1860, the Navy Department approved Superintendent Blake's suggestion that "the howitzer drill submitted by Lieut. [William H.] Parker be substituted for the one now used at the Academy, and that it be conducted by Lieut. Parker himself."[62]

On 14 January 1861, the department also approved the recommendations of the Academic Board to add topographical and hydrographical drawing to the program and to substitute Reverend Hubbard Winslow's ethics text for Wayland's tome.[63] Meanwhile, on 25 February 1861, Secretary Toucey authorized the top five students in each class to wear a metallic star on their jacket sleeves for their achievement.[64] Previously, a star was placed next to their names, but Representative William B. Maclay, Democrat, New York, suggested as an added stimulus it was to be worn on their uniforms and to be awarded at each examination.[65] It is unclear when or if the plan to give students stars was actually instituted. Park Benjamin notes that by the late nineteenth century, students at the top of a class were given stars to wear on their jackets, and "when their names are printed in the Naval Academy Register an asterisk precedes them."[66]

In response to the large new class of acting midshipmen, the academy again housed students on a school ship tied up alongside the academy. By 26 September, *Constitution* (see figure 13) was outfitted initially for the fourth class, whose students averaged 16.4 years old, but the ship later also accommodated the second and third classes at least by early 1861.[67] Superintendent Blake thought "Old Ironsides" appropriate but feared it would later be unsuitable as the summer practice ship because her draft was too great and she was unable to leave harbor easily. He estimated that it would take six weeks to refit the ship to practice-ship standards, an expensive task that would interfere with the studies of students on board. *Constitution*, a much larger ship than *Plymouth*, also needed one hundred more crew members to operate as a practice ship, because the students were learning and could not handle such a large ship all by themselves. Consequently, Blake believed that *Plymouth* remained the best vessel for the students, and he hoped she would return again to the academy.[68]

Figure 13. USS *Constitution* at anchor in the Potomac River, 1932. *(U.S. Naval Institute Photo Archives)*

Captain C. R. P. Rodgers, commandant of midshipmen, believed that *Constitution*, like *Plymouth*, the previous school ship, was the place for midshipmen to learn their craft before going to sea.[69] He concluded that "this ship endeared to every American by her glorious history, has become the threshold over which the officers of our navy are hereafter to enter their profession, and will be the standard to which they shall refer for comparison, whatever they may hereafter observe, in the equipments of ships of war." On board, the second and third classes, under the supervision of an instructor, studied the ship's rigging and other features and made sketches of their subject. In bad weather, they drilled at the battery, or one of the petty officers instructed them on things like knotting and splicing rope. The second class also had to show "upon the black board, the knowledge its members may have gleaned from the rigging and interior of the ship." Rodgers believed that the academy's goal was to instruct the midshipmen in the routines of warship operations so that they would be "prepared to enter upon the duties which shall be assigned them as midshipmen, masters, and watch officers." Rodgers also believed that the ship was a textbook: "Our young aspirants will derive their knowledge not merely from printed books or models, but from a ship of war" similar to the type they would one day command. Still, Rodgers believed that the Department of Seamanship should use a textbook that covered both seamanship and specific naval evolutions.[70] At the academy there had to be a balance between book and practical learning to create the naval officer.

On 15 September 1860, Robley D. Evans entered the *Constitution*'s world after he passed his entrance exam. Evans found it easy but explained that a candidate had to be physically fit and have "a fair foundation on which to build the education required of a sea officer," although this excluded applied science, education, and law, concentrating instead on seamanship and gunnery. Evans believed that life on *Constitution* was qualitatively better than that led by midshipmen before the academy's creation. Evans wrote that "our life on board ship was pleasant and novel, and our education on the lines that would fit us for the duties we would in the future have to perform." Although the ship was tied up next to the academy, Evans believed it isolated because it was approachable only along the long narrow wharf or by boat. All their lessons took place on board, separate from the older classes: "we never came in contact with them except when on shore for drill, or on Saturday, when we passed their quarters on our way to the town on liberty." Evans reflected that life was simple on *Constitution*, but met naval norms. He remembered that "we lived under service conditions; and while it is now the fashion to decry such training in favour of barracks on shore, I have yet to be convinced that for the conditions then existing it was not the best." Role models were important for Evans, and he felt that he owed everything to Lieutenant George W. Rodgers, captain of *Constitution*. But the midshipmen initially feared Rodgers, nephew of Oliver Hazard Perry, because the Perry-Rodgers-Slidell clan connected their mentor to the infamous Alexander Slidell Mackenzie of the *Somers* affair.[71]

Charles E. Clark also started his naval life that fall on *Constitution* and saw the Navy as an extended family. As a young boy, Charles fretted about his mother and often ran home to see if she had been kidnapped. Charles thought that Lieutenant John H. Upshur's wife appreciated his fears: "she not only was lovely to look upon, but had an unrivalled faculty for detecting the homesick, shy, and despondent among the boys and drawing them into the charmed circle about her." Meanwhile, Lieutenant Upshur, *Constitution's* executive officer, told one young man, William "Bill Pip" Pipkin, to escort his wife home after she and some other officer's wives had spent the evening on the vessel. But Pipkin replied he was unable to do so because "the last thing Dad and Ma said to me when I left home, was: 'Bill Pip, you beware of the women!'" Pipkin was about a year older than the other students and had "fallen back" into Charles' class. Charles concluded that but for the support of Mrs. Upshur, Pipkin probably would have failed at the first round of examinations. As it was, Pipkin resigned from the Navy at the outbreak of the Civil War and became a private in the Second Missouri Cavalry. He may also have served later as an enlisted man in the Confederate navy and later practiced law in Missouri until 1880, when he left his wife and children and moved to Idaho, became a miner, and died in 1919.[72]

Clark and the other students lived under *Constitution's* poop deck and in a deck house. The gun deck was refitted with three study rooms, each pupil had a locker along the berth deck wall, and the vessel had four recitation rooms. *Constitution* was stripped of her guns, except the eight to ten 32-pound guns on the quarterdeck the pupils used for practice. The young students also exercised on sails, and Clark remembered that Lieutenant Rodgers ordered him and Acting Midshipman George D. Glidden (about sixteen), to "lay aloft and overhaul down the buntlines," much to Charles' initial confusion.[73] James Morris Morgan, fifteen-year-old judge's son from Baton Rouge, Louisiana, explained that when he first arrived, the new appointees were still in their civilian cloths and the ship's officers and men treated the teenagers "almost as equals." But as soon as the pupils changed into their uniforms, the men saluted them and the officers only spoke to them "to give an order or reproof." Morgan concluded that "with the uniform I had come under naval discipline; and it was extraordinary how those soft-spoken lieutenants licked us into shape."[74]

Robley D. Evans thought that discipline on *Constitution* was strict, and despite later admiring Rodgers, he and the other boys were wary of him. Evans was a good friend with another midshipman, James Baldwin from Columbus, Mississippi. One day Baldwin got into a fight with a larger man, who attempted to hit him with a stool. Evans came to his friend's aid: "I grabbed him from behind, preventing the blow, and thus myself became part of the row." Rodgers lectured Evans on mutiny and ordered the boy locked in the wardroom. Evans, likely remembering Spencer's fate at Captain Mackenzie's hands during the *Somers* affair, was convinced that he would be hung. Evans wrote his uncle that he had better visit soon if he wished to see his nephew alive. The uncle replied simply that discipline was good for him, and he would wait for the sentence before paying a visit. Instead, Evans spent three days in confinement when another midshipman took his place in the wardroom as punishment for a different offense. Naval discipline had changed since the *Somers* affair, and the Navy protected young midshipmen from the extremes of naval law while they learned the expectations of their profession.[75]

The accuracy of statistical analysis of student behavior on *Constitution* is unclear, because the Civil War interrupted Annapolis life.[76] Still, most students were well behaved, and only a minority committed infractions: 22.7 percent of the students sampled did 52.0 percent of the misdeeds. The most common offense dealt with studying: 24.9 percent of the violations. The next highest category was those offenses—like marching out of step—that occurred in a military context, accounting for 11.6 percent. Offenses in an academic setting, like making noise in class and inattention to recitations, followed at 7.3 percent. As was the case on shore, offenses like insubordination and disrespect to superiors composed less than 2 percent of violations, while disobedience of orders equaled 2.9 percent. Finally, new violations that occurred on ship also appeared, like hammock offenses (0.4 percent) and having lost articles in the "Lucky Bag," where items found around ship were deposited (see appendix A). However, students on *Constitution* were more likely to report each other to the authorities than in previous samples: 55.9 percent of the reporting personnel were fellow students, while officers composed only 38.6 percent (see appendix A). One wonders if this was a manifestation of the deteriorating relations between students as a result of the conflicts in the country. One can only speculate that as order in the country broke down, so too did students' loyalty to each other. Still, by the end of December 1860, Superintendent Blake was confident enough in the students' conduct to agree with Lieutenant George W. Rodgers to remove a portion of the fourth class' demerits for good progress.[77]

Despite the students' general good behavior, some still misbehaved. Blake had suspended Acting Midshipman Gustavus English, a fourteen-year-old from New Jersey, for fighting and disorder in the study rooms, but he persisted in misbehaving. On the morning of 6 April 1861, English was reported for "a disgusting offence upon the berth deck of the *Constitution* last night, for which you offer no excuse." Blake regretted that he saw English so often in conduct reports and reminded the young man that if he received over 200 demerit points, he would be dismissed from the Navy "as deficient in conduct." The superintendent hoped English's conduct would improve and gave him a ray of hope: "Be assured that the authorities of the Academy desire your success, & in the hope that you will hereafter be more mindful of the obligation you assumed on entering the Institution." In the end, English failed to graduate, another potential officer expunged.[78] But by April 1861, many midshipmen had also resigned as the country disintegrated.

The Civil War broke the nation's unity and that of the armed forces. Northerners fought Southerners, and many Southern naval and Army officers resigned their commissions and returned home. Previously, for example, Skelton notes that there were few instances of sectional tensions in the Army. Occasionally at West Point, students discussed slavery and abolition, but the "authorities labored to dampen sectional loyalties" and forbade such topics of debate. Meanwhile, after 1821 the War Department "appears to have sought geographic balance in assigning newly commissioned subalterns to their units" and in the process "muted sectional friction" because officers from North and South served together. Only as the national crisis unfolded over 1860–61 did tension bubble to the surface.[79] Huntington asserted that the war was paradoxical for officers. Professionalism meant that Southern officers should defend the Union, but the North was a society many felt "rejected" their military "profession" as an unproductive pursuit. The dilemma could have paralyzed Southern officers, but as states left the Union, Washington released Southerners from their commissions and thus their professional commitment, until the attack on Fort Sumter (12–13 April 1861).[80]

Skelton found that approximately 25 percent of Southern officers eventually resigned and went South, or the Union government eventually dismissed them "for disloyalty or desertion." Significantly, Skelton calculates that the region of the South that an officer was from affected resignation patterns. As one approached the border, Southern officer affiliation with the North increased: only 15.9 percent of Lower South officers remained in the U.S. Army compared with 67.4 percent from the border region.[81] However, 64 percent of those who returned South eventually became generals in the Confederate army, as the Confederacy relied on the expertise of trained professionals as the conflicted turned distinctly landward. In contrast, Huntington notes that Northern officers often found themselves sidelined by patronage appointees.[82]

From similar traditions, the effect of professionalization on Southern naval officers was similar to their comrades in the Army. Naval officers submitted their resignation request to the secretary of the Navy, who either granted it and provided an honorable discharge, or rejected it and dismissed the officer from service and struck his name from the rolls. Moreover, the president could also decide the officer's fate, but once dismissed, there was no possibility of redress. Many requests for resignation that the Navy accepted over 1860–61 occurred as states seceded from the union during President Abraham Lincoln's transition to office, although skirmishes between Federal forces occurred before the attack on Fort Sumter. Captain V. M. Randolph, Alabama, for instance led a group of rebels who seized the Pensacola Navy Yard in January 1861, yet the Navy accepted his resignation sent before the seizure, only received in Washington after the event. William S. Dudley concludes that most Army officer resignations occurred after the attack on Fort Sumter and were accepted nonetheless, but officers in the Navy suffered a different fate. After Fort Sumter, any naval officer who requested to resign faced dismissal, likely on verbal instructions from the president, who had also begun ordering all government workers to take, or reaffirm, a loyalty oath. Meanwhile, Lincoln's secretary of the Navy, Gideon Welles, took charge on 7 March 1861 from Isaac Toucey, just condemned by the House of Representatives "for his gentle treatment of resignations."[83]

Welles felt that the Navy should dismiss anyone from service who requested permission to resign with the crisis.[84] Craig L. Symonds concludes that Welles was stricter than Lincoln in holding naval officers to their professional commitments. It was the secretary who ordered that all naval officers take a "new loyalty oath" and who terminated those who resisted. Even when states like Maryland decided to stay in the Union, Welles remained wary and refused to reinstate any dismissed officers from the state. The most famous example was Captain Buchanan, former academy superintendent. He requested to resign after riots swept Baltimore and it looked like his state would secede, and Welles struck his name from the Navy rolls instead. When secession failed to materialize, Welles refused to restore Buchanan and others, because he said he felt they had failed to come to their country's defense in its time of need. Meanwhile, when Lincoln suggested that the Navy reinstate Lieutenant Augustus McLaughlin, and deferred the decision to Welles, the secretary rejected the request.[85]

Writing after the war, Welles surmised that "many of the naval officers then in Washington and about the Navy Department were of questionable fidelity. A number had already resigned and most of those who were tainted with secession soon left the service; but some of them, on a further consideration of the subject, aided perhaps by adventitious circumstances, determined to abide by the flag and the Union."[86] Welles only wanted professionals who would serve the needs of the client during the crisis; for their part, those officers who felt that they would be unable to carry out their duties as professionals because of their loyalty to their home states resigned.[87] Officers like Buchanan and McLaughlin were unwilling to uphold their professional obligations to defend the nation but knew that, as professionals, they had no choice but to follow orders or quit. Rejected, Buchanan, McLaughlin, and others joined the Confederate States Navy.[88]

James Lee Conrad calculates that by summer 1861 almost a quarter of the U.S. Navy's officers resigned their commissions. Almost 50 percent of Southern officers (126) joined the Confederate States Navy, but Symonds asserts that the rest remained loyal.[89] Of the established naval officers who resigned, their reasons varied, but many asserted that at the very least it was because their home state had seceded and it left them incapable of carrying out their duties with proper legitimacy. Lieutenant James J. Waddell, North Carolina, dismissed, wrote that he had hoped to resign in loyalty to his state rather than because of any secessionist beliefs. Similarly, the superintendent of the U.S. Naval Observatory, Commander Matthew Fontaine Maury, Virginia, explained that the "Union is gone" and he had to return home "to share" his state's fate. Robert Tansill, another Virginian and a Marine, dismissed, contended that he had taken an oath to protect the Constitution. For U.S. naval officers, their careers were both a social and professional contract with the state. But contrary to what the young midshipmen were taught at Annapolis, Tansill asserted this meant he could "interpret" the Constitution, and he believed that the Federal government had violated states' rights. Lieutenant James B. Lewis, Virginia, dismissed, exclaimed that he believed that the Federal government had turned "into a military despotism," which ignored the Constitution that he had agreed to defend. Consequently, he answered to "the higher law" and resigned because "despotism has usurped the place of constitutional liberty."[90] Still other officers, like Captain Samuel DuPont, New Jersey, asserted that they had taken an oath to defend the nation "from without or from within."[91] However, Captain Isaac Mayo, Maryland, exclaimed that he had to resign rather than participate in a war against fellow Americans—it is likely that his dismissal on 18 May 1861 precipitated his suicide that day.[92]

Obtaining precise figures and the cause for academy student resignations as the Civil War unfolded is difficult because many students might have avoided giving their real reasons. Furthermore, data are more accessible for those students who officially graduated from the Naval School or academy and resigned their commissions. Regardless, we can draw some conclusions. The Navy had intended education and training at Annapolis to instill in future officers the values of their profession. Professionals served a client, and as Wayland's *Moral Science* taught the academy pupils, this meant that professionals followed orders rather than pass judgment on the task. Importantly, as discussed, Wayland had singled out military officers for particular commentary and noted that, if they were unable to follow their orders, then they had to resign. Meanwhile, as in the Army, the Navy sought to stifle anything that might cause regional disagreements: As chapter 3 revealed, academy authorities appear to have forbidden the use of Wayland's discussion on slavery, for instance, in their classes. Still, with increased tensions over 1860–61, Annapolis students responded in a similar manner to their West Point counterparts.

Dudley discovered that 111 acting midshipmen requested permission to resign from December 1860 to December 1861, and the Navy granted permission regardless of when they requested it or the actual resignation reasons. For instance, after the academy found forty fourth-class midshipmen deficient at their

February exams, the secretary suggested they resign, and many did. Albeit, they were then prone to cause a nighttime ruckus until released formally from the facility.[93] In contrast, of eighty-seven lieutenants who submitted resignation requests, the Navy accepted only thirty-nine; the rest were dismissed because they submitted their requests after the Fort Sumter attack. Dudley concludes that the Navy handled the acting midshipmen with clemency because the Navy depended on full officers "for the accomplishment of most tasks, and they were the future source of the Navy's senior commanders."[94] Moreover, as with its overall application of naval law and discipline with academy students, the Navy also likely realized that the pupils were still youths, rather than full naval officers with the same professional responsibilities.

From academy alumni records, 138 students listed their birthplace as one of the eventual Confederate states. Seventy-one (or 51 percent) of these resigned and officially "went South" during the conflict; fifty others resigned without a stated reason. Only seventeen (12 percent) Southern students remained in the Navy to death or retirement after 1860, and most were from Virginia, close to the seat of the Union government.[95] Like their older counterparts, their resignation reasons varied. W. E. Yancey, Alabama, left because his father threatened to disown him otherwise. Robley D. Evans, Virginia, wanted to stay in the U.S. Navy, found his mother resigned on his behalf, but eventually was reinstated. Other Southerners, who also taught at the academy, like Maryland-born Lieutenant Charles W. Flusser, appointed from Kentucky, remained in the U.S. Navy and died in battle in 1864, unable to contemplate firing on the national flag.[96] The 20 percent sample of offenses from the conduct roll for the 1860–61 academic year revealed only one related to the sectional divide. On 14 October 1860, authorities awarded Acting Midshipman J. E. Fiske (probably James E. Fisk, '57 Date, of a New Jersey merchant family background) four demerit points for flags with electioneering emblems displayed in his room. As at West Point, the administrators wanted to suppress anything that might fracture the institution's unity. Moreover, it went beyond the officer's duty to pass judgment on their client (the state) and openly take sides in the debate.

The professional indoctrination that Northerners and Southerners received at the academy likely contributed to the orderly unwinding of the relations at the facility, although the youngest students had little understanding of the issues. Harry Taylor, future rear admiral from D.C., and other students, thought that all the states were becoming their own nations and Taylor wanted the join the future navy of New York because he felt that state had the largest commerce and would need a big navy to protect it. Meanwhile, James Morris Morgan believed that Louisiana had "no right to secede," because it had been "purchased by the money of other States just as a man buys a farm."[97] Mahan exclaimed that the "Southern flavor" was ever present at the academy: "every Southerner was convinced that the justice was on their side, that their rights as well as interests were being attacked." Meanwhile, Northerners were divided over slavery, yet seemed willing to do anything to save the Union. But Mahan opined that "at our age, of course, we simply re-echoed the tones of our homes."[98] Nevertheless, rather than fight each other, the young officer-recruits voiced their concerns and departed, while those who remained prepared to defend the institution in accordance with their professional allegiance.

Charles Clark also observed the unrest that spread across the country but remembered no real fights between Northerners and Southerners, simply some "wrangling"; the Northerners were unsure of the strength of their position. By December Clark found that his Southern fellows became surer of themselves. Some stated that because New York had the Military Academy at West Point, it was natural that the Naval Academy, located farther south, belonged to the South. They declared that the Seventh Regiment in New York City, and New York City, in general, was on their side and would fight with them if the time came. As for places closer to Annapolis, Baltimore would never let Federal reinforcements pass through the city on the way to Washington to defend the capitol. Clark recalled, perhaps embellishing a little, that one day William T. Sampson, future hero of the Spanish-American War and the "ranking cadet officer," passed by a group of Southerners. Sampson replied that if Baltimore failed to let Federal troops through, troops would "march *over* [emphasis in original] Baltimore—or the place where it stood!" Clark concluded that the North would face a daunting task; six months with his Southern compatriots revealed that they were firmly a military class.[99]

Academy life started to break down in early January 1861, but rather than simply abandon the academy, Southern students followed the rules and the expectations of a naval officer. Eighteen members of the first class, for example, petitioned the secretary of the Navy to give them their graduation certificates in the event they were forced to withdraw or resign from the academy if their states withdrew from the Union.[100] Superintendent Blake rejected the request but forwarded the petition to the secretary nonetheless, who also declined their request.[101] Nevertheless, soon midshipmen from the South began to resign. George Dwight Bryan, from South Carolina, was one of the first to go, and he later wrote to his former classmates that he was now a real midshipman serving on *Excel* in Charleston harbor. Shortly thereafter, midshipmen from the Gulf States left, like William Earle Yancey, the son of an Alabama secessionist. The final bell tolled with Abraham Lincoln's inauguration as president in March 1861. Clark recalled that fort after fort fell, until the loss of Harper's Ferry virtually cut off the academy from the North. Rumors then circulated that Maryland was about to secede and take the academy, her vessels, and armaments, with her. Consequently, the academy's guns were removed and stored on *Constitution*. The professional training and ethos instilled in those who remained then rose firmly to the surface; they prepared to defend the grounds when word circulated of an impending attack.[102]

Early in April 1861, word came that the steamer *Maryland* was en route with troops from the 8th Massachusetts Regiment. The governor of Maryland, although a Unionist, wanted a minimal show of force and feared that anything larger would escalate secessionist sentiments. The landing of the troops was delayed, and the academy's officers used the time and the extra men—mainly sailors and seamen from Massachusetts—to help move *Constitution* to a safer location in the bay. Ten of Clark's class remained on board to assist, while the rest were put ashore. Clark believed that the academy had little to repel an attack, because old Fort Severn was only used for battery exercises and was useless for defense. Moreover, "we numbered less than two hundred in all, and the average age of the midshipmen in the four classes was eighteen years."[103] Superintendent Blake was so afraid for the academy that he voiced his concerns to Secretary Welles. The situation in the country was "threatening," and despite the gusto of the boys, Blake explained that "the only force at my command consists of the students of the Academy, many of whom are little boys, and some of whom are citizens of the seceded states." Blake proposed that if the academy were attacked by a force it could not repel, then he would embark the students and officers on *Constitution* and put to sea.[104]

In this atmosphere, Superintendent Blake sent Lieutenant Stephen B. Luce to Washington to meet with the chief of the Bureau of Ordnance and Hydrography and present the superintendent's views. Because of the situation, Blake recommended that they move *Constitution* to a northern port and that *Plymouth* replace her at Annapolis. In *Constitution's* present location, she could not swing on her anchor, and Luce opined that if she remained at Annapolis, she should be moored outside the bar, where she could swing freely. If worse came to worse, she would defend herself to the end, but they would scuttle her rather than let the ship fall into enemy hands. If the situation worsened, Fort Severn was in a vulnerable position if nearby Fort Madison fell into enemy hands and was armed. Blake recommended that the first-class students be immediately graduated, while the others put on leave, because they were too young to be reliable officers. Luce reported that the chief of the bureau thought that decisions affecting the academy would need time to be considered—time, however, that was rapidly running out. Blake's request, Luce was told, would be forwarded to the secretary of the Navy for consideration, but the chief took a nonchalant attitude. He reasoned that there would be plenty of warning if there was an attack and any mob would be surely repelled. Luce explained that this would only be true if the academy were not taken by surprise or treachery, so he suggested that more Marines be stationed there. The chief replied that if a requisition was sent by telegraph—Luce had no authority on his own to request Marines—they would be sent.[105]

As states left the union, William Parker noted that the academy was in a "constant state of excitement" and it was difficult for the students to study. Nevertheless, as an instructor, he thought that "so good was the discipline that everything went on as usual, and the midshipmen were kept closely to their duties." Moreover, resigning midshipmen and their friends maintained proper decorum. "Their departures were very quietly taken, and the friendships they had contracted at the school remained unimpaired." Only when Southern forces attacked Fort Sumter did the academy assume "more the appearance of a garrison." Although born in New York, Parker resigned on 19 April 1861, after Virginia seceded. Still, Parker remained committed to his duty until the Navy approved his resignation. It placed him in an awkward position when alarm was raised of a potential rebel attack on the academy. Despite his Southern sympathies, Parker commanded the academy's howitzers and "like many of the midshipmen manning it who had [also] resigned and were waiting to hear from Washington, [they all] had either to refuse to do duty or fire on our friends." The attack never came, but Parker asserted that "had we been attacked I should have stood by my guns and performed my duty to the school. I was still an officer of the navy." Parker left the U.S. Navy, joined the Confederate States Navy, and eventually became superintendent of its naval academy, while his brother Foxhall remained with the North.[106]

By 22 April, all life at the academy was centered on the Civil War, and no educational activities were accomplished. There were rumors that the people of Maryland wanted *Constitution* to be "the first ship of the war to hoist the flag of the Confederate States," and Blake thought that all communications over their telegraph were falling into enemy hands.[107] The academic routine was "completely broken up by the occupation of the grounds and a portion of the buildings of the Academy by National troops;—and it will be a long time, in any event, before it will be possible to resume a regular course of instruction at this place." Consequently, Blake ordered the acting midshipmen to *Constitution* and planned to send her to New York under the command of Lieutenant George W. Rodgers, who would "preserve organization and discipline until further orders," while Blake and some of the other officers remained behind to mind the academy's property. Blake recommended that the academy be moved somewhere north of the Delaware, probably to Fort Adams, Rhode Island. He concluded, "the officers & students of the Academy will constitute an efficient peace garrison to any fort they may occupy."[108]

Tension continued to build as more troops arrived, like the 71st New York Regiment; the 69th Irish, a German regiment; and the 1st Rhode Island Regiment.

Nevertheless, Charles Clark and his friends, just mere children, threw their books from the academy windows and they celebrated the cancellation of classes. But their joy was short-lived, and academy authorities ordered the students to board *Josephine* and depart for *Constitution* so that they and Old Ironsides could be taken out of harm's way. When they arrived on board, the students found a change in the old girl: their study rooms were no more and the guns had been moved from the spar deck. The crew was now composed of students from the four classes, two companies of the 8th Massachusetts regiment, and about twenty-five other sailors. Evans recalled that Captain C. R. P. Rodgers told them all, "My boys, stand by the old flag!" and then broke into tears.[109] On 27 April, the secretary of the Navy ordered the academy to Fort Adams, Newport, Rhode Island "with as little delay as possible."[110]

Constitution departed Annapolis under tow by *R. R. Cuyler* and headed down the Chesapeake, escorted as far as the Capes by *Harriet Lane*. Once clear, *Constitution* sailed to New York, where the midshipmen enjoyed the sights and sounds of the city and then departed for Newport, where the Naval Academy stayed until the end of the Civil War.[111] On 6 May, Colonel Abel Smith wrote Captain Blake that "a proper guard has & will be kept over the buildings containing the instruments & apparatus belonging to the U.S. government until such time as the proper dept. send for them."[112] And on 8 May, *Constitution* and the steam ship *Baltic*, carrying academy material, arrived at Fort Adams. It was almost like starting all over again; there were no quarters and only some casements, which were damp and unused for eighteen months, but they were safe at their new home.[113]

Early in its development, supporters of the U.S. Navy, like John Paul Jones, believed that a careful approach to naval officer education was important. Then, during the antebellum era, the Navy established scattered shore schools to help midshipmen prepare for their lieutenant's examinations. However, the needs of the Navy and the controversy over the *Somers* mutiny stirred a more serious consideration of how to provide a secure and controlled atmosphere in which to train and indoctrinate young naval officers. Secretary of the Navy Upshur recognized this in 1842, but it took George Bancroft's bureaucratic finesse to create the consolidated Naval School at Annapolis in 1845. Bancroft shared the belief that the Navy needed a well-regulated educational program for its officers, and the Navy turned to West Point for inspiration. There, the Army indoctrinated its cadets, trained them, and then dispatched the young men on summer encampments to show the students what army life was really like.

Naval officer education at Annapolis was similar and represented what the Navy believed was the ideal means of professionalizing officer recruits into the demands of their career. Rather than train new officers first at sea, the Navy gradually introduced them to their profession in a controlled environment. Over the 1849–51 period, this involved the creation of a four-year training program on shore after the Army's triumph in the Mexican-American War proved the utility of the West Point system, an institution that scholars also conclude exhibited early signs of professionalism. In turn, the Navy educated its young officers and taught them the moral ethos and discipline that an adult officer required. Critical to the program, however, was the establishment of the summer practice cruises in 1851. There, the Navy taught the young midshipmen, without any prior sea experience, the practical aspects of seamanship and an officer's duties on an active warship.

For this purpose, the academy selected vessels that represented operational warships as closely as possible. Then, after the initial selection and an academic year on shore, instructors at sea taught and evaluated the pupils in practical seamanship, vessel management, and naval operations like evolutions, gunnery, and teamwork. Beyond such practical aspects, the instructors maintained the pupils under a disciplinary system that aided their professional development and indoctrination. Furthermore, the academy weeded out unsatisfactory elements, instilled respect for proper shipboard order, and tracked student progress as they applied their skills. Increasing sectional tensions caused a professional quandary in the officers and students between loyalty to their home state and upholding the officer's ethos that the institution had instilled in them. The Navy's objective was to increase a young midshipman's professionalism from the outset of his career. The outbreak of the Civil War tested the midshipmen, and in the end, loyalty to one's home state outweighed affinity to the nation. Still, the professional ethics that the academy gave its students meant that Northerners and Southerners largely maintained their gentlemanly deportment, and if they were unable to continue their duties, they often followed the resignation etiquette expected of a professional who found themselves no longer able to serve their client.

CONCLUSION

Naval education at Annapolis had ended for the time being, and for a large portion of the students, the Navy had been only part of their lives before they were weeded out or later decided a professional officer's life was unappealing because of the slow promotion rates. Park Benjamin attended the Naval Academy from 1863 to 1867 and knew many of the students who attended before and after him. Writing in 1900, Benjamin concluded that during the academy era, "the school was no longer adapting itself to its students, but requiring its students to adapt themselves to it." It would be safer to conclude that by the outbreak of the Civil War, the academy and its students met each other halfway. The academy expected a certain type of student and gathered them from commercial and mercantile families. Meanwhile, the Navy changed the school to the academy to make the institution more like West Point. The academy expected its students to accept the academy's style of education and introduction to sea life, while this study has shown the academy authorities also used a gradual approach to discipline to professionalize young midshipmen into the demands of their career. Benjamin was correct when he stated that the midshipmen of the old Navy were no more when the final "Oldsters" left the academy.[1]

William B. Skelton's analysis of U.S. Army officers, a similar group, provides a glimpse of how long they stayed in the Army and their postservice lives. Of 594 Army officers Skelton found on the 1830 Army Register, 47.3 percent died in service, 36.9 percent resigned, 3.5 percent were dismissed or dropped, while 12 percent retired. Natural causes, rather than war or other conflicts, caused most deaths in service. Meanwhile, many who resigned were "junior officers, and their departure was easily offset by the annual influx of West Point graduates." Skelton calculates that the resignation rate from 1823 to 1859, "a rough measure of officers' commitment to their profession," was only about 4 percent and fell further in the 1840s and 1850s and that fluctuations likely correlated with the "economic depressions after 1837 and 1857, which restricted employment opportunities outside the army." From 1797 to 1860, the Army officer's median career length increased from ten to twenty-three years and remained stable at twenty-two to twenty-three years from 1830 to 1860. Of those who became officers during the 1792–94 period, 3.5 percent served for more than twenty years; of those who graduated West Point from 1841 to 1843, greater than one-third stayed longer than twenty years and one-fifth stayed for at least thirty years. Skelton concludes that because so many officers served together for so long, they shared experiences and developed "institutional loyalties" that were "certainly the most important ingredient in building a corporate identity." After leaving West Point, most officers entered garrison life, often in remote areas, where their only activities were regulated marches, parades, and drill with little outside contact.[2] Undoubtedly, this only further cemented their group solidarity and identity as professionals, separate from the rest of society.

The Naval Academy reflects a similar pattern (see tables 11 and 12). From 1845 to 1861 and the academy's retreat to Rhode Island, alumni records show that 1,030 students passed through its doors.[3] But only 55.5 percent of those who attended the school or academy actually graduated. The remainder, 44.5 percent, must have gone on to other things. Meanwhile, 132, or 23 percent, resigned or were dismissed from the Navy, although not over official sympathy to the Southern cause. The average service time of those who resigned or were dismissed was 12.8 years; 53 of these, or 40.5 percent, resigned after 10 years or less service, while 214 graduates (37.4 percent) died while serving their country.[4] Decomposed annually (see figure 14), there is a similar dip in resignation and dismissal rates during the

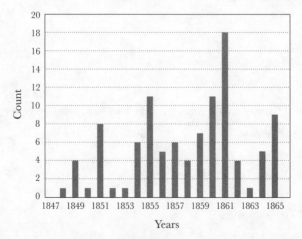

Figure 14. Resignation/Dismissal Numbers for Annapolis Graduates Appointed 1840–60. *(Calculated from Register of Alumni)* Note: Count is minus those who officially resigned because they "went South."

late 1850s that Skelton found in Army resignation rates. As with Skelton's study, this is undoubtedly linked in part to the economic downturn during this period. Still, the highest resignation and dismissal rate, even after subtracting those who officially "went South," occurred in 1861 (see figure 14), as discussed in chapter 6. Still, the resignation rates for Annapolis graduates were lower than for their West Point counterparts.

It is likely that the naval resignation rates, however, also reflect the poor chances for promotion within the Navy. In this period, promotion was seniority based, advancing from midshipman to lieutenant could take years, and the highest rank was usually captain, with the rank of commodore for anyone commanding a fleet.[5] With slow promotion, many midshipmen left the Navy to seek other careers. Lieutenant Matthew F. Maury, writing in 1840 under the pseudonym of Harry Bluff, concluded that a midshipman appointed in 1839 would probably only reach the rank of lieutenant in 1870.[6] Most of those 132 alumni who resigned after Annapolis graduation resigned "quickly," within about thirteen years of service, and of 572

Table 11. Attrition of Annapolis Graduates Appointed 1840–60

Type of Attrition	Number	Percentage
Death	214	37.4
Resigned/Dismissed	132	23.1
"Went South"	71	12.4
Retired	150	26.2
Missing Cases	5	0.9
Total	572	100

Source: Calculated from Register of Alumni.

Table 12. Naval Career Lengths Among Antebellum Annapolis Graduates

Service Time	Number	Percent	Years
Average of Retirees	150		38.9
Retired after 20 Years or Less	17	11.3	
Retired after 21 to 30 Years	12	8.0	
Retired after 31 to 49 Years	121	80.7	
Average of Resigned/Dismissed	132		12.8
Resigned/Dismissed after 10 Years or Less	54	40.9	

Source: Calculated from Register of Alumni.

graduates, only 150, or 26.2 percent, retired from the Navy. But their average service time was 38.9 years. Of these, 17, or 11.3 percent, stayed for 20 years or less; 12, or 8 percent, worked for between 21 and 30 years; while 121, or 80.7 percent retired after 31 to 49 years service. Nevertheless, while over 40 percent of naval school or academy students failed to graduate, those who actually did stayed in the Navy longer (table 12) than their Army counterparts stayed in the Army. These naval officers established the professional corps of officers after the Civil War. Using Skelton's framework, the long service time of over 80 percent of academy graduates indicates a much greater commitment to their career.

Officers left the Navy early, for whatever reason, or never graduated from Annapolis, and had postservice careers, perhaps motivated by better opportunities in the civilian world. For the Army, Skelton tacked the postservice careers of officers on the 1830 Army Register. Generally, most former Army officers later worked in the commercial/manufacturing sector (44.6 percent). Others moved into professional (19.3 percent), agricultural (18.7 percent), and government service (17.5 percent) careers. Some West Point graduates used their military training to move up the corporate ladder from civil engineers to company managers. Meanwhile, other former Army officers transitioned into banking, law, business, education, and the civil service careers. Delving deeper into these statistics, Skelton found that a large number (28.3 percent) of former officers became civil engineers. Skelton concludes that the "transportation revolution made civil engineering a booming field during most of the antebellum era" and West Point provided most of the needed workers.[7]

Unfortunately, postservice histories of Annapolis graduates are more difficult to assess than for West Point. The list of officers of the U.S. Navy, as contained in Edward W. Callahan's work, does not contain postservice information for this study's period, like that used by Skelton.[8] Nor does the academy's Register of Alumni contain any postservice data, therefore the only alternative would be to comb U.S. census records or obituaries for the years after each graduate's retirement, resignation, or dismissal for their name. This would be a time-consuming process, but it will become easier as computerization of historical records continues. One important question to ask is whether the graduate's final occupation was similar to their parents'. What skills did they bring from the Navy to civilian life? Were they specialized skills like those of the West Point civil engineers? For now we can only speculate, especially about those who never became the Navy's famous heroes.

The naval careers of those officers who resigned and "went South" during the Civil War ended abruptly in 1865. Such officers were unwelcome in the U.S. Navy and had to seek employment elsewhere. William Parker, for instance, spent time in commercial fleets, then used his teaching experience to parlay a job with the Maryland Agricultural College and eventually became its president. There, he modeled the institution after the U.S. and Confederate naval academies, even deploying a vessel for summer cruises for the students. After leaving Maryland, Parker spent a short period as U.S. ambassador to Korea in 1886, as Southerners returned to public life. By then, an alcoholic and embarrassment, Parker was soon removed from his post by Washington.[9] Meanwhile, Park Benjamin offers another glimpse of life that reveals that many academy alumni took similar postservice careers as some of their West Point counterparts.

By 1900 Benjamin found there were about five hundred academy alumni from all eras working in the civilian world. Many had fought in the Spanish-American War, but Benjamin only recorded those graduates who "have achieved high reputations" in civilian life. From the Date of '51, for example, was John S. Barnes, who by 1900 was a New York banker. Benjamin also found others: Harvard University professor Ira N. Hollis (class of 1878); physicist Professor Albert A. Michelson (class of 1873); John Hopkins University professor of electricity Louis Duncan (class of 1880); the head of the Crescent Ship Yard, Lewis Nixon (class of 1882); railway man Frank J. Sprague (class of 1878); war correspondent Joseph L. Stickney (class of 1867); authors Winston Churchill (class of 1894) and Reverend Cyrus Townsend Brady (class of 1883); Orford Copper Company president Colonel Robert M. Thompson (class of 1868); and yachtsmen S. Nicholson Kane (class of 1866) and William Butler Duncan Jr. (class of 1881). It would be a significant avenue of research to compare their fates with those of the less-famous Annapolis graduates.[10]

Like West Point, the Naval School and academy provided a cadre of workers for both the Navy and the civilian sector. In the Navy, those who stayed for a long period formed a corporate body with a *mentalité* similar to that of the Army, and many became famous individuals like George Dewey. It was this core that formed the leaders of the American Navy as it truly took the world stage after the Civil War. In-depth analysis of the long-term service careers of U.S. naval officers is beyond the focus of this present study. But a brief comment on their *mentalité* toward the business world may shed light on why some stayed in the Navy, while others left for the civilian world. Those who remained were committed to a naval career and were instilled with similar views. One can only speculate whether it was indeed caused by their similar backgrounds or subconscious absorption of "Moral Science."

Naval officers were wary of, or even outwardly hostile toward, businessmen and stock exchanges. Yet, as professionals, they defended American business interests, because they saw it in the nation's interest and had been instilled with the ethos that professionals carried out their tasks regardless. In 1845 businessman Samuel Coues attacked the Navy, and a future academy superintendent, Commander Louis Goldsborough, returned fire and criticized the "malice" and "covetousness" of the business world. One can only imagine that Goldsborough's young academy students must have later heard his views on the business world and concluded that it was the opinion that naval officers must hold. Still, Mahan later wrote his famous works that American business leaders liked, yet he too was critical of the business world and its obsession with material wealth. Peter Karsten asserts that Mahan was "a true son of Annapolis, with all the Academy disdain for those who 'attach to the making and having money' a value in excess of what Mahan thought proper."[11] One wonders if those who resigned or retired early from the Navy held a different view. Did this make them more prone to seek a job in the same business world that Mahan and Goldsborough despised? Regardless, for the civilian world Annapolis undoubtedly provided the United States with a core, educated elite to help run the country and defend its interests—typically economic—overseas with few questions. The Naval Academy provided the country with a professional officer corps that led the U.S. Navy in the postbellum era.

Karsten concludes that education and rituals at Annapolis gave young officers a common outlook and the academy became their spiritual home.[12] Yet, scholars debate when professionalism arose in the U.S. armed forces. Huntington believed that military professionalism was fleeting in the antebellum period. West Point and the Naval Academy existed, but military journals were short-lived and the era remained tied to the philosophy of the citizen-soldier. For Huntington, the armed forces only became professional in the late nineteenth century. Millet, meanwhile, asserts that the U.S. military only professionalized after the Civil War, which allowed professionals to assert dominance after the deaths of so many amateurs. In contrast, Skelton contends that the military exhibited signs of a professional culture in the antebellum period. Despite their differences, a common definition of a professional has emerged. A professional is separate from the rest of society, the client they serve. Professionals are recruited into their field and trained in the specific knowledge required to carry out their tasks. Generally, training happens in a structured setting, like a college or university: we often think of medical or engineering schools churning out students to fill skilled positions in hospitals or businesses. The professional designs the things we need, or provides a service that we cannot provide because it would be too expensive—or dangerous—for everyone to acquire the skills necessary.[13] A mature profession selects its recruits, and established members of the profession weed out those novices it feels are unsuitable.

During training, the professional is indoctrinated into a job culture and its technical requirements. Established members of the profession instill into the new recruit the ethos of their field, and the initiates develop an esprit de corps. As students, they learn to avoid giving their opinion on the task assigned to them by their client, however grim the assignment. Meanwhile, the novice grows accustomed to the behavioral expectations of their career. Those who fail to learn the technical, ethical, or "subculture" requirements of their profession leave the profession willingly or are expelled. The result of the professionalization process during the selection and training of the individual leaves the profession with only those truly committed. These common themes in the establishment of a profession gives us a litmus test by which to assess how far these criteria have been met by a career during its historical development.[14]

In exchange for protection, Western society gradually relinquished its right to private exertion of violence to increasingly professional armed forces in exchange for taxation. Rather than have private armies or armed merchant ships, economies of scale allow the state to provide efficient protection to businesses and citizens against a variety of threats domestic and foreign.[15] In turn, careers related to the sea provide a unique set of circumstances to judge the growth of a profession. Charles P. Kindleberger notes that orders on ships must be followed intelligently because of the nature of the environment.[16] Historically, on land, in the event of large-scale war, virtually anyone could be given a firearm and basic training on how to discharge the weapon, without knowing the relationship between that weapon and the environment beneath their feet. But the ocean is different. Officers responsible for coordinating the ship's movements with tactics and strategy must understand how to manage the ship, its crew, and its weapons with precision. Consequently, Huntington opined that "technicism" was felt the greatest in staff organization and education, especially in the navy as navies evolved.[17] By 1845 the U.S. Navy concluded that the best place to professionalize its young officers into the increasing demands of a far-flung Navy was at Annapolis.

The U.S. Navy's officer-training philosophy reflected the young nation's colonial ties and European tradition and changing the system was a slow process. Nevertheless, early in American history, the new nation's naval pioneers, like John Paul Jones, advocated a system of officer education that would make the Navy's leaders efficient and instill them with the ethos becoming of a leader. But the U.S. Navy's early history held onto Royal Navy traditions and role models—older established officers—molded new officer recruits into the type of person that could lead men and manage the ship. The older officers cared for their young charges and taught them shipboard life and the officer's duties. In the context of the small American Navy, wherein many vessels only needed a few officers, it was difficult to teach young officers the skills and teamwork needed to become officers on larger capital ships. Still, for young men like Stephen B. Luce, who went to sea at the tender age of fourteen, it was like being suddenly thrust into an alien world and culture.

Further officer education on land was directed at officers with sea experience, studying for their promotion exams, and relegated to a patchwork of ad hoc shore establishments at places like the Boston Naval Yard, Norfolk, and Philadelphia.

Each of these facilities gave young officers greater training in seamanship, languages, science, and naval theory. Role models at sea had already instilled the values of their career into the officers who attended these shore schools; the schools were intended to provide further training rather than to select or weed out those the profession felt were unsuitable. Consequently, as Benjamin Sands noted, the onus was on the students to study, and the trainees had greater freedom to come and go from the facilities. The Philadelphia Naval School was the most structured of the institutions, with greater restrictions on midshipman movements about the city and their schedule. With many of the Philadelphia's instructors going on to work at the Naval Academy in Annapolis, the former served as a template, along with the Army's West Point, for a fully developed program that would professionalize young naval officers into their career.

By the 1840s, the demands on the U.S. Navy were growing substantially. The force was responsible for overseas expeditions, policing piracy near the nation's shores, and relating with other nations—like Britain and France—along the West African coast while stopping the slave trade and advancing American commercial links.[18] The Navy had also begun adopting greater use of steam-powered vessels and, simultaneously, the nation became concerned when the secretary of War's young son was executed after a supposed mutiny on the *Somers*. The result of the inquiry advocated greater control over how young midshipmen were educated and recommended the creation of a naval academy. Moreover, naval supporters, like Secretary of the Navy Abel P. Upshur, asserted that the Navy would benefit from its own academy like the Army's West Point. Still, Congress often opposed a formal and centralized naval academy because of traditional American fears of creating an institution that would breed an aristocratic class. Consequently, Secretary of the Navy George Bancroft used the existing training budget for the Navy and recruited Philadelphia's instructors to centralize naval education at Annapolis. Moreover, Bancroft dispatched Passed Midshipman Samuel Marcy to West Point to study their system and how it could be adapted to naval education.

By using the Navy's present assets, Bancroft could show the country—and Congress—that a naval academy would not threaten the nation's values. Instead, Annapolis would provide a safe and structured environment, with a clear management and disciplinary system, which would indoctrinate young recruits into the demands of their profession and the needs of the society. Bancroft appointed Franklin Buchanan the first superintendent of the new Naval School at Annapolis, choosing him from a list of senior naval officers. Buchanan managed day-to-day operations, and drew up the institution's first rules. An Examining Board provided oversight for midshipmen training standards, while Bancroft and Buchanan emphasized the school's role in instilling both the technical skills and professional ethos required of a naval officer. Like a true profession, with Annapolis, the Navy sought to select only those officer recruits whose character matched the qualities held in high regard for a naval officer: academic and seafaring skills, but also good moral character and conduct. Consequently, the school examined midshipmen regularly and took into consideration both their academic accomplishments and personal deportment when deciding their suitability as potential officers.

When the Naval School opened in 1845, it represented a transition from the old style of professionalizing new officers into the Navy and a more structured approach. The old recruits continued their training at the new Naval School in a manner similar to that which they would have obtained at the older shore schools. But the Navy implemented a more systematic approach to the recruitment of new students. Statistical sampling in this study showed that the new students were increasingly in their midteens and from the professional and commercial sector of American society. These young men hoped for a naval officer career for a variety of reasons, but typically a naval life was an opportunity for a predictable career where they would meet their economic needs and see the world. Where other professional career options, like a doctor, might have high barriers to entry where the initiate was responsible for funding his training, the government paid for the naval officer's education. Bancroft hoped to enroll students with basic education and keep the entry qualifications reasonable, so that even a poorer boy might rise to the top of the profession. Under this system, the Navy could shape students into the desired career naval officers even if they had little or no sea experience.

Annapolis gave its students a combination of the liberal and practical education a naval officer required. Its objective was to make them gentlemen, able to carry out their duties on ship, in respectable society at home, and relate with nations and peoples abroad. Accordingly, midshipmen learned history, English, French, and Spanish, alongside courses in chemistry, mathematics, ordnance, and new steam technology. Annapolis also acclimatized new midshipmen to the routine of naval life. The new Naval School regulated the lives of students with clockwork efficiency, including their ability to go into the city. Superintendent Buchanan even asserted during the new facility's first year that authorities should regulate the pupils' leisure time to encourage the direction of their activity toward the development of their career. Like a mature profession, the superintendent's objective was to ensure that the pupils were ready for their examinations, where senior naval officers assessed how far the midshipmen had progressed toward fulfilling the knowledge requirements of their profession.

The early years of the new Naval School at Annapolis met with mixed results. The institution had to juggle the training requirements of existing midshipmen with sea experience, and who were set in their ways, with the demands of mentoring young boys new to the profession. The Mexican-American War also disrupted training at Annapolis, and by the late 1840s, the institution's leaders believed they should restructure education into a full four-year officer training program that would only deal with new recruits taken directly from the civilian world and train them systematically rather than be subject to the Navy's daily needs. The Army's success in the Mexican-American War gave Annapolis renewed impetus to further adapt the West Point system to the training needs of naval officers. The result, during the early 1850s, was the reorganization of the Naval School into the Naval Academy and even greater care in the selection and education of potential naval officers.

As an institution for a maturing profession, the Naval Academy carefully selected its young pupils. Academy regulations meant that students ranged between thirteen and eighteen years old and typically needed a solid public school education to pass the Annapolis entrance exam and be successful at their academy studies. Furthermore, during the academy era, like their West Point counterparts, the Navy drew its new officer recruits largely from professional and commercial families, albeit midshipmen received their appointments on the recommendation of their congressmen. Nevertheless, the academy was geographically representative of the nation, with demographics closely matching national averages for fifteen- to twenty-four-year-old white males, with fairly equal representation from North and South. Many fathers and teachers who wrote on behalf of young boys hoping to join the academy noted their honesty, integrity, and desire for a professional career.

It was during the academy era that many famous postbellum officers passed through its doors: Thomas O. Selfridge Jr., George Dewey, Alfred Thayer Mahan, among others. The academy offered such students greater academic rigor and imposed an almost scientific points system to track their progress toward acquiring officer skills. During this period, the academy grew to resemble more closely West Point and civilian colleges, with nine academic departments devoted to professional topics and liberal education. Moreover, regulations stipulated that instructors had to track their teaching endeavors closely as students made their way toward their February and June exams. The academy also soon forced students who had joined the Navy prior to 1845 to finish their studies. For those who remained, the Navy used "moral science" to indoctrinate the young initiates into the ethos of their profession and its relationship with the civilian world.

Moral science, taught with the help of Francis Wayland's *Elements of Moral Science*, provided young officers with a navigational aide to help them serve their client. The academy's Department of Ethics and English Studies instilled in them rigors of logical thinking, steeped in Christian religious beliefs and moral values taken from the Bible. One important object of teaching the midshipmen moral science was to show them that people served a higher purpose, for the students to be more than self-centered individuals. Within the context of the Naval Academy and the role of the naval officer, Wayland's moral science showed the pupils that their profession was a contract between themselves and society and that the armed forces were subservient to the civilian world, their client. As military officers, Wayland emphasized that the professional officer's duty was to carry out their orders; if they objected, they had to leave policy debates to others or resign their commission.

Moral science taught academy pupils the ethics of a professional naval officer, while their other classes gave the would-be officers more practical skills. But the most important instrument the Navy used to indoctrinate its potential officers into their future roles was discipline. The antebellum Naval Academy operated within the context of Navy-wide law and discipline, which had undergone reform during this period with the eventual elimination of such traditions as flogging. Instead, the Navy subjected its men to more measured responses to misbehavior and failures to obey orders. Mutiny remained the gravest offense, which could lead to capital punishment, but officers were subjected to formal proceedings, such as courts of inquiry and courts martial, where a panel of their peers assessed their conduct and its relationship with the Navy's laws and meted out the appropriate punishment. The Navy used similar formal processes at Annapolis.

During both the school and academy eras, the U.S. Navy realized that its officer recruits needed to be introduced gradually to naval law and discipline. Therefore, Annapolis subjected its students to a continuum of disciplinary procedures that depended on the youth of the offender and the seriousness of his offense. Students were subject to demerit points and suspension for various periods, and only as a last resort would Annapolis convene a court martial to deal with the most serious breaches of the Navy's rules. The Navy's objective was to instill in the midshipmen the behavioral expectations of their career, give the pupils an opportunity to reform their conduct, and if they refused, then disciplinary procedures gave the Navy a method by which they could expel those unsuitable for the profession. In its earliest days, Annapolis emphasized the conduct demanded of its future officers.

Professors were responsible for classroom discipline, but ultimately students were responsible to the superintendent and the commandant of midshipmen. The authorities regulated the students strictly and recorded their conduct levels with almost scientific precision in demerit records books. If a midshipman received too many demerit points, the Navy could dismiss him from the service. In turn, most midshipmen responded well to the Navy's rules, with infractions largely limited to breaking liberty regulations and other minor offenses. Significantly, subjecting young students to naval discipline within a graduated context also help instill comradeship in the young officers. Statistical analysis reveals that students reported on one another infrequently. Moreover, when confronted by authorities, the students stuck together and would even petition the Navy for the reinstatement of a dismissed peer. Often only personal disputes of honor between midshipmen affected their degree of corporateness as they learned to work as a team and bonded as colleagues.

The U.S. Naval Academy represented an integrated method to recruit potential officers and instill them with the skills and values of their profession. By the 1850s, the summer training cruises and school ships symbolized these efforts. *Preble*, *Plymouth*, and *Constitution* became the physical textbooks where the students learned the practical aspects of their career, ship management, and how to relate with the rest of a warship's crew. Sociologically, the summer-cruise ships were total institutions, cut off from the rest of society, for the specific purposes of educating young officers. The ships introduced the pupils to their future environment as they interacted with foreigners and regions that affected America. As on shore, the academy regulated the students' lives strictly and recorded their response to education and discipline to quantify their suitability to the Navy. The summer cruises tested the midshipmen's potential as future officers and the success of the academy's shore-based introduction to naval life.

Annapolis in 1845 was not a dramatic break from the past, but by the 1850s the academy was a four-year officer training program with summer training cruises clearly intended to professionalize officer-recruits into the Navy. The numerous vignettes in this study show the goals of the students on applying for midshipmen warrants, how they were treated at the school and academy, and their experiences under the institution's laws and discipline. Taken as a whole, Annapolis authorities conceptualized the students as young, often inexperienced pupils they would turn into professional officers. The students were taught in a methodical environment, their progress in academic subjects, practical seamanship, and discipline measured in a way to train and select those who would go on to become officers. With this in mind, the academy used many of the criteria that scholars look for in a professional organization. This philosophy was evident in how the students were educated and disciplined on shore as well as at sea during the summer. The Civil War interrupted the Naval Academy's activities and tested the professional values the Navy sought to instill in the young initiates.

There was no open fighting between Northern and Southern pupils, but as the country disintegrated, the stresses affected them nonetheless. Still, the midshipmen had assimilated many of the values of a professional officer. Wayland's *Moral Science* instructed readers that officers had to follow their orders, rather than pass judgment on their legitimacy. If they felt at odds with the terms of their service, professionals were committed to resign their posts. Significantly, as the United States edged toward Civil War and states left the union, rather than mutiny or simply leave the Navy without formal approval, many Southern academy students asked for permission to return to their home states. Moreover, the Navy respected the Southern students' rights and rather than arrest potential rebels on sight, the Navy permitted students to resign. But for many students, instructors, and officers the outbreak of Civil War was a professional and personal conundrum as they struggled with professional commitments, personal friendships, and loyalty to home. Some of those who remained left the Navy after several years and were still young men, while others, if they were not killed in action, went on to long years of service. It was these men, like Alfred Thayer Mahan, who laid the groundwork for the spectacular American naval expansion in the late nineteenth and early twentieth centuries.

Disciplinary Records

A n analysis of midshipman conduct was conducted using the Registers of Delinquencies. This analysis was done by taking a 20 percent random sample of midshipmen housed on shore, based on the name index for each section of the rolls, usually an academic year after 1853. Unfortunately, there is a gap in the records from 1850 to 1853, and the records from 1846 to 1850 only contain the name of the students and a basic description of their offense. The records sampled from 1853 to the end of the 1860 academic year contained such information as the offense, reporting personnel, and demerit point issued. Because the specific name an offense was given often changed from day to day, the offenses were reclassified into the general headings shown in the detailed analysis.

Table 13. Counted Offenses for 1846–50

Offense	Total
Breaking Liberty	50
Disobedience of Orders	7
Drunkenness	1
Inattention to Studies	1
Neglect of Duty	24
Tardy at Recitation	26
Unofficerlike Conduct	2

Source: Calculated from Registers of Delinquencies ("Conduct Roll," "Conduct Roll of Cadets"). 1846–50, 1853–82, volumes 346–55, Records of the United States Naval Academy, NA, RG 405. Hereafter, Registers of Delinquencies.

Table 14. Tardiness Breakdown for 1846–50

Recitation	Total
French	15
English	7
Math	3
Mechanics	1

Source: Calculated from Registers of Delinquencies.

Table 15. Offense Analysis for Academic Years 1853–54 and 1854–55

Offense	Count	Percent
Absences	250	22.7
Room Order and Cleanliness	107	9.7
Military Offense (poor marching, etc.)	100	9.1
Visiting	99	9.0
Class Offenses (disorder, etc.)	95	8.6
Lateness	61	5.6
Dereliction of Assigned Duty	51	4.6
Study Hour Violations (receiving visits, etc.)	43	3.9
Skylarking	43	3.9
Mess Hall Offense (noise, throwing bread, etc.)	35	3.2
Using Tobacco in Some Form	32	2.9
Specific Academy Regulation violations	25	2.3
General Noise	22	2.0
Leave Violations	16	1.5
Disobedience of Orders	16	1.5
Dress Uniform Violation	15	1.4
Broken Property	14	1.3
Playing Games (billiards, cards, chess)	12	1.1
After Taps Violations	9	0.8
Making Some Form of Mess	7	0.6
Throwing Objects	5	0.5
Hands in Pockets	5	0.5
Church Offense	4	0.4
Disrespect to Superior	4	0.4
Swearing or Profanity	4	0.4
Insubordination	4	0.4
Poor Conduct (unbecoming of an officer, etc.)	3	0.3
Fighting	2	0.2
Drinking	2	0.2
Unclassifiable Offenses	12	1.1
Missing Cases (offenses)	2	0.2
Total Number of Offenses in 20% Sample	1,099	
Total Number of Midshipmen in 20% Sample	40	
Missing Cases (midshipmen)	1	
Size of Population Sampled	196	

Source: Calculated from Registers of Delinquencies.

Table 16. Detailed Analysis for Academic Years 1853–54 and 1854–55

Absence Breakdown	Count	Percent
Military	190	76.0
Academic	41	16.4
Room (not in study hours specifically)	12	4.8
Military and Academic, Joint	6	2.4
Church	1	0.4
Lateness Breakdown		
Military	33	54.1
Academic	19	31.1
Mess	8	13.1
Military and Academic, Joint	1	1.6
Leave Violations		
From Academic Function Without Permission	5	31.3
From Grounds Without Permission	4	25.0
From Military Function Without Permission	4	25.0
From Church Without Permission	2	12.5
Overstaying Leave	1	6.3
Dereliction of Duty Breakdown		
Other	32	62.7
Permitting Midshipmen to Break Rules	15	29.4
Not Reporting Fellow Midshipmen	4	7.8
Reporting Personnel		
Midshipmen	434	39.5
Officers	286	26.0
Unable to Identify	191	17.4
Professors	181	16.5
Missing Cases	7	0.6
Excuses Recorded		
No Excuse Made	817	74.3
Rejected	141	12.8
Accepted in Full or in Part	95	8.6
Missing Cases	41	3.7
Remitted or Withdrawn	5	0.5
Demerit Point Analysis		
Average	4	
Maximum	18	
Minimum	0	
Standard Deviation	2.44	
Number of Offenses that Received Demerits	1,093	
25.6% of the Midshipmen Committed 52.2% of the Offenses		

Source: Calculated from Registers of Delinquencies.

Table 17. Analysis of Aggregate of Offenses for Academic Years 1855–60

Offense	Count	Percent
Dereliction of Assigned Duties	378	9.6
Study Hour Violations (visiting, etc.)	378	9.6
Room Order and Cleanliness	376	9.5
Absences	374	9.5
Class Offenses (disorder, etc.)	359	9.1
Military Offense (poor marching, etc.)	318	8.0
Lateness	269	6.8
Tobacco Related Offenses	251	6.3
Visiting (outside study hours)	178	4.5
Dress Uniform Violations	129	3.3
Leave Violations	123	3.1
Visiting (outside study hours)	104	2.6
Mess Hall Offense (throwing bread, etc.)	103	2.6
Broken Property	81	2.1
Unclassifiable Offenses	67	1.7
Skylarking	66	1.7
General Noise	63	1.6
After Taps Violations	46	1.2
Making Some Form of Mess	32	0.8
Specific Academy Regulation Violations	29	0.7
Visiting	27	0.7
Lounging About (outside study hours)	26	0.7

(continues on next page)

Table 17. Analysis of Aggregate of Offenses for Academic Years 1855–60 (continued)

Offense	Count	Percent
Poor Conduct (unofficerlike, etc.)	25	0.6
Playing Games (cards, chess, fiddle, etc.)	23	0.6
Throwing Things (snowballs, water, rocks)	17	0.4
Disobedience of Orders	16	0.4
Disrespect to Superior	14	0.4
Regulations Not Complied With (unspecified)	14	0.4
Church Offenses	11	0.3
General Talking	9	0.2
Swearing or Profanity	9	0.2
Drinking	9	0.2
Insubordination	8	0.2
Fighting or Threatening to Fight	8	0.2
Committing Improper Acts or Improprieties	6	0.2
Hands in Pockets	5	0.1
General Disorder	2	0.1
Disorderly (location not specified)	2	0.1
Not Guilty	1	0.0
Offenses Related with North-South Conflict	1	0.0
Missing Cases (offenses)	1	0.0
Total Aggregate Cases	**3,958**	

Source: Calculated from Registers of Delinquencies.

Table 18. Analysis of Aggregate of Offenses for Academic Years 1855–60

Absence Breakdown	Count	Percent
Military	318	85.0
Academic	37	9.9
Church	7	1.9
Military and Church	6	1.6
Academic and Military	4	1.1
Mess	1	0.3
Military and Mess	1	0.3
Lateness Breakdown		
Military	219	81.4
Academic	35	13.0
Mess	14	5.2
Church	1	0.4
Dereliction of Duty Breakdown		
Other (unclassifiable)	228	60.3
Permitting Midshipmen to Break Rules	118	31.2
Not Reporting Fellow Midshipmen	32	8.5
Reporting Personnel		
Officers	2,028	51.2
Midshipmen	1,386	35.0
Professors	413	10.4
Unidentifiable	111	2.8
Doctor	6	0.2
Asst. Librarian	2	0.1
Missing cases	12	0.3
Excuses Recorded		
No Excuse Made	2,754	69.6
Rejected	689	17.4
Accepted in Full or in Part	466	11.8
Missing Cases	42	1.1
Withdrawn/Mistaken	3	0.1
Delinquency Acknowledged	2	0.1
No Such report	2	0.1

Source: Calculated from Registers of Delinquencies.

Table 19. General Summary Statistics for Academic Years 1855–60

Year	1855–56	1856–57	1857–58
Sample Size (mids.)[a]	25	29	36
Pop. Size	126	147	179
Missing (mids.)	0	0	0
Offenses[b]	552	882	784
Missing (offenses)	0	1	0
% Mids. / ~50%[c]	28.0/50.4	24.1/50.6	27.8/49.9
Year	**1858–59**	**1859–60**	**1860–61**
Sample Size (mids.)	39	27	34
Pop. Size	193	137	168
Missing (mids.)	0	1	2
Offenses	587	332	821
Missing (offenses)	0	0	0
% Mids. / ~50%	23.15/51.8	29.6/53.6	31.1/50.3

a 20% sample of population.
b Number of offenses committed by 20% sample of midshipmen.
c Percent of midshipmen who committed approximately 50% of the recorded offenses.

Source: Calculated from Registers of Delinquencies.

Table 20. Demerit Point Analysis for Academic Years 1855–60

Year	1855–56	1856–57	1857–58
Average	3.7	4.0	4.1
Maximum	10	24 [a]	10
Minimum	0	0	0
Standard Deviation	2.04	2.29	2.54
Offenses Given Demerits	546	872	777
Year	**1858–59**	**1859–60**	**1860–61**
Average	4.6	4.6	3.6
Maximum	10	10	10
Minimum	0	1	1
Standard Deviation	2.48	2.29	2.30
Offenses Given Demerits	583	330	813

a P. S. Sanderson was given twenty-four demerit points for being absent from parade, all section formations and recitations on 4 March 1857. This was analyzed as one offense because the authorities dealt with them all at once.

Source: Calculated from Registers of Delinquencies.
Note: Not all offenses were issued demerits. Analysis does not count demerits later removed by superintendent.

Table 21. Offense Analysis for School Ship Academic Year 1859–60

Offense	Count	Percent
Study hours or Study Room Offenses	64	34.0
Absence	17	9.0
Class Offense	15	8.0
Military Offenses	13	6.9
Swearing	12	6.4
Dress Uniform Violations	10	5.3
Dereliction of Assigned Duties	10	5.3
After Taps Violations	7	3.7
Mess Offenses	6	3.2
General Noise	6	3.2
Throwing Objects (books, etc.)	3	1.6
Broken or Defaced Property	3	1.6
Articles in Lucky Bag	2	1.1
Lateness	2	1.1
Fighting	2	1.1
Skylarking	2	1.1
General Talking	2	1.1
Church Offenses	1	0.5
Making Some Form of Mess	1	0.5
Tobacco-related Offenses	1	0.5
Disobedience of Orders	1	0.5
Poor Conduct	1	0.5
Off Ship Without Permission	1	0.5
Specific Academy Regulation Violations	1	0.5
Unclassifiable Offenses	5	2.7
Total Number of Offenses	188	
Missing Cases (offenses)	0	
Size of Population Sampled	92	
Number of Midshipmen in 20% Sample	18	
Missing Cases (midshipmen)	0	

Source: Calculated from Registers of Delinquencies.

Table 22. Detailed Analysis for School Ship Academic Year 1859–60

Absence Breakdown	Count	Percent
Military	9	52.9
Academic	4	23.5
Prayers	3	17.6
Hammocks	1	5.9
Lateness Breakdown		
Academic	1	50.0
Mess	1	50.0
Dereliction of Duty Breakdown		
Other	4	40.0
Not Reporting Fellow Midshipmen	4	40.0
Permitting Midshipmen to Break Rules	2	20.0
Reporting Personnel		
Officers	104	55.3
Midshipmen	74	39.4
Professors	10	5.3
Excuses Recorded		
No Excuse Made	140	74.5
Rejected	27	14.4
Accepted in Full or in Part	20	10.6
Missing Cases	1	0.5
Demerit Point Analysis		
Average	4.6	
Maximum	10	
Minimum	2	
Standard Deviation	2.24	
Offenses Given Demerits	188	
22.2% of the midshipmen committed 58.5% of the offenses		

Source: Calculated from Registers of Delinquencies.

Table 23. Offense Analysis for School Ship Academic Year 1860–61

Offense	Count	Percent
Study Hour/Room Offenses	122	24.9
Military Offenses	57	11.6
Academic Offenses	36	7.3
Lateness	31	6.3
Dereliction of Assigned Duties	25	5.1
Mess Offenses	24	4.9
Absences	22	4.5
Dress Uniform Violations	21	4.3
Disobedience of Orders	14	2.9
Tobacco-related Offenses	13	2.7
Skylarking	12	2.4
General Talking	10	2.0
Swearing or Profanity	10	2.0
Fighting	8	1.6
Room Order and Cleanliness	8	1.6
General Noise	7	1.4
Throwing Things	7	1.4
General Disorder	5	1.0
Disrespect to Superior or Other Officers	4	0.8
After Taps Violations	4	0.8
Making Some Form of Mess	4	0.8
Leave Violations	3	0.6
Playing Games (pennies)	3	0.6
Insubordination	3	0.6
Broken or Defaced Property	3	0.6
Lounging About	3	0.6
Visiting (outside study hours)	2	0.4
General Hammock Offenses	2	0.4
Drinking	1	0.2
Church Offenses	1	0.2
Articles in Lucky Bag	1	0.2
Specific Academy Regulation Violations	1	0.2
Unclassifiable Offenses	23	4.7
Total Number of Offenses	490	
Missing Cases (offenses)	0	
Size of Population Sampled	130	
Number of Midshipmen in 20% Sample	26	
Missing Cases (midshipmen)	4	

Source: Calculated from Registers of Delinquencies.
Note: This analysis covers the period to the end of this academic year, after *Constitution* left Annapolis, because the name index from which the sample was composed covers this entire period.

Table 24. Detailed Analysis for School Ship Academic Year 1860–61

Absence Breakdown	Count	Percent
Military	15	68.2
Academic	3	13.6
Surgeon's Call	2	9.1
Church	1	4.5
Hammocks	1	4.5
Leave Violation Breakdown		
Absent from Building w/o Permission	2	66.7
Absent from Quarterdeck w/o Permission	1	33.3
Dereliction of Duty Breakdown		
Other	20	80.0
Not Reporting Fellow Midshipmen	1	4.0
Permitting Midshipmen to Break Rules	4	16.0
Lateness Breakdown		
Late for Military Function	18	58.1
Late for Hammock Formation	9	29.0
Late for Academic Function	4	12.9
Reporting Personnel		
Midshipmen	274	55.9
Officers	189	38.6
Professors	22	4.5
Doctor	1	0.2
Unidentifiable	4	0.8
Excuses Recorded		
No Excuse Made	346	70.6
Rejected	104	21.2
Accepted in Full or in Part	37	7.6
Missing Cases	3	0.6
Demerit Point Analysis		
Average	3.7	
Maximum	10	
Minimum	1	
Standard Deviation	1.95	
Offenses Given Demerits	485	

Source: Calculated from Registers of Delinquencies.

APPENDIX B.

Summer Cruise Assessments

Craven's 1860 report ranked the students from poor to excellent, and his rankings are reflected in the columns Aptitude and Attention. I assigned each grade a value from 0 and 6, then conducted a statistical analysis. In the tables, Excellent = 6; Very Good = 5; Good = 4; Fair = 3; Tolerable = 2; Indifferent = 1; Poor/None/Very Little = 0.

Table 25. Summer Cruise 1860, First Class

Name	Aptitude	Value	Attention	Value
Armstrong	Good	4	Very Good	5
Backus	Tolerable	2	Good	4
Banche	Excellent	6	Excellent	6
Carnes	Fair	3	Tolerable	2
Comestock, J. H.	Good	4	—	—
Cromwell	Very Good	5	Excellent	6
Cushing	Good	4	Good	4
Dexter	Good	4	Very Good	5
Fiske	Tolerable	2	Tolerable	2
Holden	Very Good	5	Very Good	5
Hudgins	Fair	3	Good	4
Ingraham	Very Good	5	Very Good	5
King	Very Good	5	Very Good	5
McFarland	Very Good	5	Excellent	6
McKay	Very Good	5	Very Good	5
Mullen	Good	4	Very Good	5
Philip	Good	4	Tolerable	2
Picking	Very Good	5	Very Good	5

(continues on next page)

Table 25. Summer Cruise 1860, First Class (continued)

Name	Aptitude	Value	Attention	Value
Rodgers	Fair	3	Fair	3
Ryan	Good	4	Good	4
Sampson	Excellent	6	Excellent	6
Snell	Good	4	Very Good	5
Spencer	Very Good	5	Good	4
Steece	Fair	3	Excellent	6
Stove	Excellent	6	Very Good	5
Sturdivant	Excellent	6	Excellent	6
Wilson	Good	4	Very Good	5
	Average	4.31		4.59
	Standard Dev.	1.12		1.19
	Missing Cases	1		0

Source: Calculated from Craven's aptitude report, in Craven to Blake, 30 September 1860, letters received.

Table 26. Summer Cruise 1860, Second Class

Name	Aptitude	Value	Attention	Value
Duer	Fair	3	Tolerable	2
Higgingson	Good	4	Good	4
Leonard	Indifferent	1	Poor	0
Moore, T. S.	Indifferent	1	Indifferent	1
Rowland	Good	4	Good	4
Smith, N. Y.	Good	4	Good	4
Swift	Good	4	Fair	3
Tyson	Good	4	Very Good	5
	Average	3.13		2.88
	Standard Dev.	1.27		1.62
	Missing	0		0

Source: Calculated from Craven's aptitude report, in Craven to Blake, 30 September 1860, letters received.

Table 27. Summer Cruise 1860, Third Class

Name	Aptitude	Value	Attention	Value
Abbott	Very Good	5	Good	4
Adams	Good	4	Good	4
Alexander	Fair	3	Very Good	5
Anderson	Excellent	6	Excellent	6
Bacot	Good	4	Good	4
Barker	Good	4	Good	4
Bartlett	Good	4	Good	4
Batchellor	Fair	3	Good	4
Beirne	Good	4	Very Good	5
Blake, C. F.	Very Good	5	Very Good	5
Bridgman	Very Good	5	Very Good	5
Brown	Very Good	5	Good	4
Camm	Very Good	5	Very Good	5
Carroll	Good	4	Good	4
Chew F. T.	Very Good	5	Very Good	5
Chew, R. S.	Excellent	6	Very Good	5
Claybrook	Good	4	Very Good	5
Dalton	Tolerable	2	Tolerable	2
Floyd	Very Good	5	Very Good	5
French	Good	4	Good	4
Gregory	Good	4	Good	4
Halcombe	Good	4	Very Good	5
Hammett	Very Good	5	Very Good	5
Haskins	Very Good	5	Good	4
Haswell	Excellent	6	Very Good	5
Hazeltine	Very Good	5	Very Good	5
Hunt	Very Good	5	Very Good	5
Hutter	Good	4	Good	4
Jackson	Good	4	Good	4
Johnson, H. S.	Very Good	5	Very Good	5
Johnson, M. S.	Very Good	5	Excellent	6
Jones	Very Good	5	Very Good	5
Lowry	Good	4	Very Good	5

(continues on next page)

Table 27. Summer Cruise 1860, Third Class (continued)

Name	Aptitude	Value	Attention	Value
McCormick	Excellent	6	Excellent	6
McDermott	Good	4	Very Good	5
Mason	Fair	3	Good	4
Miller	Good	4	Good	4
Naile	Very Good	5	Very Good	5
Pearson	Very Good	5	Very Good	5
Porter	Very Good	5	Excellent	6
Preble	Good	4	Good	4
Price	Fair	3	Tolerable	2
Read, J. H.	Fair	3	Fair	3
Rumsey	Tolerable	2	Fair	3
Sanders	Good	4	Good	4
Scales	Fair	3	Fair	3
Shepard	Good	4	Good	4
Tracy	Good	4	Good	4
Trigg	Good	4	Fair	3
Turner	Very Good	5	Good	4
Walker	Good	4	Good	4
Wallace	Very Good	5	Very Good	5
Wood	Good	4	Very Good	5
Woodward	Very Good	5	Very Good	5
	Average	4.33		4.43
	Standard Dev.	0.90		0.87
	Missing Cases	0		0

Source: Calculated from Craven's aptitude report, in Craven to Blake, 30 September 1860, letters received.

Table 28. Summer Cruise 1860, Fourth Class

Name	Aptitude	Value	Attention	Value
Chester	Tolerable	2	Good	4
Cook	Very Good	5	Very Good	5
Craig	Excellent	6	Very Good	5
Dana	Very Little	0	Indifferent	1
Danton	Good	4	Very Good	5
Flournoy	Good	4	Good	4
Fortune	Fair	3	Good	4
Health	Tolerable	2	Fair	3
Long	Tolerable	2	Fair	3
Ludlow	Good	4	Good	4
Mallory	Good	4	Good	4
McClure	Tolerable	2	Fair	3
McDaniel	Good	4	Good	4
Pipkin	Good	4	Good	4
Poor	Good	4	Fair	3
Robinson	Tolerable	2	Tolerable	2
Sands	Fair	3	Fair	3
Sigsbee	Good	4	Good	4
Stafford	Good	4	Good	4
Thomas	Fair	3	Fair	3
Van	Fair	3	Very Good	5
Vance	Very Good	5	Excellent	6
Wheeler	Indifferent	1	Fair	3
Wilkinson	Very Good	5	Tolerable	2
Wyman	Very Little	0	Fair	3
Young	Fair	3	Good	4
	Average	3.19		3.65
	Standard Dev.	1.47		1.07
	Missing Cases	0		0

Source: Calculated from Craven's aptitude report, in Craven to Blake, 30 September 1860, letters received.

NOTES

Introduction

1. Samuel P. Huntington, *The Soldier and the State: The Theory and Politics of Civil-Military Relations* (Cambridge, Mass.: Harvard University Press, reprint 1964), 8–9. For the relationship between society and the armed forces, see also Jan Glete, *War and the State in Early Modern Europe: Spain, the Dutch Republic and Sweden as Fiscal-Military States, 1500–1660* (London and New York: Routledge, 2002), 1–4. Peter Karsten deals with this wider issue in the Navy. For example, the apparent animosity of officers toward businessmen that, in his view, was instilled during their time at Annapolis (Karsten, *The Naval Aristocracy: The Golden Age of Annapolis and the Emergence of Modern American Navalism* [New York: The Free Press, 1972], 186–89).

2. Allan R. Millett, *The General: Robert L. Bullard and Officership in the United States Army, 1881–1925* (Westport, Conn.: Greenwood Press, 1975), 3–4; and Allan R. Millett, "Military Professionalism and Officership in America," *A Mershon Center Briefing Paper* 2 (May 1977): 2–7.

3. Morris Janowitz, *The Professional Soldier: A Social and Political Portrait* (Glencoe, Ill.: The Free Press, 1960), 6. For a further discussion of the origins of sociological research on the armed forces, see James Burk, "Morris Janowitz and the Origins of Sociological Research on Armed Forces and Society," *Armed Forces and Society* 19, no. 2 (1993): 167–85.

4. Donald Chisholm, *Waiting for Dead Men's Shoes: Origins and Development of the U.S. Navy's Officer Personnel System, 1793–1941* (Stanford, Calif.: Stanford University Press, 2001), 12–13.

5. Huntington, *Soldier and the State*, 237–43, 250.

6. William B. Skelton, "Samuel P. Huntington and the Roots of the American Military Tradition," *The Journal of Military History* 60, no. 2 (April 1996): 326. The literature on the development of late-nineteenth-century scientific management practices is vast. See, for example, Jack Shulimson, "Military Professionalism: The Case of the U.S. Marine Officer Corps, 1880–1898," *The Journal of Military History* 60, no. 2 (April 1996): 232–33. Alfred D. Chandler Jr. wrote an influential work on the emergence of scientific management. Chandler contends that "modern business enterprise" developed in response to "the rapid pace of technological innovation and increasing consumer demand in the United States" after the Civil War. He theorizes that managerial capitalism emerged because of the size and growth of the American market to 1914, the population's economic homogeneity, and antitrust laws. In this atmosphere, Chandler describes the institutional responses to these demands by companies like Standard Oil, General Motors, and DuPont as companies merged, developed managerial hierarchies, and instituted scientific management practices to lower costs and increase profits (*The Visible Hand: The Managerial Revolution in American Business* [Cambridge, Mass.: Harvard University Press, 1977], 12, 415–22, 457, 497–99).

7. Andrea Gabor, *The Capitalist Philosophers: The Geniuses of Modern Business—Their Lives, Times, and Ideas* (New York: Crown Business, 2000), 3.

8. Frederick Winslow Taylor, *The Principles of Scientific Management* (New York: Harper & Row, Publishers, 1911), 36–37, in Taylor, *Scientific Management* (New York: Harper & Row, Publishers, 1947).

9. Millett, "Military Professionalism," 4, 8–12, 17–18, and Millett, *Bullard*, 7, 9–10. Through this prism, Jack Shulimson shows that the Marine Officer Corps' professionalization after the Civil War was tied to the rise of scientific management practices in the civilian world. He concludes that "whether called a 'search for order,' the 'visible hand,' or the 'organizational revolution,' the dominant feature of this entire process was its avowed emphasis upon rationality and control" (Shulimson, "Military Professionalism," 232–33). For an example of professionalization in the civilian world, see Monte A. Calvert, *The Mechanical Engineer in America, 1830–1920: Professional Cultures in Conflict* (Baltimore: Johns Hopkins Press, 1967), 44–51, 62–70, 278–81.

10. Skelton, "Samuel P. Huntington," 326–33.

11. William B. Skelton, *An American Profession of Arms: The Army Officer Corps, 1784–1861* (Lawrence: University Press of Kansas, 1992), 163–66.

12. Millett, "Military Professionalism," 16–17. For examples of such U.S. Navy operations, see Mark C. Hunter, "Anglo-American Political and Naval Response to West Indian Piracy," *International Journal of Maritime History* 13, no. 1 (June 2001): 63–93; and Hunter, *Policing the Seas: Anglo-American Relations and the Equatorial Atlantic, 1819 to 1865* (St. John's, NL: International Maritime Economic History Association, 2008), chapters 3, 4, and 7. See also John H. Schroeder, *Shaping a Maritime Empire: The Commercial and Diplomatic Role of the American Navy, 1829–1861* (Westport, Conn.: Greenwood Press, 1985), 3–5, 39–41.

13. Janowitz, *Professional Soldier*, 127.

14. I compiled a database of over one thousand midshipmen, and if I was unable to clearly identify a midshipman's first name from documents, only their last name appears. The reader should also note that sometimes U.S. documents from this era used British spellings, for example "endeavour" rather than "endeavor." Personal names in notes also appear as in the original documents, including abbreviated ranks and initials.

15. James Calvert, "The Fine Line at the Naval Academy," *United States Naval Institute Proceedings* 96, no. 10/812 (October 1970): 63.

Chapter 1. The Foundation of a System

1. Harvey J. Graff, *Conflicting Paths: Growing Up in America* (Cambridge, Mass.: Harvard University Press, 1995), 32.

2. The Naval Academy, under engineering teacher Robert H. Thurston, only began producing true engineers after the Civil War. The Morrill Land-Grant Colleges Act (1862) was one impetus for the creation of engineering schools from 1868 to 1872. The act, to fund agricultural and mechanical colleges, gave some states land to sell. Other schools were founded, like the Stevens Institute of Technology in New Jersey in 1870. The school attracted Thurston from the Naval Academy to teach engineering. Thurston helped establish technical training, and the Stevens' model was followed by schools like Indiana land-grant college Purdue University. Meanwhile, from 1879 to 1896, the Naval Engineer Corps sent mechanical engineers to civilian schools, like St. John's College next to the Naval Academy in Annapolis, to teach (Calvert, *Mechanical Engineer in America*, 44–51).

3. H. W. Dickinson, *Educating the Royal Navy: Eighteenth- and Nineteenth-Century Education for Officers* (New York: Routledge, 2007), 9; and Michael Lewis, *England's Sea-Officers: The Story of the Naval Profession* (London: George Allen & Unwin, Ltd., 1948), 17–31.

4. Norbert Elias, *The Genesis of the Naval Profession*, René Moelker and Stephen Mennell, eds. (Dublin: University College Dublin Press, 2007), 31.

5. Ibid., 17, 30–32.

6. Charles Consolvo, "The Prospects and Promotion of British Naval Officers 1793–1815," *Mariner's Mirror* 91, no. 2 (May 2005): 137.

7. N. A. M. Rodger, *The Command of the Ocean: A Naval History of Britain, 1649–1815* (London: Allen Lane and the National Maritime Museum, 2004), 112–14, 121–22.

8. Consolvo, "British Naval Officers," 137; and Rodger, *Command of the Ocean*, 381.

9. Consolvo, "British Naval Officers," 138–40.

10. Jaap R. Bruijn, *The Dutch Navy of the Seventeenth and Eighteenth Centuries* (Columbia: University of South Carolina Press, 1993), 69–70.

11. Elias, *Naval Profession*, 103–12; Bernard Lutun, "Le Plan d'Estaing de 1763 ou L'Impossible reforme de la Marine," *Revue historique* 292, no. 1 (1994): 3–29. For a detailed discussion of French naval officers in the ancien régime, see Michel Vergé-Franceschi, "Les officiers généraux de la Marine royale (1669–1774)," *Revue historique* 278, no. 2 (1987): 335–60; and Pierre Lévêque, "Le Destin des Officiers de Marine de L'Ancien Regime a L'Empire," *Historique des Armées* 2 (2001): 101–12. Many French officers opposed the American Revolution, and during the French Revolution the new regime put the navy under local port control, further exacerbating tensions (Gilbert Bodinier, "Les Officiers de la Marine Royale a L'Epoque de la Guerre d'Amerique," *Revue Historique des Armées* 1995 [4]: 3–12; and William S. Cormack and Norman E. Saul, "Revolutionary Conflict in the French Navy: The Court Martial of Captain Basterot," *Consortium on Revolutionary Europe 1750–1850: Proceedings* 20 [1990]: 753–59).

12. Bruijn, *Dutch Navy*, 41–40, 69–70, 111–12, 173–74, 180.

13. Dickinson, *Educating the Royal Navy*, 33.

14. Jacob Seerup, "The Royal Danish Naval Academy in the Age of Enlightenment," *Mariner's Mirror* 93, no. 3 (August 2007): 327–34.

15. Dickinson, *Educating the Royal Navy*, 18–32; Lewis, *England's Sea Officers*, 87–90.

16. Dickinson, *Educating the Royal Navy*, 33–56; Lewis, *England's Sea Officers*, 87–90; F. B. Sullivan, "The Royal Academy at Portsmouth, 1729–1806," *Mariner's Mirror* 63, no. 4 (November 1977), 311–26; Rodger, *Command of the Ocean*, 387. See also, H. W. Dickinson, "The Portsmouth Naval Academy, 1733–1806," *Mariner's Mirror* 89, no. 1 (February 2003): 17–30.

17. Dickinson, *Educating the Royal Navy*, 57–75, and Lewis, *England's Sea Officers*, 90–94, 99–102.

18. Henry L. Burr, "Education in the Early Navy" (Ph.D. diss., Temple University, 1939), 43–44, 175–77, 179–82, 185; and Chisholm, *Dead Men's Shoes*, 29–30, 56–58, 130, 142. For a history of the early organization of the U.S. Navy officer corps, see Chisholm, *Dead Men's Shoes*, 51–76.

19. Burr, "Education in the Early Navy," 8–9.

20. A detailed individual biographical discussion of naval officers is beyond the scope of this study and has been covered admirably in James C. Bradford, ed., *Command Under Sail: Makers of the American Naval Tradition, 1775–1850* (Annapolis: Naval Institute Press, 1985);

Bradford, ed., *Captains of the Old Steam Navy: Makers of American Naval Tradition, 1840–1880* (Annapolis: Naval Institute Press, 1986); and Bradford, ed., *Quarterdeck and Bridge: Two Centuries of American Naval Leaders* (Annapolis: Naval Institute Press, 1997).

21. Christopher McKee, *A Gentlemanly and Honorable Profession: The Creation of the U.S. Naval Officer Corps, 1794–1815* (Annapolis: Naval Institute Press, 1991), 169.

22. Ibid., 194, and Burr, "Education in the Early Navy," 16.

23. Burr, "Education in the Early Navy," 18–20.

24. Huntington, *Soldier and the State*, 8–9; and David Edwin Lebby, "Professional Socialization of the Naval Officer: The Effect of Plebe Year at the U.S. Naval Academy" (Ph.D. diss., Columbia University, 1968), 23, 39–40. The "team" concept is associated mostly with Nelson and his fellow officers, but probably has a longer tradition. Captains traditionally consulted their crews and fellow captains and ideally only made decisions if there was consensus. Eventually, this led to the naval officer class seeing itself as a family. As midshipmen at Annapolis will reveal, this led to fellow midshipmen rarely "ratting" on each other.

25. Burr, "Education in the Early Navy," 84–88.

26. Ibid., 102–3.

27. McKee, *Gentlemanly and Honorable Profession*, 156. Arthur N. Gilbert found that in the eighteenth-century Royal Navy, the class-like separation of officers and men may have led to officers thinking that severe discipline was appropriate. In a unique psychoanalysis, Gilbert concludes that RN midshipmen, while in training aboard ship, saw the vices of the common men below decks, while striving for the ideals of the ordered, gentlemanly society of officers above deck. Although I fail to grasp the psychological nuances that support the study, somehow the midshipman's exposure resulted in the grown officer imposing severe discipline on the men in an attempt to impose gentlemanly order below (Gilbert, "Crime as Disorder: Criminality and the Symbolic Universe of the 18th Century British Naval Officer," in Robert William Love Jr., ed., *Changing Interpretations and New Sources in Naval History: Papers from the Third United States Naval Academy History Symposium* [New York and London: Garland Publishing, Inc., 1980], 110–22).

28. Albert Gleaves, *Life and Letters of Rear Admiral Stephen B. Luce, U.S. Navy, Founder of the Naval War College* (New York: G. P. Putnam's Sons, 1925), 6–8.

29. Ibid., 8.

30. Ibid., 9–10.

31. Ibid., 13.

32. Ibid., 22.

33. Robert J. Schneller Jr., *A Quest for Glory: A Biography of Rear Admiral John A. Dahlgren* (Annapolis: Naval Institute Press, 1996), 3–7.

34. Ibid., 8, 10–11. For more on Samuel Francis DuPont, see James M. Merrill, *Du Pont, the Making of an Admiral: A Biography of Samuel Francis Du Pont* (New York: Dodd, Mead, 1986).

35. Schneller, *Quest for Glory*, 17, 19, 21–23, 30–31, 36–37, 78. Foote supported temperance and slave trade suppression, for instance (Spencer C. Tucker, *Andrew Hull Foote: Civil War Admiral on Western Waters* [Annapolis: Naval Institute Press, 2000], 39–51, 55–60, 68).

36. McKee, *Gentlemanly and Honorable Profession*, 203–5 and Burr, "Education in the Early Navy," 147–48. Naval chaplains doubled at sea as teachers and the captain's secretary, so it is no surprise that one was asked to teach navigation and mathematics. The chaplain was only given time away from serving the captain to teach midshipmen and other crew members,

if their captains, like Captains David Porter or Thomas Truxtun, believed in classroom-style education (McKee, *Gentlemanly and Honorable Profession*, 201).

37. Ibid., 205–8.

38. Burr, "Education in the Early Navy," 151–54.

39. Ibid., 161–64.

40. Benjamin F. Sands, *From Reefer to Rear-Admiral: Reminiscences and Journal Jottings of Nearly Half a Century of Naval Life* (New York: Frederick A. Stokes Company, 1899), 1, 6–7, 9–10.

41. Ibid., 70–71, 73–74, 78; Edward W. Callahan, ed., *List of Officers of the Navy of the United States and of the Marine Corps from 1775 to 1900* (New York: Haskell House, reprint 1969), 145. Revised edition available online at <http://www.history.navy.mil/books/callahan/index.htm>.

42. Burr, "Education in the Early Navy," 149–57.

43. Ibid., 159–60.

44. Frank M. Bennett, *The Steam Navy of the United States: A History of the Growth of the Steam Vessels of War in the U.S. Navy, and of the Naval Engineer Corps* (Westport, Conn.: Greenwood Press, reprint 1972), 34–35, 53–60, 62–67, 652–53, and appendix B, "A List of Steam Vessels of War That Have Been Built for the United States Navy . . . "; David L. Canney, *The Old Steam Navy, Volume One: Frigates, Sloops, and Gunboats, 1815–1885* (Annapolis: Naval Institute Press, 1990), 27–30; and William H. Thiesen, *Industrializing American Shipbuilding: The Transformation of Ship Design and Construction, 1820–1920* (Gainesville: University Press of Florida, 2006), 140–68. For details of how steam warships were used on some stations, see for instance, Hunter, "West Indian Piracy," 63–93.

45. A. P. Upshur, "Report of the Secretary of the Navy," 4 December 1841, *Cong. Globe*, 27th Cong., 2nd sess., appendix, 22 (1841).

46. F. M. Brown, "A Half Century of Frustration: A Study of the Failure of Naval Academy Legislation Between 1800 and 1845," United States Naval Institute *Proceedings* 80, no. 6 (June 1954): 631–35; and Chisholm, *Dead Men's Shoes*, 75–77. Federalists were conservative and wanted a strong central government, while anti-Federalists, like Thomas Jefferson's Republicans, preferred a weaker central government, more power to the states, and individual freedom. For a further discussion, see Gordon S. Wood, *The Creation of the American Republic 1776–1787* (Chapel Hill: University of North Carolina Press, 1969), 474–75, 508, 510, 544–45; and Joyce Appleby, *Inheriting the Revolution: The First Generation of Americans* (Cambridge, Mass.: Belknap Press, 2000), 26–27.

47. Chisholm, *Dead Men's Shoes*, 30–31. James Roger Sharp notes that Federalist and Republican views could be paradoxical and inconsistent. Moreover, by the early nineteenth century, Republicans split between those suspicious of banking and those who advocated federal involvement in the nation's growth. Moreover, U.S. politics became more confused as Federalists disappeared from the political stage or joined other parties, Republican and Democrat (James Roger Sharp, *American Politics in the Early Republic: The New Nation in Crisis* [New Haven: Yale University Press, 1993], 8–10, 279–84).

48. Senate, 8 August 1842, *Cong. Globe*, 27th Cong., 2nd sess., 859 (1842). Congressional biographical information from United States, Congress, *Biographical Directory of the United States Congress, 1774–1989* (Washington, D.C.: GPO, 1988; updates at http://bioguide.congress.gov), Senate Document 100-34.

49. Ibid., 859–60 (1842).

50. Senate, 9 August 1842, *Cong. Globe*, 27th Cong., 2nd sess., 864 (1842).

51. Ibid.

52. Ibid.

53. Senate, 8 August 1842, *Cong. Globe*, 27th Cong., 2nd sess., 859–60 (1842).

54. Senate, 9 August 1842, *Cong. Globe*, 27th Cong., 2nd sess., 864 (1842), and House, 13 August 1842, *Cong. Globe*, 27th Cong., 2nd sess., 888 (1842).

55. Frances Seward to Lazette Worden, 23 December 1842, in Judith A. Nientimp, "The *Somers* Mutiny," *University of Rochester Library Bulletin* 20, no. 1 (Autumn 1964): <http://www.lib.rochester.edu/index.cfm?PAGE=2477>; Craig L. Symonds, *Confederate Admiral: The Life and Wars of Franklin Buchanan* (Annapolis: Naval Institute Press, 1999), 69–70; John P. Lovell, *Neither Athens nor Sparta? The American Service Academies in Transition* (Bloomington and London: Indiana University Press, 1970), 28; Jack Sweetman, *The U.S. Naval Academy: An Illustrated History* (Annapolis: Naval Institute Press, 1979), 3–5. See also *Proceedings of the Court of Inquiry . . . Mutiny on Board the United States Brig of War Somers* (New York: Greeley & McElrath, 1843) and *Proceedings of the Naval Court Martial: In the Case of Alexander Slidell Mackenzie* (New York: Henry G. Langley, 1844).

56. A. P. Upshur, "Report of the Secretary of the Navy, Navy Department," December 1842, *Cong. Globe*, 27th Cong., 3rd sess., appendix, 41 (1842).

57. Ibid., appendix, 42 (1842).

58. Lilian Handlin, *George Bancroft: The Intellectual as Democrat* (New York: Harper & Row, Publishers, 1984), 18–34, 92–181.

59. Chisholm, *Dead Men's Shoes*, 199–200. Chisholm admits that his extensive study of the U.S. officer corps omitted any substantial analysis of the Naval Academy and its curriculum but suggests that it "would provide a great window into thinking about what naval officers should be" (40–41).

60. Sweetman, *Naval Academy*, 12–16.

61. George Bancroft to Franklin Buchanan, 7 August 1845, in *Plan and Regulations of the Naval School at Annapolis* (Washington, D.C.: C. Alexander, Printer, 1847), 3–4.

62. James L. Morrison Jr., *"The Best School in the World": West Point, the Pre-Civil War Years, 1833–1866* (Kent, Ohio: Kent State University Press, 1986), ix–x, 2–3.

63. Ibid., 32–35.

64. Ibid., 4, 23–30, 73–74, 121.

65. Ibid., 39–43, 64–71.

66. Ibid., 44–55.

67. Ibid., 59, 91–94, 114–15, and 122–25.

68. Park Benjamin, *The United States Naval Academy* (New York and London: G. P. Putnam's Sons, 1900), 144–45.

69. Ibid., 146–48.

70. Symonds, *Confederate Admiral*, 71. See also Henry Francis Sturdy, "The Establishment of the Naval School at Annapolis," *United States Naval Institute Proceedings* 72 (April 1946, part II): 10–12.

71. S. Marcy to Hon. Geo. Brancroft, 18 July 1845, reprinted in John D. Hayes, "Influence of West Point on the Founding of the Naval Academy," *Assembly* 19 (Winter 1961): 10–11.

72. Ibid., 11.

73. George Bancroft to Franklin Buchanan, 7 August 1845, in *Plan and Regulations of the Naval School at Annapolis*, 5–6.

74. Symonds, *Confederate Admiral*, 67–68, 72; and Buchanan, "Plan of the Naval School at Fort Severn, Annapolis, Md.," in *Plan and Regulations of the Naval School at Annapolis*, 9–10.

75. Buchanan, "Plan of the Naval School at Fort Severn, Annapolis, Md.," in *Plan and Regulations of the Naval School at Annapolis*, 10–11.

76. Franklin Buchanan to George Bancroft, "Rules to Govern Examinations at the Naval School at Fort Severn, Annapolis, Maryland," 14 August 1845, approved 28 August 1846, in *Plan and Regulations of the Naval School at Annapolis*, 18–19.

77. Ibid., 19–20.

78. Buchanan, "Rules and Regulations for the Internal Government of the Naval School," 10 October 1845, Letters received by the superintendent of the U.S. Naval Academy, 1845–1887, Records of the United States Naval Academy, National Archives (NA), Record Group (RG) 405. Hereafter, letters received.

79. Franklin Buchanan, 15 October 1845, letters received.

80. Bancroft, "Report of the Secretary of the Navy 1845," 1 December 1845, *Cong. Globe*, 29th Cong., 1st sess., appendix, 17 (1845).

81. Ibid.

82. Ibid.

Chapter 2. The Naval School, 1845–1849

1. Walter C. Ford and J. Buroughs Stokes, "The Selection and Procurement of Better Candidate Material for the Naval Academy," United States Naval Institute *Proceedings* 71 (April 1946, part II): 19; Chisholm, *Waiting for Dead Men's Shoes*, 191; and "An Act Making Appropriations for the Naval Service . . ." 3 March 1845, Section 5, *Statutes at Large*, 28th Cong., 2nd sess., 794 (1845).

2. U.S. Naval Academy Alumni Association, *Register of Alumni, Graduates and Former Naval Cadets and Midshipmen*, 91st Edition (Annapolis: The Naval Academy Alumni Association, 1976). Hereafter, Register of Alumni; and United States Naval Academy, Registers of Candidates for Admission to the Academy, Oct. 1849–Oct. 1860, Records of the United States Naval Academy, NA, RG 405. Hereafter, Registers of Candidates for Admission. Percentage of white males between fifteen and twenty-four calculated from Ben J. Wattenberg, *The Statistical History of the United States from Colonial Times to the Present* (New York: Basic Books, Inc., 1976), Series A 195–209, "Population: Population of States, by Sex, Race, Urban-Rural Residence, and Age: 1790 to 1970," 24–37; and McKee, *Gentlemanly and Honorable Profession*, table 2.

3. McKee, *Gentlemanly and Honorable Profession*, 69, 82, 88.

4. Ibid., 111–15.

5. George Twiggs to George Bancroft, 13 June 1846, miscellaneous letters received by the secretary of the Navy, Naval Records Collection of the Office of Naval Records and Library, Records of the Office of the Secretary of the Navy, NA, RG 45. Hereafter, misc. letters received by the secretary.

6. Chisholm, *Dead Men's Shoes*, 179, and Hunter, *Policing the Seas*, 122–26.

7. H. Nutes to secretary of the Navy, 16 May 1846, misc. letters received by the secretary.

8. Buchanan, "Plan of the Naval School at Fort Severn, Annapolis, Md.," in *Plan and Regulations of the Naval School at Annapolis*, 9–10.

9. John Parrish Jr. to secretary of the Navy, 17 April 1846, misc. letters received by the secretary.

10. Marcus L. Dadley to secretary of the Navy, 16 September 1845, misc. letters received by the secretary.

11. James Van Allen to secretary of the Navy, 30 January 1846, misc. letters received by the secretary.

12. Richard G. Parker to secretary of the Navy, 27 May 1846, misc. letters received by the secretary.

13. Robert Taylor to secretary of the Navy, 24 November 1845, misc. letters received by the secretary.

14. Lawrence J. Reiss to secretary of the Navy, 26 March 1846, misc. letters received by the secretary.

15. Isaiah Townsend to D. S. Dickinson, 27 March 1846, misc. letters received by the secretary.

16. Paul Dillingham Jr. to secretary of the Navy, 12 March 1846, misc. letters received by the secretary.

17. Washington Haxtun to secretary of the Navy, 16 December 1845, misc. letters received by the secretary.

18. John W. Davis to secretary of the Navy, 7 January 1846, misc. letters received by the secretary.

19. John Lawrence to secretary of the Navy, 13 February 1846, misc. letters received by the secretary.

20. John Davis to secretary of the Navy, 13 May 1846, misc. letters received by the secretary.

21. George Springer to the president of the United States, 16 May 1846, misc. letters received by the secretary.

22. Midshipmen were referred to by their date of appointment to the Navy, which might be different from the year in which they first attended the Naval School or academy if they first went to sea. Hence '41 Date, or Date of 1841, refers to midshipmen appointed in 1841.

23. McKee, *Gentlemanly and Honorable Profession*, 89–95.

24. Craig L. Symonds, "Introduction," in William Harwar Parker, *Recollections of a Naval Officer 1841–1865* (Annapolis: Naval Institute Press, reprint 1985), ix–xiii.

25. Ibid., 130–31, 137.

26. Ibid., 134, 137.

27. Gleaves, *Stephen B. Luce*, 23–35.

28. Ibid., 39.

29. The secretary of the Navy to Lieutenant A. J. Dallas, 17 October 1837, in Gardner W. Allen, ed., *The Papers of Francis Gregory Dallas. United States Navy. Correspondence and Journal, 1837–1859* (New York: De Vinne Press, reprint 1917), 1. Hereafter, Dallas Papers.

30. The secretary of the Navy to F. G. Dallas, 2 April 1838, Dallas Papers, 2.

31. Hon. Samuel Cushman to Lieutenant A. J. Dallas, 24 June 1839, Dallas Papers, 3–4.

32. The secretary of the Navy to Acting Midshipman F. G. Dallas, 8 November 1841, Dallas Papers, 5.

33. The secretary of the Navy to Acting Midshipman Dallas, 24 November and 25 December 1841; Downes to Dallas, 28 December 1841; the secretary of the Navy to Midshipman Dallas, 21 March 1943; the secretary of the Navy to Midshipman Dallas, 11 January 1845, Dallas Papers, 6–9.

34. The secretary of the Navy to Midshipman Dallas, 7 April 1845 and 10 March 1846; Captain F. H. Gregory to Midshipman Francis G. Dallas, 19 March 1846, Dallas Papers, 10–12.

35. Assistant Surgeon Taylor to Midshipman Dallas, 15 May 1848, Dallas Papers, 24.

36. Midshipman Dallas to Surgeon Hulse, 3 June 1846; Commodore Conner to Midshipman Dallas, 4 June 1846; Midshipman Dallas to Commodore Conner, 4 July 1846; Commodore Conner to Midshipman Dallas, 4 July 1846; Midshipman Dallas to Commodore Conner, 16 September 1846; Commodore Conner to Midshipman Dallas, 18 September 1846, Dallas Papers, 12–18.

37. The secretary of the Navy to Midshipman Dallas, 4 November 1846 and 6 January 1847; Midshipman Dallas to the secretary of the Navy, 2 March 1847; The secretary of the Navy to Midshipman Dallas, 10 March 1847; Commodore Matthew C. Perry to Midshipman Dallas, 20 November 1847; Commander Upshur to Midshipman Dallas, 6 May 1848, Dallas Papers, 18–22.

38. United States, Abstracts of Service Records of Naval Officers ("Records of Officers"), 1798–1893, Naval Records Collection of the Office of the Naval Records and Library, Records of the Bureau of Naval Personnel, NA, RG 45. Hereafter, Abstracts of Service Records.

39. Abstracts of Service Records.

40. Benjamin, *Naval Academy*, 155–156.

41. Lt. Ward to Franklin Buchanan, 7 October 1845, letters received.

42. Ibid.

43. Ibid.

44. Ibid.

45. Prof. Chauvenet, Prof. Coffin, and Prof. W. F. Hopkins. "Courses of Studies Recommended to Be Pursued at the Academy," fall 1845, letters received.

46. Ibid.

47. Ibid.

48. Robert Marr et al., to Professor Lockwood, 5 December 1845, letters received.

49. Quarterly reports contained a cover letter with any comments from the superintendent, followed by the professors' grade reports on each subject.

50. Buchanan to Bancroft, 30 January 1846, Letters sent by the superintendent of the U.S. Naval Academy 1845–65, Records of the United States Naval Academy, NA, RG 405. Hereafter, letters sent.

51. Ibid.

52. Ibid., 16 April 1846, letters sent.

53. Lt. Ward to Franklin Buchanan, 25 April 1846, letters received.

54. Register of Alumni.

55. Lt. Ward to Commander Buchanan, 11 July 1846, letters received.

56. Register of Alumni.

57. Board of Examiners, Naval School, to secretary of the Navy, 11 July 1846, letters received.

58. Ibid.

59. Bennett, *Steam Navy*, 652–53.

60. Lt. Ward to Commander Buchanan, 13 August 1846, letters received.

61. Ibid. Ward was likely referring to Professor Denison Olmsted's *Rudiments of Natural Philosophy and Astronomy: Designed for the Younger Classes in Academies, and for Common Schools* (New York: Collins & Brother, 1846).

62. Lt. Ward to Commander Buchanan, 13 August 1846, letters received. Most likely Nathaniel Bowditch's *The New American Practical Navigator* (New York: E. & G. W. Blunt, 1846).

63. Lt. Ward to Commander Buchanan, 13 August 1846, letters received.

64. Ibid.

65. Buchanan to Bancroft, "Rules to Govern Examinations at the Naval School at Fort Severn, Annapolis, Maryland," 19–20.

66. James Russell Soley, *Historical Sketch of the United States Naval Academy* (Washington, D.C.: GPO, 1876), 85–86; and Bennett, *Steam Navy*, 653.

67. Buchanan to J. Y. Mason, 14 January 1847, letters sent.

68. Callahan, ed., *List of Officers*.

69. Buchanan to J. Y. Mason, 14 January 1847, letters sent.

70. Buchanan to J. Y. Mason, 26 April 1847, letters sent.

71. William Chauvenet to Commander Upshur, 11 October 1847, letters received.

72. G. P. Upshur to J. Y. Mason, (undated November) 1847, letters sent.

73. William Chauvenet to Commander Upshur, 30 Oct 1847, letters received.

74. Louis H. Bolander, "The Naval Academy in Five Wars," United States Naval Institute *Proceedings* 71 (April 1946, part II): 35–36.

75. Ibid., 36.

76. George P. Upshur to J. Y. Mason, 20 January 1848, letters sent.

77. J. Y. Mason to Chas. W. Copeland, 18 February 1848, letters received.

78. G. P. Upshur to J. Y. Mason, 6 May 1848, letters sent.

79. G. P. Upshur to William B. Preston, 26 March 1849, letters sent.

80. G. P. Upshur to William Ballard Preston, 28 April 1849, letters sent.

81. G. P. Upshur to William B. Preston, 26 March 1849, letters sent.

82. Register of Alumni.

83. Benjamin, *Naval Academy*, 186.

84. G. P. Upshur to Chauvenet, 22 December 1848, letters sent.

85. J. Y. Mason, "Report of the Secretary of the Navy," 4 December 1848, *Cong. Globe*, 30th Cong., 2nd sess., appendix, 24–25 (1848), and Soley, *Naval Academy*, 89.

CHAPTER 3. THE NAVAL ACADEMY, 1850–1860

1. Soley, *Naval Academy*, 88–89, 90.

2. William Branford Shubrick to William Ballard Preston, 22 August 1849, letters received; and Benjamin, *Naval Academy*, 188. Benjamin suggests this was the Academic Board, while Soley contends it was a special board the secretary composed to review the school (Soley, *Naval Academy*, 89), but my research indicates it was really the Examining Board, also tasked to study the situation at Annapolis.

3. William Branford Shubrick to William Ballard Preston, 22 August 1849, letters received.

4. Soley, *Naval Academy*, 91. Although a sloop of war was ordered attached to the school since at least 1847, it was only instituted in practice in 1851 (see chapter 6).

5. United States Naval Academy, *Regulations of the United States Naval Academy* [1849] (Washington, D.C.: GPO, 1849). It is unclear from the documentation when these regulations started. Although called the 1849 regulations, it seems the Navy only implemented them fully in 1850, when the Academy was instituted formally (Soley, *Naval Academy*, 89). Still, age profiles of the 1849 academic-year students are dramatically lower than previous years, and meet the 1849 regulations. Consequently, it seems likely that some recommendations were implemented in 1849.

6. Soley, *Naval Academy*, 98.

7. Charles Todorich, *The Spirited Years: A History of the Antebellum Naval Academy* (Annapolis: Naval Institute Press, 1984), 68–70; and United States Naval Academy, *Regulations of the U.S. Naval Academy at Annapolis, Maryland* (Washington, D.C.: A. O. P Nicholson, Printer, 1855), 5–6, 13–19. Hereafter, Regulations, 1855.

8. Todorich, *Spirited Years*, 81–84; and Regulations, 1855, 21–22.

9. Regulations, 1855, 23.

10. Benjamin, *Naval Academy*, 216–17.

11. Regulations, 1855, 19–20.

12. Ibid., 21–22.

13. J. H. C. Coffin, Henry H. Lockwood, and William Chauvenet to Cdr. L. M. Goldsborough, 28 June 1855, letters received.

14. A. E. K. Benham et al., to the gentlemen of the Academic Board, 20 November 1852, letters received.

15. Francis Wayland, *The Elements of Moral Science* (Cambridge, Mass.: Belknap Press of Harvard University Press, reprint 1963). Wayland's revised 1835 edition was republished in 1837 and sold about 75,000 copies. The 1835 and 1837 editions were also used at other colleges. Joseph L. Blau, "A Note on the Text," in Wayland, *Moral Science*.

16. J. E. Nourse to G .S. Blake, 8 December 1858, letters received.

17. Graham to Stribling, 15 September 1851, letters received.

18. Wayland, *Moral Science*, 18–19.

19. Ibid., 71–74.

20. Ibid., 74.

21. Ibid., 134–35.

22. Ibid., 183, 187–88, 191.

23. Ibid., 329–32.

24. Ibid., 332.

25. A. E. K. Benham et al., to the gentlemen of the Academic Board, 20 November 1852, letters received.

26. According to organ dealer Henry Erben, who provided an estimate on the best type of organ for the chapel, it was fifty-five feet long and twenty-five feet high. Erben's son, Henry Jr., attended Annapolis with the Date of '49, served the Navy for forty-five years, and retired as a rear admiral (Register of Alumni). His father wrote, "I feel disposed to do as much as I possibly can [regarding the organ], feeling an interest in the Institution on an account of my son having been there and also the interest I take in the Navy" (Henry Erben to William Chauvenet, 16 July 1853, letters received).

27. Karsten, *Naval Aristocracy*, 31.

28. Regulations, 1849, Sections 12 and 24.

29. G. S. Blake, 20 January 1859, letters received.

30. G. S. Blake to H. H. Wiling (illegible), 26 February 1859, letters sent.

31. M. C. Perry, president of Board of Examiners to William A. Graham, 10 June 1852, letters received.

32. C. K. Stribling to John P. Kennedy, 22 November 1852, letters sent.

33. C. S. McCauley, president of the Board of Examiners to J. C. Dobbin, 17 June 1853, letters received.

34. United States Naval Academy, *Revised Regulations of the U.S. Naval Academy at Annapolis, Maryland* (1853) (Washington, D.C.: Robert Armstrong, Printer, 1853). Hereafter, Regulations, 1853.

35. L. M. Goldsborough to J. C. Dobbin, 10 July 1854, letters sent.

36. Ibid.

37. Regulations, 1855, 1–4.

38. Skelton, *American Profession of Arms*, 163–66.

39. Ibid., 158–59.

40. Ibid., 163–66.

41. Mr. Chase et al., "Sons of Officers who Reported and were rejected, admitted, or Subsequently Rejected" in "Portfolio of Statistics . . . ," 1 September 1899, letters received.

42. Ford and Stokes, "Better Candidate Material for the Naval Academy," 19–20, and "An Act Making Appropriations for the Naval Service . . . ," 31 August 1852, *Statutes at Large*, 32nd Cong., 1st sess., 102 (1852).

43. Isaac Toucey to George Blake, 27 February 1861, letters received.

44. Coffin and Lockwood to Blake, 4 March 1861, letters received.

45. John W. Faires to Benjamin Etting, 26 February 1851, letters received.

46. Register of Alumni.

47. Biographical information from Register of Alumni and Registers of Candidates for Admission; educational background from U. D. Lathrop to Naval Academy, 8 August 1854, letters received.

48. William B. Preston to George P. Upshur, 14 May 1850, letters received.

49. William A. Graham to C. K. Stribling, 5 October 1850, letters received.

50. Register of Alumni.

51. J. A. Webber to C. K. Stribling, 2 October 1851, letters received.

52. William A. Graham to C. K. Stribling, 3 October 1951, letters received.

53. Registers of Candidates for Admission and Register of Alumni.

54. C. K. Stribling to John P. Kennedy, 31 January 1853, letters sent.

55. Register of Alumni; Registers of Candidates for Admission; and Callahan, ed., *List of Officers*, 484. It is unclear why so many of these examples of students I found in the records failed to graduate. It is likely that the administration better maintained documents related to such students in case of appeal.

56. Thomas O. Selfridge Jr., *What Finer Tradition: The Memoirs of Thomas O. Selfridge Jr., Rear Admiral, U.S.N.* (Columbia: University of South Carolina Press, reprint 1987), 3–6.

57. Ibid., 8–10.

58. George Dewey, *Autobiography of George Dewey: Admiral of the Navy* (New York: AMS Press, reprint 1969), 3–7.

59. Ibid., 8.

60. Ibid., 10–13.

61. Ibid., 14–15.

62. Ibid., 16–20.

63. Alfred Thayer Mahan, *From Sail to Steam: Recollections of Naval Life* (New York: Da Capo Press, reprint 1968), 47, 72–73.

64. Ibid., 54–56.

65. Charles E. Clark, *My Fifty Years in the Navy* (Annapolis: Naval Institute Press, reprint 1984), 1–3.

66. Ibid., 4–5.

67. Ibid., 5–6, and Register of Alumni.

68. Robley D. Evans, *A Sailor's Log: Recollection of Forty Years of Naval Life* (Annapolis: Naval Institute Press, reprint 1994), 10–12.

69. Ibid., 16–20.

70. Ibid., 22–23, 30–39. The concluding chapter will detail more about Clark's and Evans' experiences at the academy.

71. Registers of Candidates for Admission.

72. Joseph Smith to C. K. Stribling, 27 September 1851, letters received.

73. A. H. Wilcox to superintendent, Naval Academy, 12 May 1858, letters received.

74. Registers of Candidates for Admission and Register of Alumni.

75. C. K. Stribling to William A. Graham, 21 May 1852, letters sent.

76. L. Howard Newman et al., to Cdr. L. M. Goldsborough, superintendent, 2 November 1853, letters received.

77. W. R. Butt et al., to Isaac Toucey, 13 December 1858, letters sent.

78. L. Howard Newman et al., to Cdr. L. M. Goldsborough, superintendent, 2 November 1853, letters received.

79. Midshipmen E. Keanry et al., to L. M. Goldsborough, 1 November 1853, letters received.

80. Midshipman C. M. Garland et al., to C. K. Stribling, 22 October 1853, letters received.

81. H. H. Lockwood to C. K. Stribling, 24 October 1853, letters received.

82. Mahan, *Sail to Steam*, 61–62.

83. S. A. Smith to L. M. Goldsborough, 18 April 1854, letters received.

84. J. W. Hester et al., to J. C. Dobbin, 19 January 1854, letters sent.

85. E. Simpson to L. M. Goldsborough, 20 January 1854, letters sent.

86. L. M. Goldsborough to J. C. Dobbin, 21 January 1854, letters sent.

87. James L. Taylor et al., to Cdr. T. T. Craven, 14 October 1859, letters received.

88. George S. Blake to president of the Board of Visitors, 13 June 1859, letters received.

89. "An Old Salt," "Naval Academy," name of newspaper illegible, c. 1860, letters received.

90. Blake, undated note, possibly to the secretary of the Navy, attached to anonymous newspaper article, c. 1860, letters received.

91. C. T. Houpt, "Graduation Exercises at the Naval Academy, 1854–1914," United States Naval Institute *Proceedings* (April 1946, part II): 131–32, and Register of Alumni.

Chapter 4. Discipline and Law in the School Era

1. Regulations, 1855, chapter XI, paragraph 18.

2. James E. Valle, *Rocks & Shoals: Order and Discipline in the Old Navy, 1800–1861* (Annapolis: Naval Institute Press, 1980), 29, 36.

3. Harold D. Langley, *Social Reform in the United States Navy, 1798–1862* (Chicago: University of Illinois Press, 1967), 39–40.

4. Ibid., 161–88 and fn. 63, 188.

5. Ira Dye, *Uriah Levy: Reformer of the Antebellum Navy* (Gainesville: University Press of Florida, 2006), 171, 204.

6. Valle, *Rocks & Shoals*, 3–4, 41, 45–47.

7. Langley, *Social Reform*, 43.

8. "An Act for the Better Government of the Navy of the United States," 23 April 1800, *Statutes at Large*, 6th Cong., 1st sess., 45–53 (1800), article I, III.

9. Ibid., article V, VI, XIII, XIV, XV, XVI, XVII.

10. Ibid., article XIX, XX, XXI, XXII.

11. Ibid., articles XXXV–XLII, and Valle, *Rocks & Shoals*, 50. James E. Valle concludes that courts martial, or other disciplinary actions, had little effect on an officer's career because promotion was seniority based. Even with a disciplinary record, an officer could still advance and a record did not carry the same "stigma" then as today. Additionally, "junior officers who were suspended often resigned from the Navy, especially midshipmen who were young enough to start over again in some other profession" (*Rocks & Shoals*, 51–58).

12. Valle, *Rocks & Shoals*, 53–55.

13. George Bancroft to Franklin Buchanan, 7 August 1845, in *Plan and Regulations of the Naval School at Annapolis*, 4.

14. Franklin Buchanan to Naval School, 10 October 1845, letters sent.

15. Buchanan, "Rules and Regulations for the Government of the U.S. Naval School at Fort Severn, Annapolis," article 10, 11, and 12 in *Plan and Regulations of the Naval School at Annapolis.*

16. Ibid., articles 14, 15, 16, and 17.

17. Ibid., article 19.

18. Ibid., article 23.

19. Ibid., article 20.

20. Ibid., articles 10, 11, and 12.

21. Symonds, *Confederate Admiral*, 38; and Buchanan to J. Y. Mason, 5 December 1846, letters sent.

22. Buchanan to J. Y. Mason, 5 December 1846, letters sent.

23. Ibid., letters sent.

24. Buchanan, "Rules and Regulations for the government of the U.S. Naval School at Fort Severn, Annapolis," article 3.

25. Benjamin, *Naval Academy*, 164, 175–79. Chorus lyrics based on "To the West Point Cadets & Graduates. Benny Havens, Oh! A Favorite Song as Sung at West Point," (Buffalo: J. Sage and Sons, 1855). American 19th-Century Sheet Music. Copyright Deposits, 1820–60, Library of Congress. Music Division, DIGITAL ID sm1855 600840 <http://hdl.loc.gov/loc.music/sm1855.600840>. See also, Todorich, *Spirited Years*, 54–55.

26. For example, see Todorich, *Spirited Years*, 36–37.

27. Benjamin, *Naval Academy*, 163, 167–68.

28. It is difficult to conclude based on the conduct rolls alone that they were more (or less) inclined to follow school or naval regulations than later students. If anything, the types of offenses committed shows that the midshipmen tended to act more grown-up than in later periods, as will be seen.

29. I have used the headings contained in the academy records: "Breaking Liberty," "Disobedience of Orders," "Drunkenness," "Inattention to Studies," "Indecorous Conduct," "Neglect of Duty," "Tardy at Recitation," and "Unofficerlike Conduct."

30. The final "Disobedience of Orders" infraction was unclear, and was simply reported by Lieutenant Ward.

31. Symonds, *Confederate Admiral*, 79.

32. Register of Alumni and Callahan, ed., *List of Officers.*

33. Benjamin, *Naval Academy*, 167–68.

34. Ibid., 174.

35. Lt. John Ward to George P. Upshur, 2 May 1847, letters received.

36. George P. Upshur, 4 May 1847, letters received.

37. Register of Alumni.

38. J. H. Ward to H. C. Hunter, 29 May 1847; J. H. Ward to H. C. Hunter, 1 June 1847; and J. H. Ward to J. Y. Mason, 1 June 1847, letters sent.

39. Register of Alumni.

40. G. P. Upshur to J. Y. Mason, 19 June 1847, letters sent.

41. Register of Alumni and Registers of Candidates for Admission.

42. G. P. Upshur to William B. Preston, 30 October 1849, letters sent.

43. Register of Alumni.

44. G. P. Upshur to William Ballard Preston, 24 July 1849, letters sent.

45. Register of Alumni and Callahan, ed., *List of Officers*.

46. G. P. Upshur to J. Y. Mason, 25 January 1848, letters sent.

47. Ibid.

48. Ibid., 27 January 1848, letters sent.

49. Register of Alumni and Callahan, ed., *List of Officers*.

50. G. P. Upshur to J. Y. Mason, 9 February 1848, letters sent.

51. Register of Alumni and Callahan, ed., *List of Officers*.

52. J. Y. Mason to George P. Upshur, 23 February 1848, letters received.

53. G. P. Upshur to J. Y. Mason, 1 March 1848, letters sent.

54. Register of Alumni and Callahan, ed., *List of Officers*.

55. Franklin Buchanan to George Bancroft, 17 and 18 February 1846, letters sent. McLaughlin was then listed as a deserter.

56. Franklin Buchanan to secretary of the Navy, 19 February 1846, letters sent.

57. Register of Alumni.

58. G. P. Upshur to J. Y. Mason, 25 November 1847, letters sent.

59. Ibid.

60. Ibid.

61. Register of Alumni.

62. Valle, *Rocks & Shoals*, 91.

63. For a brief overview see Charles Todorich, "The Lockwood Incident," United States Naval Institute *Proceedings* 104, no. 6/904 (June 1978): 71–73.

64. Upshur to J. Y. Mason, 24 March 1848, letters sent.

65. Ibid.

66. J. Y. Mason, "Charges and specification of charges preferred by the secretary of the Navy against Midshipman J. McLeod Murphy of the Navy," 8 April 1848, in Office of the Judge Advocate General (Navy), Records of General Courts-Martial and Courts of Inquiry of the Navy Department, 1799–1867, case 1081, Records of the Office of the Judge Advocate General (Navy), NA, RG 125. Hereafter, JAG and case number.

67. Upshur to J. Y. Mason, 24 March 1848, letters sent.

68. JAG 1081, File JMLM No. 1.

69. Ibid., File JA No. 1.

70. Ibid., File JMLM No. 1.

71. JAG 1081.

72. J. Y. Mason, "Charge and specifications of a charge preferred by the secretary of the Navy against Midshipman John Gale of the Navy," 24 April 1848, in JAG 1082.

73. JAG 1082, File JG No. 1.

74. Ibid., File JG No. 1.

75. Ibid.

76. JAG 1082, 7–8.

77. Ibid., 22–24.

78. Ibid., 24–30.

79. Ibid., 27–33.

80. JAG 1082, File JG No. 2.

81. JAG 1082, 34–35.

82. J. Y. Mason, "Charge and specifications of a charge preferred by the secretary of the Navy against Midshipman Edward Hunter Scovell of the Navy," 23 April 1848, in JAG 1083.

83. JAG 1083, 4–5.

84. Ibid., 13–16. The records indicate William Law, but it was more likely Richard L. Law, Date of '41 (Register of Alumni).

85. Ibid., 19–21.

86. Ibid., 22–26.

87. Ibid., File EHS No. 1.

88. Ibid., 1.

89. JAG 1083, 26–27.

90. G. P. Upshur to J. Y. Mason, 13 November 1848, letters sent, Register of Alumni, and Callahan, ed., *List of Officers*.

91. Register of Alumni and Callahan, ed., *List of Officers*.

92. Appleby, *Inheriting the Revolution*, 30, 244. Given the social backgrounds of midshipmen and their desire to be true naval officers, it should not be surprising that duels occurred at the Naval School. James R. Webb, screenwriter of *How the West Was Won* (1963) and historical commentator, concludes that generally few school boys graduate without an "I'll see you after school" fight, usually fought "in the immediate heat of anger." But Webb also concludes that duels were matters of honor tending to "be an occupational hazard of the military, lawyers, politicians, gay young blades of the southern landowning class, and newspaper editors." Moreover, he contends that dueling was most common in the Navy: "possibly because of the frictions created by the close quarters of shipboard life" (Webb, "Pistols for Two . . . Coffee for One," *American Heritage* 25, no. 2 [1975]: 66 and 70. Also available online at <http://www.americanheritage.com/articles/magazine/ah/1975/2/1975_2_66.shtml>). For extreme examples dueling in society, see Ute Frevert, *Men of Honour: A Social and Cultural History of the Duel* (Cambridge, UK: Polity Press, English Translation, 1995). In particular chapter 3, "The Honour of Officers." Duels were a regular occurrence at the German naval college in Kiel to the early twentieth century. A senior officer supervised the events, "which means that they were afforded quasi-recognition as an institutional means of settling conflicts of honour" (Frevert, *Men of Honour*, 75). Dueling only ended in Germany when postwar de-Nazification purged military ethos from society (Frevert, *Men of Honour*, 228–31).

93. McKee, *Gentlemanly and Honorable Profession*, 403–4.

94. Ira Dye, *Uriah Levy*, 163–65.

95. Schneller, *Quest for Glory*, 21.

96. Register of Alumni and Registers of Candidates for Admission. I have not been able to uncover their ages.

97. G. P. Upshur to J. Y. Mason, 12 May 1848, letters sent.

98. J. Y. Mason to Cdr. George P. Upshur, 24 May 1848, in JAG 1091.

99. JAG 1091, 30–35.

100. Ibid., 36–40.

101. Ibid., 57–59.

102. G. P. Upshur to J. Y. Mason, 8 June 1848, letters sent.

103. Commander Upshur to the secretary of the Navy, 8 June 1848, in Dallas Papers.

104. Midshipman Dallas to Midshipman Harrison, 24 May 1848; Midshipman Dallas to Midshipman Dibble, 24 May 1848; Midshipman Gale to Midshipman Dallas, 6 June 1848; Certificate of Dr. Palmer, 7 June 1848, in Dallas Papers, 25–30.

105. Capt. Chas. W. Morgan to Passed Midshipman Dallas, 4 July 1848; the secretary of the Navy to Passed Midshipman Dallas, 6 July 1848; Passed Midshipman Dallas to the secretary of the Navy, 3 September 1848; the secretary of the Navy to Late Passed Midshipman Dallas, 9 September 1848; late Passed Midshipman Dallas to the secretary of the Navy, 12 September 1848, with note attached from Mason returning the letter, in Dallas Papers, 45–49. Meanwhile, Lieutenant Colonel de Russy wrote Dallas and explained that he "trespass[ed] against the Rules of the Service" to lobby his congressman to take up his cause. On 25 September 1848, Mason wrote Dallas again and told him that his record, until then, was fine and that "there was nothing in the report which affected your character, or made you subject to a dishonorable discharge." Despite letters from friends, and former commanders, to the president and the secretary of the Navy, nothing worked to get Dallas reappointed. By May 1849, frustrated, Dallas courted the German navy and received a commission as a lieutenant, 2nd class, on 3 August 1849. Dallas served about four years and then reapplied to be reinstated in the U.S. Navy. On 23 February 1853, Secretary of the Navy John P. Kennedy informed Dallas that because of personal testimonies on his behalf, and his service record in the German navy, he had been reinstated as a passed midshipman and given leave until 1 January 1854 to prepare to assume his new duties (Capt. Foxhall A. Parker to the president, 8 December 1848; Abbott Lawrence, Esq., to the president, 11 December 1848; Lieutenant Colonel de Russy to the secretary of the Navy, 29 December 1848, in Dallas Papers, 51–57; the secretary of the German navy to late Passed Midshipman Dallas, 3 August 1849, in Dallas Papers, 63–64; late Passed Midshipman Dallas to the secretary of the Navy, 17 February 1853; the secretary of the Navy to Passed Midshipman Dallas, 23 February 1853; the secretary of the Navy to Passed Midshipman Dallas, 23 February 1853, in Dallas Papers, 108–11).

106. As noted in G. P. Upshur to J. Y. Mason, 14 June 1848, letters sent.

107. Register of Alumni and Registers of Candidates for Admission.

CHAPTER 5. DISCIPLINE AND LAW IN THE ACADEMY ERA

1. Langley, *Social Reform*, 161–88, 192, and fn. 63.

2. Valle, *Rocks & Shoals*; and Gilbert, "Crime as Disorder," 110–12.

3. Robert Smith, secretary of the Navy, in Dye, *Uriah Levy*, 21.

4. Ibid., 21–22, 66–67, 71.

5. Ibid., 163–74, 186–87, 194, 196–97.

6. Ibid., 198–201.

7. Langley, *Social Reform*, 200–201.

8. Dye, *Uriah Levy*, 204–3.

9. Langley, *Social Reform*, 202–5; and "An Act to Provide a More Efficient Discipline for the Navy," 2 March 1855, *Statutes at Large*, 33rd Cong., 2nd sess., 627–29 (1855).

10. "An Act to Provide a More Efficient Discipline for the Navy," Section 2 and 3.

11. Langley, *Social Reform*, 202–5.

12. Valle, *Rocks & Shoals*, 55.

13. "An Act to Provide a More Efficient Discipline for the Navy," Section 4.

14. Ibid., Sections 5–8.

15. Ibid., Section 7.

16. Ibid., Section 10.

17. Ibid., 17 July 1862, *Statues at Large*, 37th Cong., 2nd sess., 600–610 (1862).

18. Langley, *Social Reform*, 202–5.

19. Dye, *Uriah Levy*, 198.

20. Benjamin, *Naval Academy*, 190–91.

21. Regulations, 1849, Section 12 and Section 24.

22. John P. Kennedy to C. K. Stribling, 14 October 1852, letters received.

23. William Wallard Preston to George P. Upshur, 27 May 1850, letters received, and Register of Alumni and Registers of Candidates for Admission.

24. Stockton's biographical information from Registers of Candidates for Admission. The other midshipman's name is almost illegible. It could be Rufus A. Whittier, Date of '50. It is unclear why Whittier would have been at the academy in July 1850, although he was appointed an acting midshipman in March 1850 (Callahan, ed., *List of Officers*).

25. C. K. Stribling to secretary of the Navy, 27 July 1850, letters sent.

26. Henry H. Lockwood to C. K. Stribling, July 1852, letters received.

27. C. K. Stribling to John P. Kennedy, 12 October 1852, letters sent.

28. The Register of Alumni and Registers of Candidates for Admission show Vultee with the 1853 Date, and if actually appointed in 1853, he would have arrived at the academy that fall. One must conclude that Vultee eventually fell back a year and then never graduated. The names of the last two midshipmen were not sufficiently legible to identify.

29. J. C. Dobbin to C K. Stribling, 21 May 1853, letters received.

30. Benjamin, *Naval Academy*, 193–94, 200–201, 219.

31. Register of Alumni and Registers of Candidates for Admission.

32. J. Taylor Wood to Captain G. S. Blake, 12 October 1857, letters received.

33. Register of Alumni and Registers of Candidates for Admission.

34. Lt. R. H. Wyman to T. T. Craven, 31 October 1859, letters received.

35. Register of Alumni.

36. Ibid.

37. Mahan, *Sail to Steam*, 56.

38. Ibid., 57–58.

39. Regulations, 1849, Section 11, and Regulations, 1853, 21–23.

40. Chief of Bureau of Ordnance and Hydrography to L. M. Goldsborough, 19 January 1855, letters received.

41. Graham to Stribling, 6 May 1851, letters received; Register of Alumni and Registers of Candidates for Admission.

42. Callahan, ed., *List of Officers*, and Register of Alumni.

43. J. C. Dobbin to L. M. Goldsborough, 17 May 1854, letters received.

44. C. K. Stribling to C. S. McCauley, 14 June 1853, letters sent.

45. Anne Marie Drew, ed., "Those Demerits Are a Perfect Humbug: The Letters of Josiah G. Beckwith Jr.," in Drew, ed., *Letters from Annapolis: Midshipmen Write Home 1848–1969* (Annapolis: Naval Institute Press, 1998), 12–30; J. G. Beckwith Jr. to J. G. Beckwith Sr., March 1853, and J. G. Beckwith Jr. to J. G. Beckwith Sr., 23 January 1855, in Drew, ed., *Letters from Annapolis*, 15, 28–29.

46. C. K. Stribling to John P. Kennedy, 2 December 1852, letters sent; Callahan, ed., *List of Officers*; and Register of Alumni.

47. Register of Alumni and Registers of Candidates for Admission.

48. C. K. Stribling to John P. Kennedy, 4 December 1852, letters sent.

49. C. K. Stribling to T. T. Craven and Samuel P. Carter, 9 December 1852; C. K. Stribling to Hammond, Haralson, W. H. Smith, and Barrett, 9 December 1852, letters sent.

50. Kennedy to Stribling, 9 December 1852, letters received.

51. John P. Kennedy to C. K. Stribling, 16 December 1852, letters received; and Callahan, ed., *List of Officers*.

52. Register of Alumni and Registers of Candidates for Admission.

53. "Proceedings of a Board of Inquiry . . ." 8 December 1852, letters received.

54. Ibid.

55. Ibid.

56. Ibid.; Register of Alumni; and Registers of Candidates for Admission.

57. John P. Kennedy to C. K. Stribling, 16 December 1852, letters received.

58. John P. Kennedy to C. K. Stribling, 17 January 1853, letters received.

59. C. K. Stribling to John P. Kennedy, 17 January 1853, letters sent.

60. L. M. Goldsborough to J. C. Dobbin, 5 December 1853, letters sent.

61. Ibid., letters sent; and Register of Alumni.

62. Callahan, ed., *List of Officers*.

63. L. M. Goldsborough to Commodore Charles Morris, 13 March 1854, letters sent.

64. Ibid.

65. Ibid.

66. Ibid.

67. L. M. Goldsborough to Charles Morris, 20 March 1854, letter 1, letters sent.

68. Ibid.

69. Regulations, 1855, Chapter XI, Discipline, paragraphs 34–42.

70. Ibid.

71. Register of Alumni and Registers of Candidates for Admission.

72. There were five missing cases (of suspension end dates) for this sample because the Navy either dismissed those students or they resigned before their suspension ended. The standard deviation of the total suspension time for the sample was 6.39 (United States Naval Academy, Orders for the Suspensions of Acting Midshipmen, NA, RG 405. Hereafter, Orders for the Suspensions of Acting Midshipmen).

73. Register of Alumni and Registers of Candidates for Admission.

74. The exact identity of the other midshipman is illegible.

75. Orders for the Suspensions of Acting Midshipmen; Register of Alumni; and Registers of Candidates for Admission.

76. George M. Bache to G. S. Blake, 22 April 1858, letters received.

77. J. A. Miller to T. T. Craven, 22 April 1858, letters received.

78. George M. Bache to G. S. Blake, 22 April 1858, letters received.

79. T. T. Craven to G. S. Blake, 22 April 1858, letters received.

80. The midshipmen's behavior is similar to that discovered by N. A. M. Rodger for another period. Rodger's naval men only mutinied or protested if authorities violated their rights (Rodger, *The Wooden World: An Anatomy of the Georgian Navy* [London: Collins, 1986], 243–44).

81. Pledge to superintendent, 17 January 1853, letters received.

82. John P. Kennedy to C. K. Stribling, 19 January 1853, letters received, and Callahan, ed., *List of Officers*.

83. E. Furber et al., to superintendent, 14 December 1857, letters received; Register of Alumni; and Registers of Candidates for Admission.

84. Green to Blake, 16 January 1858, letters received, and Register of Alumni.

85. W. K. Mayo to L. M. Goldsborough, 27 December 1854, letters received. Cheever, appointed in 1849, was likely still at the school under the old rules, or had fallen back a year at some stage (Register of Alumni and Registers of Candidates for Admission).

86. There were several Charles Cushmans attending Annapolis at this time, and it was impossible to identify which one was involved in the incident with Mayo.

87. W. K. Mayo to L. M. Goldsborough, 27 December 1854, letters received.

88. Ibid.

89. P. Loyall to L. M. Goldsborough, 31 December 1854, letters received.

90. Ibid.

91. Register of Alumni and Callahan, ed., *List of Officers*.

92. Dobbin to Goldsborough, 7 February 1855, letters received.

93. JAG 2015, 1–3; Register of Alumni; and Registers of Candidates for Admission.

94. JAG 2015, 3–6.

95. Ibid., 14–16.

96. Ibid., 23, and attachment B.

97. Register of Alumni.

98. JAG 1264, 1–2. I have not been able to identify Moffitt's or Lynch's first names.

99. Ibid., 29–32.

100. Ibid., 32–33.

101. A. J. Dallas to W. A. Graham, 12 May 1851, JAG 1264.

102. Graham to Stribling, 6 June 1851, letters received.

103. Register of Alumni and Callahan, ed., *List of Officers*.

104. Valle, *Rocks & Shoals*, 92.

105. Alfred Thayer Mahan to Sam Ashe, 5 December 1858, in Robert Seager II and Doris D. Maguire, eds., *Letters and Papers of Alfred Thayer Mahan*, vol. 1 (Annapolis: Naval Institute Press, 1975).

106. Registers of Candidates for Admission.

107. Hicks, 11 March 1858, letters received. The letter, a written excuse for a disciplinary infraction, was likely sent to the commandant of midshipmen.

108. Clark to the commandant of midshipmen, 14 March 1858, letters received.

109. Green to Blake, 20 March 1858, letters received.

110. United States, Naval War Records Office, *Official Records of the Union and Confederate Navies in the War of the Rebellion*, vol. 16 (Washington, D.C.: GPO, 1903), 738.

111. G. W. Hayward et al., to Isaac Toucey, 8 April 1859, letters sent.

112. Charles Todorich claimed that the other students tarred and feathered Foot. Unfortunately, Todorich's source for this information is unclear, and I have been unable to confirm his description, although his assertion seems logical (Todorich, *Spirited Years*, 153).

113. T. T. Craven to G. S. Blake, 3 April 1859, letters sent, and G. W. Hayward et al., to Isaac Toucey, 8 April 1859, letters sent.

114. Isaac Toucey to George S. Blake, 6 April 1859, letter 1, letters received.

115. Isaac Toucey to George S. Blake, 27 April 1859, letters received.

116. Isaac Toucey to George S. Blake, 20 May 1859, letters received.

117. This behavior matches Jana Lynn Pershing's finding, for 1992–93 students, that peer pressure can override reporting a comrade. See Jana Lynn Pershing, "Balancing Honor and Loyalty: Social Control at the United States Naval Academy" (Ph.D. diss. University of Washington, 1997).

CHAPTER 6. SUMMER CRUISES, SCHOOL SHIPS, AND THE OUTBREAK OF CIVIL WAR

1. Todorich, *Spirited Years*, 68 and 74–79.

2. Erving Goffman, *Asylums: Essays on the Social Situation of Mental Patients and Other Inmates* (Chicago: Aldine Publishing Co., 1962), xiii and 5; Chisholm, *Dead Men's Shoes*, 7; and Heide Gerstenberger, "Men Apart: The Concept of 'Total Institution' and the Analysis of Seafaring," *International Journal of Maritime History* 8, no. 1 (June 1996): 173–82. For a wider discussion of institutions, see also Chisholm, *Dead Men's Shoes*, 6–13.

3. Mark C. Hunter, "Youth, Law, and Discipline at the U.S. Naval Academy, 1845–1861," *The Northern Mariner/Le Marin du nord* 10, no. 2 (April 2000): 30–31.

4. Buchanan, "Plan of the Naval School at Fort Severn, Annapolis," in *Plan and Regulations of the Naval School at Annapolis*, 10–11; and Regulations, 1849, Section 6, paragraphs 1–6.

5. Mahan, *Sail to Steam*, 94. For West Point's influence on the Naval Academy, see also Hayes, "Influence of West Point," 8–11.

6. D. Conner, president of Board of Examiners, to William A. Graham, 10 October 1851, letters received.

7. C. K. Stribling, 1 October 1851, letter 2; and C. S. McCauley, president of the Board of Examiners to J. C. Dobbin, 15 June 1853, letters received.

8. Robert H. Wyman to L. M. Goldsborough, 25 November 1854, letters received.

9. G. S. Blake to T. T. Craven, 22 June 1859, letter 1, letters sent.

10. Schroeder, *Shaping a Maritime Empire*, 3–10, 17–28, 50–65; and Howard I. Chapelle, *The History of the American Sailing Navy: The Ships and Their Development* (New York: W. W. Norton & Company, Inc., 1949), 400–403, 436–42, 549.

11. Millett, "Military Professionalism," 5, 7.

12. Bureau of Ordnance and Hydrography, "Regulations for the Practice Ship . . .," 18 July 1851, letters received.

13. L. M. Goldsborough to J. C. Dobbin, 21 February 1855, and L. M. Goldsborough to Joseph F. Green, 22 June 1855, letters sent.

14. L. M. Goldsborough to J. C. Dobbin, 2 April 1856, letters sent.

15. L. M. Goldsborough to J. C. Dobbin, 11 May 1856; L. M. Goldsborough to J. C. Dobbin, 6 June 1856; and L. M. Goldsborough to J. C. Dobbin, 10 June 1856, letters sent.

16. Peter Burroughs, "Defence and Imperial Disunity," *Oxford History of the British Empire*, vol. 3 (Oxford, UK: Oxford University Press, 1999), 325. For more details on Anglo-French naval rivalry during this period, see also C. I. Hamilton, *Anglo-French Naval Rivalry, 1840–1870* (Oxford, UK: Clarendon Press, 1993); and Andrew Lambert, "Politics, Technology and Policy-Making, 1859–1865: Palmerston, Gladstone and the Management of the Ironclad Naval Race," *The Northern Mariner/Le Marin du nord* 8, no. 3 (July 1998): 9–38.

17. Millett, "Military Professionalism," 7.

18. "Extract from the proceedings of the Academic Board, 26 June 1851," in C. K. Stribling to William A. Graham, 27 June 1851, letters sent.

19. Todorich acknowledges the limited experience the midshipmen obtained on *John Hancock* before they transferred to *Preble* (Todorich, *Spirited Years*, 167), but Sweetman states that the time on *John Hancock* was a "coastal cruise" before embarking on *Preble* (Sweetman, *Naval Academy*, 42). Meanwhile, "List of Ports the Practice Ship Visited," in Mr. Chase et al., "Portfolio of Statistics . . . ," 1 September 1899, letters received, wrongly lists *John Hancock* as the practice ship for 1851.

20. Samuel Flagg Bemis, *A Diplomatic History of the United States*, 5th Edition (New York: Holt, Rinehard, and Winston, Inc., 1965), 314–16; Charles Brown, *Agents of Manifest Destiny: The Lives and Times of the Filibusters* (Chapel Hill: University of North Carolina Press, 1980), 17–18; and Hunter, "West Indian Piracy," 240–48.

21. Craven to Stribling, 1 October 1851, letter 2, letters received.

22. William A. Graham to C. K. Stribling, 10 June 1852; and Craven to Stribling, 1 October 1852, letters received. For details on *Pennsylvania*, see Chapelle, *American Sailing Navy*, 370–74.

23. Craven to Stribling, 1 August 1853 and 1 October 1853, letters received.

24. Dobbin to Goldsborough, 9 June 1854 and 10 June 1854; and Craven to Goldsborough, 28 June 1854, letters received.

25. J. F. Green, quoted in L. M. Goldsborough to J. C. Dobbin, 30 September 1856, letters sent; and Mr. Chase and Others, "Portfolio of Statistics . . . ," 1 September 1899, letters received.

26. (unsigned), "U.S. Practice Ship Preble off Naval Academy, Annapolis Md.," 21 June 1858, letters sent, and Craven to Blake, 20 September 1858, letters received.

27. Isaac Toucey to G. S. Blake, 14 September 1858, letters sent; and Isaac Toucey to George S. Blake, 14 September 1858, letters received. Tension between the United States and Paraguay were high since 1855, when the latter country fired on USS *Water Witch*, conducting research in the area. By 1858 Washington dispatched a flotilla to South America to settle the issues between the countries, whereupon Paraguay agreed to American terms (Frederick Moore Binder, *James Buchanan and the American Empire* [Selensgrove, Pa.: Susquehanna University Press, 1994], 259–61).

28. (unsigned), "U.S. Ship 'Plymouth' off Naval Academy, June 11th 1860," 11 June 1860, letters sent; and Edward Simpson, 17 June 1860, letters received.

29. Craven to Blake, letter 1, 15 September 1860; and Craven to Blake, 30 September 1860, letters received.

30. L. M. Goldsborough to J. C. Dobbin, 20 June 1854, letters sent; and Todorich, *Spirited Years*, 80.

31. Craven to Stribling, 1 October 1851, letter 2; and Craven to Stribling, 1 October 1852, letters received.

32. Craven to Goldsborough, 28 June 1854, letters received.

33. Craven to Blake, 20 September 1858, letters received.

34. Craven to Stribling, 1 October 1853, letters received.

35. Craven to Blake, 27 September 1859, letters received. The journals of George M. Bache and George P. Ryan, for example, are housed in the Nimitz Library, Special Collections and Archives Division, U.S. Naval Academy, Annapolis, Md.

36. Charles P. Kindleberger, *Mariners and Markets* (New York: New York University Press, 1992), 48.

37. C. K. Stribling to T. T. Craven, 21 June 1853, letters sent.

38. L. M. Goldsborough to J. F. Green, 26 June 1856, letters sent.

39. L. M. Goldsborough to Joseph F. Green, 22 June 1855, letters sent.

40. C. K. Stribling to Commodore Lewis Warrington, chief of the Bureau of Ordnance and Hydrography, 17 July 1851, letters sent.

41. Lt. W. Wilcox to Commander Joseph F. Green, 27 September 1856, letters sent. Jefferson Slam, '60 Date, is the Register of Alumni's only Slam. It is possible that he fell back a year and then failed to graduate (Register of Alumni).

42. W. R. Butt, S. H. Hackett, H. F. Condict, J. L. Taylor, and S. L. French to J. F. Green, 28 September 1856, letters sent. Park Benjamin believes that, generally, students behaved poorly to protest their living conditions, because the academy "starved" them while on the summer cruises (Benjamin, *Naval Academy*, 220–21). The argument could be stretched to conclude that the boys' actions were like the safety-valve misbehaviors that Rodger describes (Rodger, *Wooden World*, 243–44). In reality, it is more likely that these were, as Benjamin initially began to speculate, simply boys acting out in "boy fashion," thinking that the cruise was almost over and they justified their actions in the words of the adults they emulated.

43. L. M. Goldsborough to J. C. Dobbin, 30 September 1856, letters sent.

44. Register of Alumni; Registers of Candidates for Admission; and Charles Welsh to L. M. Goldsborough, 10 October 1856, letters received. Taylor, '56 Date, probably fell back a year, and later graduated.

45. Craven to Stribling, 5 August 1851, 1 October 1851, letters 1 and 2; and Craven to Stribling, 1 October 1852, letters received.

46. Craven to Goldsborough, 30 September 1854, letters received.

47. Ibid.

48. Drew, ed., *Letters from Annapolis*, 31.

49. G. S. Blake to Isaac Toucey, 27 September 1859, letters sent. G. S. Blake to Isaac Toucey, 19 November 1859, letters sent. He reiterated his call on 9 May 1860 (G. S. Blake to Isaac Toucey, 9 May 1860, letters sent).

50. Craven to Blake, 30 September 1860, letters received. On the marline spike, see George P. B. Nash et al., *The Visual Encyclopedia of Nautical Terms Under Sail* (New York: Crown Publishers, 1978), 10.08.

51. Edward Simpson, 17 June 1860, letters received.

52. Craven's aptitude report, in Craven to Blake, 30 September 1860, letters received.

53. Craven to Blake, 30 September 1860, letters received. See also, Todorich, *Spirited Years*, 179.

54. Parker, *Recollections*, 215–16.

55. Girault to Isaac Toucey, 7 July 1860, letters received.

56. Winlock to Blake, 21 July 1860, letters received.

57. H. E. Nourse to Blake, 30 July 1860, letters received.

58. Toucey to Blake, 6 September 1860, letters received.

59. Winlock, 6 October 1860, letters received.

60. Ibid.

61. Ibid.

62. Isaac Toucey to Capt. George S. Blake, 12 December 1860, letters received.

63. Ibid.

64. Isaac Toucey to George S. Blake, 25 February 1861, letters received.

65. W. B. Maclay to Isaac Toucey, 21 February 1861, letters received.

66. Benjamin, *Naval Academy*, 397.

67. Of the 114 cases of students appointed in 1860, there were thirty missing cases. The standard deviation was 1.06 (G. S. Blake to Isaac Toucey, 20 September 1860, letters sent).

68. G. S. Blake to Isaac Toucey, 26 September 1860, letters sent.

69. A reminder to the reader not to confuse the school ships (*Constitution* and *Plymouth*) and the summer practice ships (*Preble* and *Plymouth*). The school ships remained tied up at the academy from October to June, while the practice ships went to sea summertime.

70. C. R. P. Rodgers, commandant of midshipmen and instructor in seamanship to Capt. G. S. Blake, superintendant, 23 February 1861, letters received.

71. Evans, *Sailor's Log*, 41–43, 46–48; Clark, *Fifty Years*, 15; and James Morris Morgan, *Recollections of a Rebel Reefer* (Boston and New York: Houghton Mifflin Company, 1917), 27–28.

72. Clark, *Fifty Years*, 7–8, and editor's note fn. 10; and Morgan, *Recollections*, 24–25.

73. Clark, *Fifty Years*, 11–12; Register of Alumni; and Registers of Candidates for Admission.

74. Morgan, *Recollections*, 1–2, 22.

75. Evans, *Sailor's Log*, 47–48; and Morgan, *Recollections*, 27–28.

76. The academy put many students on the ship when disorder erupted in Maryland, and the ship housed several classes, unlike *Plymouth* the year before. Therefore a direct comparison between the two years is impossible. To make matters worse, the conduct roll continues after *Constitution* and the remaining students sailed north to Rhode Island without those who resigned. The name index thus covers the period until the end of the academic year in June, rather than to the outbreak of war. Because the name index was used to gather the 20-percent random sample, the sample also covers the entire period (Registers of Delinquencies).

77. G. S. Blake to G. W. Rodgers, 31 December 1860, letters sent.

78. G. S. Blake to Gustavus English, 6 April 1861, letters sent; Register of Alumni; and Registers of Candidates for Admission.

79. Skelton, *American Profession of Arms*, 349.

80. Huntington, *Soldier and the State*, 212–13.

81. Skelton, *American Profession of Arms*, 348, 355–56.

82. Huntington, *Soldier and the State*, 213.

83. William S. Dudley, *Going South: U.S. Navy Officer Resignations & Dismissals on the Eve of the Civil War* (Washington, D.C.: Naval Historical Foundation, 1981), 4–6, 9, 11–13, 21. Also available online at <http://www.history.navy.mil/library/online/going_south.htm>.

84. Gerard A. Patterson, "Confederates from Annapolis," *American History* 40, no. 3 (2005): 63.

85. Craig L. Symonds, *Lincoln and His Admirals* (Oxford, UK: Oxford University Press, 2008), 54–55.

86. Gideon Welles, *Diary of Gideon Welles*, vol. 1 (Boston and New York: Houghton Mifflin Company, 1911), 5.

87. For a recent discussion of Lincoln's naval policy during the Civil War, see Symonds, *Lincoln and His Admirals*, 3–36.

88. Ibid., 55.

89. James Lee Conrad, *Rebel Reefers: The Organization and Midshipmen of the Confederate States Naval Academy* (Boulder, Colo.: Da Capo Press, 2003), 6; and Symonds, *Lincoln and His Admirals*, 55.

90. Dudley, *Going South*, 21–23.

91. Captain Samuel DuPont to Commander Andrew Hull Foote, 25 January 1861, in ibid., 4.

92. Ibid., 22.

93. Ibid., 13; and Morgan, *Recollections*, 29–31.

94. Dudley, *Going South*, 13.

95. Calculated from Register of Alumni. Conrad believes that ninety-five graduates went South. By 21 April 1861, the Confederate states established their own naval academy, CSS *Patrick Henry*, which enrolled 106 students (Conrad, *Rebel Reefers*, 6). Meanwhile, Gerard Patterson discovered sixty-four academy alumni who joined the Confederate States Navy after resigning from the U.S. Navy (Patterson, "Confederates from Annapolis," 59).

96. Gerard, "Confederates from Annapolis," 62; Register of Alumni; and Callahan, ed., *List of Officers*.

97. Morgan, *Recollections*, 32–33.

98. Mahan, *Sail to Steam*, 85–92.

99. Clark, *Fifty Years*, 14–15.

100. J. M. Spencer et al., to Isaac Toucey, 7 January 1861, letters sent.

101. G. S. Blake to Isaac Toucey, 9 January 1861, letters sent.

102. Clark, *Fifty Years*, 16–17; and Register of Alumni.

103. Clark, *Fifty Years*, 17. Although the average age of the fourth-class was much younger. See table 7, chapter 3.

104. G. S. Blake to Gideon Welles, 15 April 1861, letters sent.

105. S. B. Luce to George S. Blake, 17 April 1861, letters received.

106. Parker, *Recollections*, 216–17. Symonds concludes that Parker's "southern lineage was the source of his decision to resign" and join the Confederacy (Symonds, "Introduction," in Parker, *Recollections*, x, xvi).

107. G. S. Blake to Gideon Welles, 22 April 1861, letters sent.

108. G. S. Blake to Gideon Welles, 24 April 1861, letters sent.

109. Clark, *Fifty Years*, 18–22; and Evans, *Sailor's Log*, 53.

110. Gideon Welles to George S. Blake, 27 April 1861, letters received.

111. Clark, *Fifty Years*, 18–22.

112. Col. Abel Smith to Capt. George S. Blake, 6 May 1861, letters received.

113. C. R. P. Rodgers, commandant of midshipmen, to Capt. Andrew Harwood, chief of the Bureau of Ordnance and Hydrography, 9 May 1861, letters sent.

CONCLUSION

1. Benjamin, *Naval Academy*, 197, 209.

2. Skelton, *American Profession of Arms*, 182–89, 212–16.

3. This study's statistical analysis used a database of 1,030 students compiled from the Register of Alumni to find information about the common student. It is unclear what happened to five of the midshipmen for whom I searched for information.

4. See the previous chapter for more details about Civil War resignations and dismissals of officers.

5. For a further discussion of attempts at promotion reform, see Chisholm, *Dead Men's Shoes*, 116, 166, 305, 361.

6. Langley, *Social Reform*, 22.

7. Skelton, *American Profession of Arms*, 217–19.

8. See Callahan, ed., *List of Officers*.

9. Symonds, "Introduction," in Parker, *Recollections*, xix–xxi.

10. Benjamin, *Naval Academy*, 194–95, 422–23, and 425.

11. Karsten, *Naval Aristocracy*, 186–89.

12. Ibid., 24–30, 44.

13. Huntington, *Soldier and the State*, 8–9, 198–99, 218–20; Millett, "Military Professionalism," 2–12, 17–18; *Robert L. Bullard*, 3–4, 7, 9–10; Skelton, "Samuel P. Huntington," 326; Shulimson, "Military Professionalism," 232–33; and Janowitz, *Professional Soldier*, 6.

14. Huntington, *Soldier and the State*, 10–16; Janowitz, *Professional Soldier*, 6; Millett, "Military Professionalism," 2–7; and *Robert L. Bullard*, 3–4.

15. Glete, *War and the State in Early Modern Europe*, 1–4.

16. Kindleberger, *Mariners and Markets*, 48.

17. Huntington, *Soldier and the State*, 193.

18. See, for example, Hunter, *Policing the Seas*, 169–95.

BIBLIOGRAPHY

PRIMARY SOURCES

Georgetown University Special Collections, Washington, D.C. Regulations of the U.S. Naval Academy at Annapolis, Md. Washington, D.C.: A. O. P. Nicholson, Printer, 1855.

Library of Congress, Washington, D.C.

Music Division. American 19th-Century Sheet Music. Copyright Deposits, 1820–60. "To the West Point Cadets & Graduates. Benny Havens, Oh! A Favorite Song as Sung at West Point." Buffalo: J. Sage and Sons, 1855. DIGITAL ID sm1855 600840, <http://hdl.loc.gov/loc.music/sm1855.600840>.

Prints and Photographs Division. Frank Leslie's *Illustrated Newspaper*.

National Archives, College Park, Md.

RG 19 Records of the Bureau of Ships, 1940–66. Ship Design and Construction Drawings, compiled 1862–1909.

National Archives, Washington, D.C.

RG 45 Naval Records Collection of the Office of Naval Records and Library.

Records of the Bureau of Naval Personnel. Abstracts of Service Records of Naval Officers ("Records of Officers"), 1798–1893.

Records of the Office of the Secretary of the Navy. Miscellaneous Letters Received by the Secretary of the Navy.

RG 125 Records of the Office of the Judge Advocate General (Navy).

Records of General Courts-Martial and Courts of Inquiry of the Navy Department, 1799–1867.

RG 405 Records of the U.S. Naval Academy.

Letters Received by the Superintendent of the U.S. Naval Academy, 1845–1887.

Letters Sent by the Superintendent of the U.S. Naval Academy 1845–65; Volumes 2, 4–6, 8, 10–11, 14 Aug. 1845–Apr. 23, 1862.

United States. Registers of Delinquencies ("Conduct Roll," "Conduct Roll of Cadets"). 1846–50, 1853–82; Volumes 346–55.

William W. Jeffries Memorial Archives, Nimitz Library, U.S. Naval Academy.

RG 405 Records of the U.S. Naval Academy.

Orders for the Suspensions of Acting Midshipmen.

Registers of Candidates for Admission to the Academy. Oct. 1849–Oct. 1860.

Plan and Regulations of the Naval School at Annapolis. Washington, D.C.: C. Alexander, Printer, 1847.

Regulations of the U.S. Naval Academy (1849). Washington, D.C.: GPO, 1849.

Revised Regulations of the U.S. Naval Academy at Annapolis, Md. (1853). Washington, D.C.: Robert Armstrong, Printer, 1853.

Published Primary Sources

Allen, Gardner W., ed. *The Papers of Francis Gregory Dallas. United States Navy. Correspondence and Journal, 1837–1859.* New York: De Vinne Press, 1917, reprint.

Bowditch, Nathaniel. *The New American Practical Navigator.* New York: E. & W. Blumt, 1846.

Callahan, Edward W., ed. *List of Officers of the Navy of the United States and of the Marine Corps from 1775 to 1900.* New York: Haskell House, reprint 1969. Revised edition available at <http://www.history.navy.mil/books/callahan/index.htm>.

Clark, Charles E. *My Fifty Years in the Navy.* Annapolis: Naval Institute Press, 1917, reprint 1984.

Dewey, George. *Autobiography of George Dewey: Admiral of the Navy.* Reprint, New York: AMS Press, 1969.

Drew, Anne Marie, ed. *Letters from Annapolis: Midshipmen Write Home 1848–1969.* Annapolis: Naval Institute Press, 1998.

Evans, Robley D. *A Sailor's Log: Recollections of Forty Years of Naval Life.* Annapolis: Naval Institute Press, reprint, 1994.

Gleaves, Albert. *Life and Letters of Rear Admiral Stephen B. Luce, U.S. Navy, Founder of the Naval War College.* New York: G. P. Putnam's Sons, 1925.

Mahan, Alfred Thayer. *From Sail to Steam: Recollections of Naval Life.* New York: Da Capo Press, reprint 1968.

Marshall, Edward Chauncey. *History of the United States Naval Academy.* New York: D. Van Nostrand, 1862.

Morgan, James Morris. *Recollections of a Rebel Reefer.* Boston, New York: Houghton Mifflin Company, 1917.

Olmsted Denison. *Rudiments of Natural Philosophy and Astronomy: Designed for the Younger Classes in Academies, and for Common Schools.* New York: Collins & Brother, 1846.

Parker, William Harwar. *Recollections of a Naval Officer, 1841–1865.* Introduction, Craig L. Symonds. Annapolis: Naval Institute Press, reprint 1985.

Proceedings of the Court of Inquiry . . . . [of] mutiny on board the United States Brig of War Somers. New York: Greeley & McElrath, 1843.

Proceedings of the Naval Court Martial . . . of Alexander Slidell Mackenzie. New York: Henry G. Langley, 1844.

Sands, Benjamin F. *From Reefer to Rear-Admiral: Reminiscences and Journal Jottings of Nearly Half a Century of Naval Life.* New York: Frederick A. Stokes Company, 1899.

Seager, Robert, II, and Doris D. Maguire, eds. *Letters and Papers of Alfred Thayer Mahan.* Volume I: 1847–1889. Annapolis: Naval Institute Press, 1975.

Selfridge, Thomas O., Jr. *What Finer Tradition: The Memoirs of Thomas O. Selfridge, Jr., Rear Admiral, U.S.N.* Columbia: University of South Carolina, reprint,1987.

United States. Congress. *Biographical Directory of the United States Congress, 1774–1989.* Washington: GPO, 1988; updates at http://bioguide.congress.gov. Senate Document 100-34.

United States. Congress. *The Congressional Globe.* Washington, D.C.: Blair & Rives, 1841–1845.

———. *The Public Statutes at Large of the United States of America*. Richard Peters and George P. Sanger, eds. Boston: Little, Brown, 1800, 1845, 1856, 1862.

United States Navy. Naval War Records Office. *Official Records of the Union and Confederate Navies in the War of the Rebellion*, vol. 16. Washington, D.C.: GPO, 1903.

U.S. Naval Academy Alumni Association. *Register of Alumni, Graduates and Former Naval Cadets and Midshipmen*. 91st Edition. Annapolis: The Naval Academy Alumni Association, 1976.

Wattenberg, Ben J. *The Statistical History of the United States from Colonial Times to the Present*. New York: Basic Books, Inc., Publishers, 1976.

Wayland, Francis. *The Elements of Moral Science*. Cambridge, Mass.: Belknap Press of Harvard University Press, 1837, reprint, 1963.

Welles, Gideon. *Diary of Gideon Welles*. Boston and New York: Houghton Mifflin, 1911.

SECONDARY SOURCES

Appleby, Joyce. *Inheriting the Revolution: The First Generation of Americans*. Cambridge, Mass.: Belknap Press, 2000.

Bemis, Samuel Flagg. *A Diplomatic History of the United States*. 5th edition. New York: Holt, Rinehart, and Winston, 1965.

Benjamin, Park. *The United States Naval Academy*. New York and London: G. P. Putnam's Sons, 1900.

Bennett, Frank M. *The Steam Navy of the United States: A History of the Growth of the Steam Vessel of War in the U.S. Navy, and of the Naval Engineer Corps*. Westport, Conn.: Greenwood Press, reprint 1972.

Binder, Frederick Moore. *James Buchanan and the American Empire*. Selensgrove, Pa.: Susquehanna University Press, 1994.

Bodinier, Gilbert. "Les Officiers de la Marine Royale a L'Epoque de la Guerre d'Amerique," *Revue Historique des Armées* 1995 (4): 3–12.

Bolander, Louis H. "The Naval Academy in Five Wars." United States Naval Institute *Proceedings* 71 (April 1946, part II): 35–45.

Bradford, James, ed. *Captains of the Old Steam Navy: Makers of the American Naval Tradition, 1840–1880*. Annapolis: Naval Institute Press, 1986.

———. *Command Under Sail: Makers of the American Naval Tradition, 1775–1850*. Annapolis: Naval Institute Press, 1985.

———. *Quarterdeck and Bridge: Two Centuries of American Naval Leaders*. Annapolis: Naval Institute Press, 1997.

Brown, Charles. *Agents of Manifest Destiny: The Lives and Times of the Filibusters*. Chapel Hill: University of North Carolina Press, 1980.

Brown, F. B. "A Half Century of Frustration: A Study of the Failure of Naval Academy Legislation Between 1800 and 1845." United States Naval Institute *Proceedings* 80, no. 6 (June 1954): 631–35.

Bruijn, Jaap. *The Dutch Navy of the Seventeenth and Eighteenth Centuries*. Columbia: University of South Carolina Press, 1993.

Burk, James. "Morris Janowitz and the Origins of Sociological Research on Armed Forces and Society." *Armed Forces and Society* 19, no. 2 (1993): 167–85.

Burr, Henry L. "Education in the Early Navy." Ph.D. diss., Temple University, 1939.

Burroughs, Peter. "Defence and Imperial Disunity." In *Oxford History of the British Empire*. Vol. 3. Oxford, UK: Oxford University Press, 1999.

Calvert, James. "The Fine Line at the Naval Academy." United States Naval Institute *Proceedings* 96, no. 10/812 (October 1970): 63–68.

Calvert, Monte A. *The Mechanical Engineer in America, 1830–1910: Professional Cultures in Conflict*. Baltimore: Johns Hopkins Press, 1967.

Canney, David L. *The Old Steam Navy, Volume One: Frigates, Sloops, and Gunboats, 1815–1885*. Annapolis: Naval Institute Press, 1990.

Chandler, Alfred D., Jr. *The Visible Hand: The Managerial Revolution in American Business*. Cambridge, Mass.: Harvard University Press, 1977.

Chapelle, Howard I. *The History of the American Sailing Navy: The Ships and Their Development*. New York: W. W. Norton & Company, Inc., 1949.

Chisholm, Donald. *Waiting for Dead Men's Shoes: Origins and Development of the U.S. Navy's Officer Personnel System, 1793–1941*. Stanford, Calif.: Stanford University Press, 2001.

Conrad, James Lee. *Rebel Reefers: The Organization and Midshipmen of the Confederate States Naval Academy*. Boulder, Colo.: Da Capo Press, 2003.

Consolvo, Charles. "The Prospects and Promotion of British Naval Officers 1793–1815." *Mariner's Mirror* 91, no. 2 (May 2005): 137–59.

Cormack, William S., and Norman E. Saul. "Revolutionary Conflict in the French Navy: The Court Martial of Captain Basterot." *Consortium on Revolutionary Europe 1750–1850: Proceedings* 20 (1990): 753–59.

Dickinson, Harry W. *Educating the Royal Navy: Eighteenth- and Nineteenth-Century Education for Officers*. New York: Routledge, 2007.

———. "The Portsmouth Naval Academy, 1733–1806." *Mariner's Mirror* 89, no. 1 (February 2003): 17–30.

Dudley, William S. *Going South: U.S. Navy Officer Resignations & Dismissals on the Eve of the Civil War*. Washington, D.C.: Naval Historical Foundation, 1981. Available online at <http://www.history.navy.mil/library/online/going_south.htm>.

Dye, Ira. *Uriah Levy: Reformer of the Antebellum Navy*. Gainesville: University Press of Florida, 2006.

Elias, Norbert. *The Genesis of the Naval Profession*. René Moelker and Stephen Mennell, eds. Dublin: University College Dublin Press, 2007.

Ford, Walter C., and J. Buroughs Stokes. "The Selection and Procurement of Better Candidate Material for the Naval Academy." United States Naval Institute *Proceedings* 71 (April 1946, part II): 19–33.

Frevert, Ute. *Men of Honour: A Social and Cultural History of the Duel*. Cambridge, UK: Polity Press, English Translation 1995.

Gabor, Andrea. *The Capitalist Philosophers: The Geniuses of Modern Business—Their Lives, Times, and Ideas*. New York: Crown Business, 2000.

Gerstenberger, Heide. "Men Apart: The Concept of 'Total Institution' and the Analysis of Seafaring." *International Journal of Maritime History* 8, no. 1 (June 1996): 173–82.

Gilbert, Arthur N. "Crime as Disorder: Criminality and the Symbolic Universe of the 18th Century British Naval Officer." In *Changing Interpretations and New Sources in Naval History: Papers from the Third United States Naval Academy History Symposium*. Robert William Love Jr., ed. New York and London: Garland Publishing, Inc., 1980.

Glete, Jan. *War and the State in Early Modern Europe: Spain, the Dutch Republic and Sweden as Fiscal-Military States, 1500–1660*. London and New York: Routledge, 2002.

Goffman, Erving. *Asylums: Essays on the Social Situation of Mental Patients and Other Inmates*. Chicago: Aldine Publishing Co., 1962.

Graff, Harvey J. *Conflicting Paths: Growing Up in America*. Cambridge, Mass.: Harvard University Press, 1995.

Hamilton, C. I. *Anglo-French Naval Rivalry, 1840–1870*. Oxford, UK: Clarendon Press, 1993.

Handlin, Lilian. *George Bancroft: The Intellectual as Democrat*. New York: Harper & Row, Publishers, 1984.

Hayes, John D. "Influence of West Point on the Founding of the Naval Academy." *Assembly* (Winter 1961): 8–11.

Houpt, C. T. "Graduation Exercises at the Naval Academy, 1854–1914." United States Naval Institute *Proceedings* 72 (April 1946, part II): 131–37.

Hunter, Mark C. "Anglo-American Political and Naval Response to West Indian Piracy." *International Journal of Maritime History* 13, no. 1 (June 2001): 63–93.

———. *Policing the Seas: Anglo-American Relations and the Equatorial Atlantic, 1819 to 1865*. St. John's, NL: International Maritime Economic History Association, 2008.

———. "Youth, Law, and Discipline at the U.S. Naval Academy, 1845–1861." *The Northern Mariner/Le Marin du nord* 10 no. 2 (April 2000): 23–39.

Huntington, Samuel P. *The Soldier and the State: The Theory and Politics of Civil-Military Relations*. Cambridge, Mass.: Harvard University Press, 1957, reprint 1964.

Janowitz, Morris. *The Professional Soldier: A Social and Political Portrait*. Glencoe, Ill.: Free Press, 1960.

Karsten, Peter. *The Naval Aristocracy: The Golden Age of Annapolis and the Emergence of Modern American Navalism*. New York: The Free Press, 1972.

Kindleberger, Charles P. *Mariners and Markets*. New York: New York University Press, 1992.

Lambert, Andrew. "Politics, Technology and Policy-Making, 1859–1865: Palmerston, Gladstone and the Management of the Ironclad Naval Race." *The Northern Mariner/Le Marin du nord* 8, no. 3 (July 1998): 9–38.

Langley, Harold D. *Social Reform in the United States Navy, 1798–1862*. Chicago: University of Illinois Press, 1967.

Lebby, David Edwin. "Professional Socialization of the Naval Officer: The Effect of Plebe Year at the U.S. Naval Academy." Ph.D. diss., Columbia University, 1968.

Lévêque, Pierre. "Le Destin des Officiers de Marine de L'Ancien Regime a L'Empire." *Historique des Armées* 2(2001): 101–12.

Lewis, Michael. *England's Sea-Officers: The Story of the Naval Profession*. London: George Allen & Unwin, Ltd., 1939; reprint 1948.

Love, Robert William, Jr., ed. *Changing Interpretations and New Sources in Naval History. Papers from the Third United States Naval Academy History Symposium*. New York and London: Garland Publishing, Inc., 1980.

Lovell, John P. *Neither Athens nor Sparta? The American Service Academies in Transition*. Bloomington and London: Indiana University Press, 1970.

Lutun, Bernard. "Le Plan d'Estaing de 1763 ou L'Impossible reforme de la Marine." *Revue historique* 292, no. 1 (1994): 3–29.

McKee, Christopher. *A Gentlemanly and Honorable Profession: The Creation of the U.S. Naval Officer Corps, 1794–1815*. Annapolis: Naval Institute Press, 1991.

Merrill, James M. *Du Pont, the Making of an Admiral: A Biography of Samuel Francis Du Pont*. New York: Dodd, Mead, 1986.

Millett, Allan R. *The General: Robert L. Bullard and Officership in the United States Army, 1881–1925.* Westport, Conn.: Greenwood Press, 1975.

———. "Military Professionalism and Officership in America." *A Mershon Center Briefing Paper 2.* Columbus: Ohio State University, 1977.

Morrison, James L., Jr., *"The Best School in the World": West Point, the Pre-Civil War Years, 1833–1866.* Kent, Ohio: Kent State University Press, 1986.

Nash, George P. B., et al. *The Visual Encyclopedia of Nautical Terms Under Sail.* New York: Crown Publishers, 1978.

Nientimp, Judith A. "The Somers Mutiny." *University of Rochester Library Bulletin* 20, no. 1 (Autumn 1964). Reprint, online at <http://www.lib.rochester.edu/index.cfm?PAGE=2477>.

Patterson, Gerard A. "Confederates from Annapolis." *American History* 40, no. 3 (2005): 58–67.

Pershing, Jana Lynn. "Balancing Honor and Loyalty: Social Control at the United States Naval Academy." Ph.D. diss., University of Washington, 1997.

Rodger, N. A. M. *Command of the Ocean: A Naval History of Britain, 1649–1815.* London: Allen Lane and National Maritime Museum, 2004.

———. *The Wooden World: An Anatomy of the Georgian Navy.* London: Collins, 1986.

Schneller, Robert J., Jr. *A Quest for Glory: A Biography of Rear Admiral John A. Dahlgren.* Annapolis: Naval Institute Press, 1996.

Schroeder, John H. *Shaping a Maritime Empire: The Commercial and Diplomatic Role of the American Navy, 1829–1861.* Westport, Conn.: Greenwood Press, 1985.

Seerup, Jacob. "The Royal Danish Naval Academy in the Age of Enlightenment." *Mariner's Mirror* 93, no. 3 (August 2007): 327–34.

Sharp, James Roger. *American Politics in the Early Republic: The New Nation in Crisis.* New Haven, Conn.: Yale University Press, 1993.

Shulimson, Jack. "Military Professionalism: The Case of the U.S. Marine Officer Corps, 1880–1898." *The Journal of Military History* 60, no. 2 (April 1996): 231–42.

Skelton, William B. *An American Profession of Arms: The Army Officer Corps, 1784–1861.* Lawrence: University Press of Kansas, 1992.

———. "Samuel P. Huntington and the Roots of the American Military Tradition." *The Journal of Military History* 60, no. 2 (April 1996): 325–38.

Soley, James Russel. *Historical Sketch of the United States Naval Academy.* Washington, D.C.: GPO, 1876.

Sturdy, Henry Francis. "The Establishment of the Naval School at Annapolis." United States Naval Institute *Proceedings* 72 (April 1946, part II): 1–17.

Sullivan, F. B. "The Royal Academy at Portsmouth 1729–1806." *Mariner's Mirror* 63, no. 4 (November 1977): 311–26.

Sweetman, Jack. *The U.S. Naval Academy: An Illustrated History.* Annapolis: Naval Institute Press, 1979.

Symonds, Craig L. *Confederate Admiral: The Life and Wars of Franklin Buchanan.* Annapolis: Naval Institute Press, 1999.

———. *Lincoln and His Admirals.* Oxford, UK: Oxford University Press, 2008.

Taylor, Frederick Winslow. *Scientific Management.* New York: Harper & Row, Publishers, 1947.

Thiesen, William H. *Industrializing American Shipbuilding: The Transformation of Ship Design and Construction, 1820–1920.* Gainesville: University Press of Florida, 2006.

Todorich, Charles. "The Lockwood Incident." United States Naval Institute *Proceedings* 104, no. 6/904 (June 1978): 71–73.

———. *The Spirited Years: A History of the Antebellum Naval Academy*. Annapolis: Naval Institute Press, 1984.

Tucker, Spencer C. *Andrew Hull Foote: Civil War Admiral on Western Waters*. Annapolis: Naval Institute Press, 2000.

Valle, James E. *Rocks & Shoals: Order and Discipline in the Old Navy, 1800–1861*. Annapolis: Naval Institute Press, 1980.

Vergé-Franceschi, Michel. "Les officiers généraux de la Marine royale (1669–1774)." *Revue historique* 278, no. 2 (1987): 335–60.

Webb, James R. "Pistols for Two . . . Coffee for One." *American Heritage* 25, no. 2 (1975): 66–84. Available online at <http://www.americanheritage.com/articles/magazine/ah/1975/2/1975_2_66.shtml>.

Wood, Gordon S. *The Creation of the American Republic, 1776–1787*. Chapel Hill: University of North Carolina Press, 1969.

INDEX

Adams, Henry, 107
Adams, John (midshipman), 37, 46
Adams, John (president), 4, 79
Albany, 38
Allegheny, 11
Allen, William, 12–13, 21
American Seamen's Friend Society, 78
Ames, Sullivan D., 120
Annapolis, misbehavior in, 90–91
Archer, William Segar, 12
armed forces: professionalization of,
   ix–x, 15, 19, 156–57, 188n9; scientific
   management practices in, ix–x, 187n6,
   188n9
Armstrong, J., 115, 157, 182
Army, U.S.: career of officers in, 158–59,
   160; graduate school, establishment of,
   ix; postservice careers of officers, 161;
   professionalization of, x, xi, 19; reasons
   for joining, 59; recruitment policies, 59;
   resignation of Southern officers, 149–
   50, 151; success of during Mexican-
   American War, xi, 50, 157, 167; unity
   during Civil War, 152
Army Corps of Engineers, 17
Army War College, ix
Ashe, Sam, 125

Bache, George M., 120
Bainbridge, William, 8–9
Baldwin, James, 147

Baldwin, Thomas, 79
Baltic, 156
Bancroft, George, 16; early life
   and education of, 15; Mexican-
   American War and, 46; Naval School
   appointments, requests for, 31–33;
   Naval School, behavioral expectations
   at, 82; Naval School, discipline at, 83;
   Naval School, establishment of, 17, 20,
   21, 23, 25–26, 129, 156, 165; Naval
   School improvements, 45; Naval School
   progress report, 40–41; officers, system
   to educate, 1; school run by, 15; as
   Secretary of Navy, 17; writing of, 15
Bancroft, Sarah Dwight, 15
band of brothers relationships, 5, 81–82,
   83–84, 90–91, 98, 101–2, 106, 116,
   120–21, 127, 168–69
Barnes, John S., 162
Barrett, Clarence, 114
Barron, James, 99
Barron, Samuel, 8, 93
Bassett, S. S., 46
Beauregard, Pierre G. T., 59
Beckwith, Josiah G., Jr., 113–14
Benjamin, Park, 38, 48, 84, 86, 144, 158,
   162, 210n42
Bennett, Frank M., 43
Bennett, John W., 37
Bigelow, George A., 108
Bishop, Joshua, 121

Philadelphia Naval Asylum School
examining board, 20–21
Philip, John V., 95, 182
Philip, John Van Ness, 74
Pipkin, William "Bill Pip," 147, 186
Plymouth, 130, 131, 132, 133, 135, 139,
140–41, 144–45, 154, 169, 211n69,
212n76
Poinsett, Joel, 19
Porpoise, 88
Porter, David, 190–91n36
Powell, Jean M., 122
Preble, 37, 38, 131, 133–34, 136–37, 138,
140, 169, 209n19, 211n69
Preble, Edward, 79
Prentiss, Roderick, 119–20
Preston, William Ballard, 49, 107
Princeton, 11, 37
professionalism: in armed forces, ix–x, 15,
19, 156–57, 188n9; characteristics of,
ix; formal education for professional
careers, 1; in Navy, x–xii, 43, 48–49,
50, 75–76, 131, 142, 156–57, 163–64;
officers' duty to the state, 56, 68, 129,
149–51, 157, 168; summer cruises'
importance in teaching, 129, 131
promotion: discipline and, 200n11;
examinations for, 3, 4; resignation from
Navy and, 160; seniority as basis for, 4,
160, 200n11

Queen, Walter W., 99–100, 101

R. R. Cuyler, 156
Ragland, Eldred B., 116
Randolph, V. M., 149
Read, George C., 20
Reed, Allen V., 76–77
Ritchie, Robert, 93
Robertson, James P., 119, 126
Rodgers, C. R. P., 108, 145–46, 156
Rodgers, George W., 146, 147, 148, 155

Royal Navy, 1–2, 3, 79, 134, 164, 190n27
Ruschenberger, William S. W., 50
Sackets Harbor school, 8
St. Bibb, 38
St. Louis, 37
Sampson, William T., 153, 183
Sanders, Morton W., 120
Sands, Benjamin, 9–10
Saratoga, 37
Sawyer, George A., 65
scientific management practices, ix–x,
187n6, 188n9
Scovell, Edward, 92, 93, 96–98
sea duties, 5
Seawell, Joseph, 37
Selfridge, Thomas O., 65–66
Selfridge, Thomas O., Jr., 65–66, 115, 143,
167
service academies, x
Seward, Frances, 14
Seward, William Henry, 14
ships: design and construction of, 11;
education aboard, 5–6, 7, 14, 38; rules
and regulations, 131
ships, school and summer practice,
211n69; academy program for, 51;
Buchanan's program for, 23–24;
discipline on, 120, 137–39, 147–48,
178–81, 212n76; Norfolk Naval School,
9, 10; size of, 131, 133; success of
training on, 141–42; training aboard,
x–xi, xii, 129, 131, 133, 135–37,
145–46, 157, 169. See also *Constitution*;
Plymouth; *Preble*
shore duties, 5
shore-based naval education: activity level
for students at, 9; chaplains as teachers,
7–8, 190–91n36; curriculum taught
at, 8–9, 10, 11, 17; funding for, 25;
instructors at, 11–12; success of naval
education program, 128–29
Shubrick, William B., 50

About the Author

Mark C. Hunter is a maritime and naval historian of the Atlantic world. He specializes in nineteenth- and early-twentieth-century history with a particular emphasis on economic history, non-state actors, education, and training. Dr. Hunter received his PhD in history from the University of Hull (2004) and studied under maritime economic historian Dr. David J. Starkey.